Successful Community Sanctions and Services for Special Offenders

Proceedings of the 1994 Conference of the International Community Corrections Association (ICCA)

Barbara J. Auerbach, M.A.
and Thomas C. Castellano, Ph.D.
Editors

American Correctional Association Staff

Reginald A. Wilkinson, President
James A. Gondles, Jr., Executive Director
Gabriella M. Daley, Director, Communications and Publications
Leslie A. Maxam, Assistant Director, Communications and Publications
Alice Fins, Managing Editor
Michael Kelly, Associate Editor
Sherry Wulfekuhle, Editorial Assistant
Dana M. Murray, Graphics and Production Manager
Michael Selby, Graphics and Production Associate

Cover design by Michael Selby. Photo by Tony Garcia/Tony Stone Images.

This publication may be ordered from the:
American Correctional Association
4380 Forbes Boulevard
Lanham, MD 20706-4322
1-800-222-5646

For information on publications and videos available from ACA, contact our World Wide Web home page at:

http://www.corrections.com/aca

Printed in the United States of America by Kirby Lithographic, Co., Inc., Arlington, VA.

ISBN 1-56991-092-8

Library of Congress Cataloging-in-Publication Data
Successful community sanctions and services for special offenders / Barbara J. Auerbach and Thomas C. Castellano, editors.
p. cm.
Includes bibliographical references.
ISBN 1-56991-092-8 (pbk.)
1. Community-based corrections. 2. Alternatives to imprisonment. 3. Community service (Punishment) I. Auerbach, Barbara. II. Castellano, Thomas C. III. American Correctional Association.
HV9279.S83 1998
364.6'8—dc21 98-16876
CIP

ICCA

Richard J. Billak
President

Peter Kinzinger
Executive Director

Gary Mulhair
Conference Committee Chair

Larry Fehr
Conference Coordinator

TABLE OF CONTENTS

Section 3: What Works

Section 4: Bridging the Gap Between Research and Practice

FOREWORD

We are very pleased to be publishing this work with the International Community Corrections Association. We believe that correctional programs operating in a community setting are an integral part of a comprehensive correctional system, which offers a full range of options for affecting offender behavior and rehabilitation. This collection of essays on special needs offenders show that successful programs must be built on a structure that provides for public safety and responds to the needs of victims, offenders, and the community, as well as including a collaborative comprehensive planning process for the development of policies, programs, and services.

The individuals who wrote these chapters offer fresh insights into effective strategies that, in the end, are cost-effective for the community and the correctional system. Their ideas are well documented by research and practice. The chapters address offenders who are or have been substance abusers, violence-prone, mentally disordered, unskilled and unemployed, and sex offenders. Most of the essays discuss ensuring the integrity and accountability of community programs by establishing a reliable system for monitoring and measuring performance that is in accord with accepted standards of professional practices and sound evaluation methods.

We endorse community-based programs because they can enable offenders to work and pay taxes, make restitution, meet court obligations, maintain family ties, and develop or maintain critical support systems within the community. It is the responsibility of correctional professionals to inform the public about the mission and scope of community-based programs. The public needs to understand how offenders are selected for these programs—that they are carefully screened to evaluate their risk to public safety and their potential for success and that these are sanctions with careful monitoring and follow up.

James A. Gondles, Jr.
Executive Director
American Correctional Association

PREFACE

When our politicians appear in front of the television camera or at a public forum to talk about solutions to crime, they increasingly take the "Tough on Crime" approach. They focus on more and longer prison sentences as if that were the answer. As the result of this simplistic position, the United States has fostered the world's largest and most expensive prison system. Our incarcerated population has quintupled since 1970 to more than 1.6 million offenders at a cost exceeding thirty billion annually. Worse still are the indications that the "Tough on Crime" policy of the United States is being imitated by other countries.

Has the "Tough on Crime" approach made our communities any safer? No, we know all too well that punishment does not reduce the risk of reoffending, nor does it make our communities any safer. Punishing offenders will not make them better citizens when they return to their communities. In fact, punishment alone likely will result in higher-risk offenders reentering our communities. If we really are concerned about public safety, we should be preparing offenders to reenter society better able to function in a competitive environment. This can be accomplished best by offering interventions that have been demonstrated to reduce offender risk. After all, more than 95 percent of all offenders imprisoned will reenter the community.

Throughout this book, you will read repeatedly that offenders are a heterogeneous population. Today's offenders are in more need of complex, multidimensional interventions. Special needs offenders require specialized interventions. There is no "silver bullet." There are no simple solutions. You also will learn that there are successful interventions that can be applied in many situations and there are partial solutions to solving crime if interventions are applied appropriately.

The International Community Corrections Association entered into the "What Works" project with the initial belief that there was little scientific evidence supportive of successful community corrections interventions. In relatively short order, ICCA has come to the realization that, in fact, there exists a considerable amount of research supportive of quality interventions. However, many of the "What Works" answers are not found in neatly compiled manuals waiting to be read and implemented. Instead, "What Works" answers are painfully difficult to learn and even more difficult to implement successfully for any number of reasons. But most importantly, we as professionals can facilitate ways for offenders to succeed and we must realize that positive results are achievable if principles and policies are applied correctly.

The chapters in this book explore various special need populations and discuss what the literature has found to work. In no way are the answers conclusive; rather, they help us look at offenders in more of a problem-solving approach, providing guidance through sets of principles that have shown positive results. Learning and practicing the "What Works" strategies is a dynamic process promising the potential of dynamic results supportive of true public safety. The chapters contained in this book provide us with a foundation from which to work and upon which to build.

The ICCA has made a long-term commitment to sponsoring "What Works" conferences and publishing the conference proceedings. We have learned that the combined papers from our "What Works" events have a cumulative effect of building off one another. This is an exciting and challenging time for community corrections. Steadily, we are marrying correctional theory and practice together in ways that will deliver public safety results.

Peter Kinzinger
Executive Director
International Community Corrections Association

Section 1:
Introduction

Lessons, Prospects, and Pitfalls for Effective Treatment Programming in Community Corrections

1

Thomas C. Castellano, Ph.D.
Southern Illinois University, Carbondale, Illinois

Barbara J. Auerbach, M.A.
Carbondale, Illinois

The 1994 Conference of the International Community Corrections Association (ICCA)

Conference Overview

The papers contained in this volume were presented at the International Community Corrections Association's (formerly known as IARCA, The International Association of Residential and Community Alternatives) Eighth International Conference. The conference was held in Seattle, Washington, in November 1994. The title of the conference, "This Works! Community Sanctions and Services for Special Offenders," reflects forcefully and unambiguously the major goal of the conference: to bridge the gap between evaluation research findings and improved service delivery in community corrections. The conference—the second in a trilogy of research conferences sponsored by ICCA—was designed to build upon the more general themes established during the previous year's annual conference in Philadelphia, which had been titled "What Works in Community Corrections: A Consensus Conference." The 1993 conference examined promising assessment and classification tools, treatment and programming options, and general principles of implementation. The 1995 research conference, held in Ottawa, Ontario, in October 1995, was titled "Research to Results: The Challenge." It focused on what makes for successful program design and how program innovation can be effectively accomplished.

The 1994 Seattle conference sought to bridge the gap between research and practice by commissioning papers from distinguished researchers on what is known about effectively supervising and serving "special offenders" in the community. The papers are presented in this volume. They are among the best research in community corrections available to practitioners today.

For each of five special offender groups—violent offenders, sex offenders, chemically dependent offenders, mentally impaired offenders, and unskilled/unemployed offenders—researchers were asked to summarize findings on the following issues:

- CHARACTERISTICS AND TRENDS: What offender and policy trends and characteristics currently are occurring and what are the contributing factors influencing those trends?
- WHAT WORKS BEST: In light of the best research concerning each offender group, what are the critical factors in determining success and which interventions show the most promise?
- INCORPORATION INTO PRACTICE: How should these findings be implemented into programs so that services can work best in practice?

In addition to the commissioned papers, Dr. Paul Gendreau was invited to present the keynote address summarizing the evaluation literature on the effectiveness of community corrections. Dr. Gendreau, a professor of psychology at the University of New Brunswick, has published extensively during his more than thirty years of work and study in criminal justice settings. He is best known as one of the leaders in the academic movement to "reaffirm rehabilitation." His many important studies and publications have been influential in countering the "nothing works" perspective that has dominated the field during the last two decades.

A second keynote address was given by Dr. Kurt Neudek, senior officer of the United Nations. Dr. Neudek heads the Office for Drug, Alcohol and Crime Prevention of the Centre for International Crime Prevention of the United Nations Office in Vienna, Austria. He discussed variations among nations in the response to and management of special offenders in the community.

ICCA presented its 1994 Margaret Mead Award to Chase Riveland, former secretary of the Washington Department of Corrections. His acceptance address focused on the need to expand and improve community correctional programming.

Following these presentations, intensive workshops were held to give program participants an opportunity to explore further the research findings presented earlier. Conference response panels provided for reaction to the commissioned papers from a variety of professional perspectives including those of legislators, judges, county executives, journalists, and citizen activists. Finally, Hubert G. Locke, professor in the Graduate School of Public Affairs at the University of Washington, presented the concluding speech. Professor Locke was challenged with the formidable task of synthesizing the information that had been presented throughout the conference, to help us bridge the gap between research and practice.

Conference Goals

The Seattle conference was intended to provide community corrections practitioners with state-of-the-art knowledge on what can be done within community-based treatment services to improve public safety, and what can be done to ensure that these services become more effective and efficient. The explicit focus was on the identification of effective behavioral technologies of offender change and rehabilitation. According to Larry Fehr, the conference coordinator: "A major premise of this research conference . . . is that there is a growing body of evaluation research literature which suggests that even with some of the most problematic offenders, carefully constructed and implemented treatment services and training work better than incarceration alone in reducing future criminality" (1995). The desire was for participants to come away from the conference with increased knowledge on how to improve and expand community correctional programs and services to better promote the rehabilitative function of community corrections.

This orientation clearly marks a dramatic change in thinking within community corrections. For many years, both practitioners and researchers have been reluctant to talk about rehabilitation, in either institutional or community settings. The conventional wisdom, at least since the mid-1970s, has been that "nothing works." Instead of correctional treatment, for the last twenty years policy makers, practitioners, and academics (with few exceptions) have been focused on risk control, risk management, intensive surveillance, electronic detention, day reporting centers, smart sentencing, and the like.

Intermediate sanctions, most often premised on increasing the punitiveness, intensiveness, and potential deterrent impact of the criminal sanction, became the primary subject of innovation and research in community corrections. A "new penology" emerged, characterized by "an administrative style that seeks depersonalized efficiency in processing increasingly large hordes of inmates (offenders) in and out of the system" (Cullen, 1995: 339-340; see also Feeley and Simon, 1992). The task for community corrections officials (especially parole agents) was transformed from assisting the (re) integration of offenders in the community to discerning which offenders in the community should be (re) incarcerated (Cullen, 1995: 352; see also Simon, 1992). While the strength of these trends has varied across states and elements of the correctional system, for the most part, treatment and offender rehabilitation were banished to the outhouse of the corrections' enterprise.

Thinking is beginning to change, however, and the front door has been opened again to treatment and rehabilitative programming in community corrections. One recent example of the changes in thinking among criminal justice professionals struck us as emblematic. At a meeting on correctional options programming sponsored by the Bureau of Justice Assistance of the U.S. Department of Justice, a colleague stated unequivocally that "we know what works." Moreover, he stated that the recipe for success is quite evident and straightforward. If the recipe is followed, he argued, a successful correctional program could be guaranteed. For him, at least, the barriers to the development and implementation of successful programs resulting in "rehabilitated" offenders do not include unproven or uncertain behavioral technologies.

This statement would have been considered blasphemous even ten years ago, but today, expressions of optimism regarding the effectiveness of correctional treatment are increasingly common in academic journals, trade magazines, books, and at professional conferences. The dominant attitudes of cynicism and skepticism regarding the benefits of correctional treatment are being chipped away. ICCA's research conferences have been at the vanguard of that change.

Changing the beliefs and attitudes of skeptical and cynical correctional practitioners was a second goal of the 1994 Seattle conference. The conference organizers attempted to encourage this attitudinal change not only through the dissemination of scientific evidence, but also through the delivery of symbolic and normative messages to provide participants with encouragement and social support to "keep the faith." There is good reason to do so.

After being bombarded for decades with the notion that "nothing works" in community corrections, the organizers of the ICCA conference series felt the time was overdue for the spreading of good news. This motivating focus is evidenced in the statements by Richard Billak, ICCA's Secretary for the 1993 Research Conference:

> Like a slumbering giant, those of us in the profession of community corrections have been awakened to a clamor from the system for our services. However, after being numbed by our defensiveness during the '70s brought on by the "Nothing Works" syndrome, and still being dazed by the recent euphoria to become a remedy for overcrowding, this conference (1993) should be our wake-up call.
>
> No longer should we be cowered into a posture of being either defensive or reactive, but rather prepare to present the formidable knowledge of our field before the public in an effort to lead the way to a balanced, fair, and effective system of justice. . .
>
> No longer to be intimidated by the sociopolitical rhetoric that surrounds us, we would hope all of us exit this conference with a clear vision of what we know and what we need to know regarding "What Works" in community corrections.

Thus, the conference series was intended to mobilize constituents of community-based correctional treatment in the struggle against the dominant forces of reaction and shortsightedness that continue to adhere to the outdated and monolithic notion that nothing works. The armaments in the struggle would include the positive evaluation research evidence presented during the conferences. Together with the professional and social support provided during the meetings, the hope was that an enduring synergy would result.

Whether the available evaluation research can justify such a position, the attempt to communicate the message that "some programs do work and work well" is no doubt a worthwhile end in itself. A full-blown debate on correctional treatment effectiveness is now beginning to reemerge, and conferences such as the 1994 ICCA conference have nurtured that debate. Unlike the situation twenty years ago when this same debate began to fade from acceptable discourse, today there is a significantly increased body of literature and practical experience to better inform the contours of the debate and its eventual outcome. Some of the more relevant and telling literature and experience were presented at the 1994 ICCA conference. Moreover, despite the limits of our knowledge, the conference presenters provided the seeds of significant and well-founded hope for the future of community-based treatment programming. We encourage you to read the following sections closely and to draw your own conclusions.

Organization of this Volume and a Summary of Lessons Learned

The balance of this section introduces each of the subsequent sections and is organized to highlight "what works" for the special-offender populations examined at the conference. It also illustrates some of the limits of current knowledge, and notes some of the relevant factors found in the political and social contexts that likely will affect our ability to incorporate knowledge of "what works" into practice.

Section 2 begins with the remarks of Chase Riveland, former secretary of the Washington State Department of Corrections and the recipient of the 1994 Margaret Mead Award. Secretary Riveland is among the most respected commissioners of corrections in the nation today and his longstanding commitment to community corrections sets him apart as a significant source of inspiration for ICCA. His remarks include a set of steps for community corrections practitioners, which he believes can strengthen the field:

- He urges ICCA to do more of what it already does—resist rhetoric, show a commitment to humanity and pragmatism, and demonstrate repeatedly that things do work.

- He cautions practitioners to avoid the "generalization of numbers," to promote public knowledge of the many successes rather than the few failures.
- He urges continued research.
- He asks practitioners to educate the public and challenge policy makers as to the real issues of crime and the approaches that really do work.

Section 2 also includes the keynote remarks of Dr. Kurt Neudek, senior officer of the United Nations. Dr. Neudek is a senior officer at the Centre for International Crime Prevention of the United Nations Office in Vienna, Austria, which acts as a facilitator for governments, promoting the exchange of views and experiences in criminal justice. Dr. Neudek reviews the history of penal sanctions, describing the types and forms of community sanctions in use around the world. He notes our great national paradox: that on the one hand, the United States has the highest per capita rate of imprisonment in the world and, on the other hand, it is one of the major pioneers and exporters of alternatives to imprisonment. It is American and Canadian research, he says, that has been most rigorous and outstanding in quality.

Section 3 describes "what works" for specific offender populations. The Keynote remarks of Dr. Paul Gendreau open the chapter because his work has so clearly influenced all of the other researchers whose findings as to specific offender populations follow. Dr. Gendreau's extensive writing and work on the effectiveness of correctional treatment programming, along with those of colleagues such as James Bonta, Donald Andrews, Francis Cullen, and Ted Palmer, have been perhaps the strongest empirically based counter to the legacy of Robert Martinson's "nothing works" findings of the mid-1970s.

As a result of their evaluative research work, Dr. Gendreau and his colleagues at the University of New Brunswick at St. John and elsewhere firmly hold the view that rehabilitative programs can be successful under the right circumstances. In so doing, they have provided both some much-needed encouragement and a rich set of challenges to practitioners and researchers.

What kind of treatment programs does Dr. Gendreau find most effective? After first discussing a recent meta-analysis of the recidivism-prediction literature and identifying derivative lessons for implementation of a comprehensive protocol for offender assessment (such as focus should be placed on the assessment of "dynamic" predictors), Dr. Gendreau sets forth a series of principles of effective intervention that he believes can reduce recidivism from 10 to 60 percent. Effective programs are programs:

- With intensive services that are behavioral in nature
- That target the criminogenic needs of high-risk offenders
- That match treatment, offender, and counselor style
- Where program elements and strategies are enforced in a firm but fair manner
- Where therapists are trained and supervised appropriately
- That place the offender in situations where pro-social activity predominates
- That include relapse prevention in the community
- That include quality community-based services for offenders

Very importantly, Dr. Gendreau also identifies principles of ineffective intervention. A close review of what he writes indicates that much of the recent innovation within the field (such as "punishing smarter" strategies) and much of the traditional interventions found in corrections (including nondirective therapies aimed at reducing "personal distress") are inconsistent with principles of effective intervention. Finally, Dr. Gendreau discusses some of the barriers that must be overcome for solid and effective programming efforts to be established on a widespread basis.

Following Dr. Gendreau, the work of Drs. Prendergast, Anglin, and Wellisch on substance-abusing offenders is presented in Chapter 5. Prendergast and others, who have developed their findings at the University of California at Los Angeles Drug Abuse Research Center, state categorically that it now has been clearly established that substance abuse treatment is effective (whether voluntarily or coercively undertaken). "What works for which type of offender, under which conditions, and in which settings" is the question of interest now. They discuss a number of principles for effective treatment based on both research and clinical practice:

- Supervision is needed for an extended period of time to reduce the possibility of relapse.

- Both aversive conditions and incentives are necessary for substance-abusing offenders to be responsive to substance abuse treatment and services.

- A staged approach is best—clients should receive appropriate services at the appropriate time so they are not overwhelmed or unprepared to take advantage of the services being provided. Effective treatment involves some matching of clients to services, and no single treatment has been found to be effective for all or most drug abusers.

- Continuity of care in the community is critical. Relapse-prevention training has been the primary program approach.

- Treatment integrity is also critical. The program must be implemented and sustained over time by management and staff with adequate experience and training.

- Programs should be linked with other services to address the variety of additional problems and needs typical of substance-abusing offenders.

In Chapter 6, Dr. Jeffrey Fagan examines the treatment of violent offenders. Dr. Fagan, of New Jersey's Rutgers University, notes the difficulty in making assertions as to program effectiveness in this area given the dearth of controlled studies for violent offenders and the primary focus in those studies that do exist on juveniles rather than adults. However, he does discuss several trends that stand out regarding effective interventions. They tend to parallel the principles of effective intervention articulated by Gendreau:

- Programs that emphasize therapeutic integrity yield better results than those with eclectic treatments.

- Behavioral, cognitive-behavioral or cognitive, life skills, or skill-oriented interventions are more effective than other approaches.

- Programs should focus on specific offender groups and avoid mixing risk levels and behavior problems.

- Programs that carefully match offender risks and needs with program models do better than those with haphazard or convenience assignments.

- Structured programs with overlapping phases stressing reintegration are more effective than those seeking only intraprogram behavioral adjustments.

Chapter 7 looks at mentally disordered offenders. Drs. Grant T. Harris and Marnie E. Rice of the Mental Health Center at Penetanguishene, Ontario, discuss what the research says about effective service for this group. They argue that few data exist on what works with mentally disordered offenders as a distinct offender population. Existing research does indicate that they differ little from criminal offenders generally in terms of the prediction of their criminal and violent recidivism. The authors suggest that obstacles to program implementation lie not in our lack of knowledge, but in our lack of will to use what we already know.

- As to the reduction in recidivism of this group of offenders, the authors suggest that effective treatment should focus on the criminogenic needs of relatively high risk individuals. Services that are highly structured, behavioral or cognitive-behavioral intensive and run for offenders in their home communities work best.

- As to improving the mental disorders of such offenders, services should emphasize teaching and learning in small incremental steps. There should be opportunities to share responsibility and for frequent interaction with clinicians. The use of antipsychotic medications is supported by the authors as well.

Chapter 8 examines the issues associated with the assessment, management, and treatment of sex offenders. Dr. Vernon Quinsey of Queen's University, Kingston, Ontario, discusses the issues of the risk of recidivism and his finding is that sex offenders do not differ significantly from other offenders in this regard. Dr. Quinsey's work is aimed at more accurately appraising risk given the existence of low public tolerance for mistakes in this area. Sex-offender treatment programs have not been convincingly evaluated he says, but he suggests that some approaches to treatment are known to be more effective than others. He suggests a cognitive-behavioral approach generally. In addition, treatment programs for sex offenders should:

- Fit with what is known about the treatment of offenders in general
- Have a convincing theoretical rationale
- Have been demonstrated to produce the desired change
- Be feasible
- Allow for the measurement of program integrity

Chapter 9 is a review of the research on employment and training programs by Dr. Douglas C. McDonald of Abt Associates, Inc. He looks at community-based programs for various disadvantaged populations, including offenders. All of the programs were designed to improve the skills and training of their clients, rather than to restructure the job market. Most of the evaluative literature reviewed by Dr. McDonald is based on studies conducted in the 1970s. Little relevant research conducted in the 1980s and 1990s was identified in this review, suggesting that employment-oriented offender programming warrants greater empirical scrutiny. Based on the 1970s program evaluations, Dr. McDonald finds little that is hopeful. There are exceptions, however, including Job Corps and related programs in which comprehensive support was provided. Those programs, reported increased earnings and reduced crime.

In attempting to determine why there are so few successes in employment and training programs for offenders, Dr. McDonald points out the nationwide deterioration in employment prospects for all unskilled and poorly educated men and women. He suggests, however, that some approaches are more effective than others. Program managers and policymakers should:

- Focus on placing offenders in jobs
- Provide continuing services, even after the first job is obtained
- Create tighter linkages between prison and community-based programs
- Assess offenders to determine their readiness for employment and to identify other problems that may obstruct their attempts to enter the labor market

- Consider the potential of wage subsidies such as the earned-income tax credit
- Urge the federal government to reassert its role in supporting experimentation

In Section 4, Professor Hubert G. Locke, the conference chair and professor of the Graduate School of Public Affairs, University of Washington, summarizes the work of the conference and discusses the gap between research and practice. Professor Locke is concerned with the issue of how to put our growing but still imperfect knowledge of what works in [community] corrections into practice and into the policy arena. Conferences such as the ICCA research conferences help to improve practice. But Professor Locke is concerned that the second task—elevating the public policy debate based on our new knowledge—will be considerably more difficult. He exhorts ICCA members to seize the day, to work to educate the public, legislators, and anyone else who will listen, to change the climate of public thinking.

What Next? A Proposed Research and Action Agenda

A number of themes emerge from the chapters that follow, pointing the way toward the next set of challenges for researchers and practitioners. Two primary tasks stand out for researchers: (1) to examine more closely specialized interventions with particular offender subgroups; and (2) to conduct more research on community-based sanctions. As to the tasks facing practitioners, there are also at least two striking needs: (1) to insist in even stronger terms on the importance of therapeutic integrity in program conditions; and (2) to wholeheartedly support Gendreau's responsivity principle by demanding appropriate training for treatment providers, and by matching offender type to treatment intervention and counselor style.

The Research Agenda

Differential Efficacy

The theme of the 1994 ICCA conference was "what works" with special groups of offenders. Conference organizers recognized the tremendous diversity within the offender population, and worked on the operating assumption that what works with one group of offenders may not work well with a different group of offenders. As stated by Director Riveland, "Instead of touting singular solutions for the crime problem, we must break the issue down into its component parts. And by concentrating on what works with special offenders, we can maximize the impact of our interventions and avoid stereotypical solutions."

Nonetheless, most of the papers presented at the conference identify a common set of principles associated with effective interventions across offender subgroups. Those principles parallel strongly the principles of effective treatment identified and articulated by Dr. Gendreau. In many instances, the authors appear to have reviewed similar bodies of literature in coming to their conclusions about what works. Clearly, there is limited knowledge currently available on the types of specialized interventions that are most effective with distinct types of offenders.

Why is this the case? It may be because specialized interventions with particular offender subgroups have not been adequately tested or because such interventions have been tested and not been shown to be efficacious. It also may be the result of members within the offender population having more in common with one another than is generally assumed. Perhaps most criminal offenders exhibit underlying characteristics related to their criminality, regardless of their classification as drug, violent, or sex offenders, thus warranting a generalized form of correctional treatment interventions.

Whatever the reason or reasons for the pattern of findings, more testing of specialized interventions with particular offender subgroups clearly is needed. New evaluative efforts should be conducted in conjunction with rigorous research endeavors that examine further the interventions that seem to work with more general offender populations. In each instance, program interventions and evaluative research should be guided by a theory, or theories of criminality.

The theory of criminality that underlies the general principles of effective treatment endorsed in most of the following chapters is not fully specified in any one chapter. However, the principles and recommended intervention strategies are largely premised on a model of the criminal as impulsive, deficient, and cognitively impaired (see Andrews and Bonta, 1994, for a discussion of an underlying theoretical model consistent with this description). This view of the criminal offender appears to be valid at first glance. So, too, do the core intervention principles identified by the authors as being associated with efficacious treatment: intensive, directive behavior modification programs based on social learning models that focus on cognitive skill development, with services delivered by staff trained to be change agents and to serve as effective anti-criminal models.

Despite the intuitive appeal of these principles, however, they evidence certain limits. Except for the chapter by McDonald on offender employment and training programs, most of the interventions endorsed by the authors are focused heavily and almost exclusively on the individual offender as the target of change. The authors generally do not advocate broader interaction with the larger social systems and contexts in which offenders live, work, and play (such as family, workplace, and community). While we believe that the psychological model of criminality and the associated interventions endorsed by most of the authors are reasonable, and that they should serve as the core of any treatment-intervention strategy, we also suggest that interventions based on broader theoretical models must be explored. In particular, and as suggested by McDonald, interventions based on models of criminality that include the individual's relation to larger community and familial structures, as well as to the labor market, warrant further development and testing.

It should be remembered that community corrections evolved during the twentieth century from a supervision model that emphasized the community corrections officer as a deliverer of services to one that emphasized the officer as a broker of services. Moreover, the definition of an effective officer evolved from one who acted as a "clinician," an individual change agent, to an officer who simultaneously served as a community change agent and an individual change agent. This evolution was not accidental, nor was it based simply on increasing caseload demands. It was the result of common beliefs that the successes associated with one-on-one clinically oriented interventions were limited, especially because the target population tends to suffer from a multiplicity of needs that cannot be addressed adequately by a single individual. Further, the extant theory and interventions were seen as limited because the larger social setting in which people live and behave was not emphasized adequately, either as a locus of explanation or intervention. We doubt if the field of community corrections wants to repeat the failures of the past. Accordingly, we encourage further innovations within the field that apply the principles articulated by Gendreau and his colleagues, but which also use them as the foundation for broader interventions that attempt to impact positively on the offender's immediate social situation.

Community-based Interventions

The primary intended focus of the 1994 ICCA conference was to identify which community sanctions work most effectively with special offender populations. In short, the focus of the meeting was effective community-based interventions. Both Director Riveland and United Nations Senior Officer Neudek, in their addresses, emphasized the need to expand noncustodial sanctions. Nonetheless, many of the findings in this volume stem from prison-based programs. Very little specific guidance is offered on how to improve community-based programming in a manner consistent with the evaluation literature.

Most of the principles articulated by Gendreau and echoed by the authors are very difficult to apply in the community. For example, the first principle presented by Gendreau is that services should be intensive and behavioral. Intensive services should occupy 40 to 70 percent of the offender's time in a program and be of three to nine months duration. Clearly, the program setting to which this principle is applicable is custodial or residential in nature. It is almost impossible to deliver these intensive services in nonresidential community-based programs—the types of programs that service the vast bulk of offenders sentenced to a community-based sanction.

We need much more information on what works in community-based settings. We have a great deal of information on what does not seem to work in community corrections (such as "smart sentencing" initiatives, including intensive surveillance programs and boot camps, or nondirective counseling and employment training programs), but much more needs to be done to assess the effectiveness of treatment-oriented correctional programming in the community. What little we know about effective community-based treatment programming tends to come from evaluations of community-based substance abuse treatment programs (see Anglin and others) and community-based aftercare programs that serve offenders recently released from institutional settings. It is clearly time for rigorous evaluative research on the effectiveness of treatment interventions that typically take place in the community. Much more relevant research is needed.

The Action Agenda

We are confident that the research agenda described here can and will be achieved. Timely completion of the agenda, however, will require researchers and program staff to work together more closely and collaboratively in the design, implementation, and evaluation of programs than has been the case in the past. This close working relationship will be necessary to ensure that programs adhere to sound intervention principles and that programs are able to be evaluated and can result in generalizable findings. Moreover, such efforts can be important in helping shape larger public policy thrusts within the field.

We cannot help but be concerned that the program conditions necessary to determine what works with any real level of certainty will be difficult in today's political climate. Current public policy goals for corrections tend to de-emphasize the need for stronger and better program conditions. To the contrary, political and financial support for treatment programming in any form has dropped precipitously. Nonetheless, practitioners and treatment-oriented researchers must continue the struggle for improved treatment programming, their arguments strengthened, we hope, by the findings presented in this volume and the general literature on "what works." This is the most immediate and pressing challenge for the field of community corrections today.

It is one that has already witnessed some success. Despite a political climate that has supported the revitalization of chain gangs and the establishment of austere and Spartan correctional environments, a number of states have recently enacted Community Corrections Acts (for example, Michigan, Ohio, and Virginia) that encourage the expansion of treatment programming within community corrections. Importantly, these acts have tended to be based on the results of scientific inquiry and the knowledge that has been derived from the "what works" literature.

Therapeutic Integrity

Perhaps the most important concept in this literature, and one to which all practitioners should pay heed, is the concept of therapeutic integrity. Therapeutic integrity may be the key issue in all of correctional treatment. It relates to the quality and intensity of the service delivery system. It subsumes a number of questions that must be addressed by practitioners and researchers. For example, to what extent do treatment personnel actually adhere to the program principles and employ the techniques of therapy they purport to provide? To what extent are the treatment staff competent? How hard do they work?, and how much is treatment diluted in the correctional environment so that it becomes treatment in name only (Gendreau and Ross, 1983-1984)?

Experience repeatedly indicates that the answers to these questions tend to be negative. The correctional system is not likely to be a context in which programs with therapeutic integrity are the norm. Even Gendreau's own research with the Corrections Program Assessment Inventory indicates that only about 10 percent of adult and juvenile programs had programmatic elements that would indicate an effective service was being provided (most of these are institutional programs, however). Significantly increasing this percentage would require a major paradigm change in corrections and a tremendous influx of resources, especially in terms of well-trained, competent staff.

Nonetheless, the available research indicates that therapeutic integrity is the essence of effective treatment and that we must struggle to achieve this level of programming despite the obvious resource limitations most programs face (for example, see McEwen, 1995) if we are to be effective in our endeavors. This, perhaps more than any other issue, is the challenge facing community corrections. In effect, as is the case in most of the human services, we need to do more with less.

The Responsivity Principle

A related theme involves what Dr. Gendreau calls the "responsivity principle." It is a key principle of effective treatment. It states that treatment should be delivered in a manner that facilitates the learning of new prosocial skills by the offender. This is promoted by matching treatment to the offender type and to the counselor style. In correctional settings, this principle long has been recognized (albeit in different terms), but it has been difficult to implement and sustain.

Systematic differential treatment approaches date back at least to the work of J. Douglas Grant with court-martialed Navy personnel at the Naval Retraining Command, Camp Elliot (Grant and Grant, 1957). This experience influenced the development of Quay's classification scheme (still used in the Federal Bureau of Prisons) and therapeutic communities in corrections (Jones, 1957), among others. As Hans Toch, a longtime observer and proponent of correctional treatment programming, has written:

> The formula that evolved was a marvelous one: classify the prisoners in treatment-relevant terms and sort them into homogeneous enclaves that would be run by teams of congruent staff members. In each enclave, offenders would present comparable problems; some could be predatory

> men, for instance, and others, vulnerable. Inmates with special needs would be accommodated with tailor-made regimes, including specialized services. The staff teams would have autonomy to evolve and exercise professional expertise in working with their clients. They would get to know their inmates, and each other. They would be supported by modern resources, such as vocational and training facilities (Toch, 1993: 74).

But as Toch continues in his discussion, the formula he describes—even if endorsed by many at an earlier point in time—largely has been set aside during contemporary times: ". . .Corrections agencies have shifted from a rehabilitation-oriented philosophy to a management-oriented one." A narrowed ideological base and a management orientation to corrections, as well as directions in programming efforts that constrain prisoner voluntariness and choices in seeking responsibility, have left Toch and other rehabilitationists looking back in time as a wellspring of hope for the future. As Toch writes, "Has the time come for new adventures, such as Morgantown and Lexington—for new Camp Elliots? For the sake of staff and inmates in the system, I hope the answer will be affirmative" (p.75). This statement of hope for the future obviously does not speak well of the present. It does, however, speak to the immense challenges that are faced in all of corrections, if the field is truly earnest in its quest to deliver effective treatment programs.

What would be required for correctional programming to better adhere to the responsivity principle? The demands would be numerous and multifaceted, and parallel Toch's discussion of differential treatment programming. They would start with the implementation of meaningful offender classification systems. Classification systems within community corrections abound. During the last two decades, significant improvement has been made in the development of decision making processes that result in the rational assignment of offenders to various supervision and control levels within the community. The major trend has been toward the use of objective risk and needs assessment instruments.

Such instruments, if based on reliable data and validated with the target population, can be used to promote effective treatment programming. Risk assessments are not only appropriate for release and supervision decisions, but also for planning interventions that reduce risk. For instance, risk assessment can be used to match the intensity of services to the risk level of the offender (Bonta, 1993). Unfortunately, this is not often an explicit function of the current risk assessment processes. Similarly, needs assessments most often do not include a focus on criminogenic needs—those needs that are most directly related to the individual's offending behavior. Nor does this assessment process often inform about the intensity, duration, and types of interventions that are actually delivered.

Despite the fact that risk and needs instruments have "seldom (been) designed to reveal much about offenders as individuals . . . (and) neither did they specifically focus on the 'what' of intervention" (Palmer, 1992: 165), their use can be modified to deliver treatment services more effectively. This would require the development of instruments designed to measure how individuals within a larger subgroup differ along important treatment-relevant dimensions (for example, anxiety, intelligence, or verbal abilities). This information can suggest how a client likely will respond to various treatment providers and treatment modalities. Based on this information, clients then can be matched with therapists and the appropriate style and mode of therapy. We encourage practitioners and researchers to work collaboratively in the development of treatment classification instruments and procedures that promote adherence to the responsivity principle.

Conclusions

These final pages have highlighted some of the social and technical barriers to successful community-based interventions with offenders. While we think the social impediments are significantly more intractable than are the technical barriers, it is also clear that knowledge barriers still exist. The science of changing people remains uncertain. Nonetheless, the chapters in this volume indicate that we have learned significantly more about what works with offender populations than was the case twenty, ten, or even five years ago. Still, much more light needs to be shed on the topic of which community-based interventions work best with distinct correctional populations. Researchers and practitioners need to continue working closely together to uncover the truth about what works and what does not in community corrections. A close reading of the chapters to follow can serve as a road map for these efforts.

References

Andrews, D.A. and James Bonta. 1994. *The Psychology of Criminal Conduct.* Cincinnati, Ohio: Anderson.

Bonta, James. 1993. Risk—Needs Assessment and Treatment. Paper presented at the 1993 Conference of the International Association of Residential and Community Alternatives. Philadelphia, Pennsylvania: November 3-6.

Cullen, Francis T. 1995. Assessing the Penal Harm Movement. *Journal of Research in Crime and Delinquency.* 32(3): 338-358.

Feeley, Malcom S. and Jonathan Simon. 1992. The New Penology: Notes on the Emerging Strategy of Corrections and its Implications. *Criminology.* 30: 449-474.

Fehr, Larry. 1995. Introduction to IARCA's Research Conference. *The IARCA Journal.* February: 4.

Gendreau, Paul and Robert R. Ross. 1983-84. Correctional Treatment: Some Recommendations for Effective Intervention. *Juvenile and Family Court Journal.* 34(Winter): 31-39.

Grant, J. Douglas and Marguerite Q. Grant. 1959. A Group Dynamics Approach to the Treatment of Nonconformists in the Navy. *Annals of the American Academy of Political and Social Sciences.* 322: 126-135.

Jones, Maxwell. 1957. Commentary. *British Journal of Delinquency.* 7: 307-308.

McEwen, William. 1995. *National Assessment Program: 1994 Survey Results.* Washington, D.C.: National Institute of Justice, U.S. Department of Justice.

Palmer, Ted. 1992. *The Re-Emergence of Correctional Intervention.* Newbury Park, California: Sage Publications.

Simon, Jonathan. 1992. *Poor Discipline: Parole and the Social Control of the Underclass, 1890-1990.* Chicago: University of Chicago Press.

Toch, Hans. 1993. News of the Future. *Federal Probation.* 57(3): 73-75.

Section 2: Political and Social Context

Remarks by the Recipient of the 1994 Margret Mead Award

2

Chase Riveland

Former Secretary, Washington State Department of Corrections, Olympia, Washington

First of all, I would like to thank IARCA, not only for what you have done over the years, but what you stand for, and for bringing what you stand for to Seattle. I think that is very important. We need to hear the kind of discussion that you have had over the last few days, and that has been terribly important. I would like to particularly thank Jim for his introduction and his leadership of IARCA but I wish to thank the officers of IARCA. Particularly, I know that Gary Mulhair, Larry Fehr, and also Hubert Locke have been very important people in having, I think, the largest of IARCA's conferences in recent years be so terribly successful. And, the three of them have been the major leaders behind this whole thing, although there obviously are many, many people who have contributed to it.

I'd like to first of all thank you for allowing me to participate also, because over the years, you have been very important people to the agenda that many of us have, and you are folks who always seem to be there, and no matter what is happening throughout our society you are people who sort of keep the faith. I particularly feel, like anyone would, personally honored. But I can't accept an honor for something when so many of you have done so much more than I have for community corrections and for working in our communities. But, I quite honestly would accept it on the basis that it seems to reflect the kinds of things that happen in the State of Washington, the things that people who are not only the staff in community corrections in the State of Washington, but those people who are part of the profit and the nonprofit residential and community correctional programs in the State of Washington, which, arguably, are second to none in the country, and on behalf of all of those people who continually make that kind of contribution and have over the years. I would accept the award on behalf of them, rather than on my behalf.

I had to do a little studying on Margaret Mead and I learned, first of all, that she was a person who was a very strong woman, and was maligned for most of her professional life, and not recognized for the contributions that she made to many fields, first of all, to anthropology. She was not recognized a great deal until later in her career. As a matter of fact, if many of the laws that we have today were present then, she probably would have had many lawsuits that she could have filed. Judge Martinez would have found, I am sure, in favor of her at that point in time. I have to recognize Judge Martinez because I know that he is probably the fairest guy in the world and having sat on a panel for several days now, I think his contribution to everything here has been pretty important also.

What I found is that Margaret Mead is arguably the best-known anthropologist in the world and had a tremendous effect on American thought. She not only dispelled many of the things that people thought about the heathens, if you will, in much of the world, but she found that many parts of family life and culture that existed somewhere else were better done, if you will, than they have been in this country. She contributed a lot, obviously, in her literature about the Pacific tribes and the Native Americans in this country.

And the model she described held up a mirror to the model that we have in this country, a model of competitiveness. What she found in many of the other cultures was a sense of cooperation, that seemed to her to be a model that might be more effective long term than the competitive nature that our particular culture had at that point in time. So, she held the mirror up to our society, and she dispelled many of the myths we had about gender superiority. She found that in other cultures that there were issues of gender that were dealt with much more favorably than in our culture, and displayed again and again the virtues of a cooperative society and cooperative communities versus the competitive societies and communities that we have.

I would like to switch from that and talk a bit about colonial times and what has happened, because communities are something that we are all about. In colonial times, born of necessity in this country, our communities were generally cooperative, and frequently communal, and people were interdependent and reliant on each other, mostly for survival reasons. They were in small communities, and they had to get along. The laws and the punishments in those communities for violating those laws were community-oriented. The laws, although frequently reflecting the community's dominant religious beliefs, were nominally created to maintain social order. Lying in idleness and sex outside of marriage were not only sins, but crimes and threats to the well-being of that community.

For many crimes, the penalties were aimed not so much at punishment, but rather to teach a lesson to the offender. And, the penalties were intended to shame the individual within the community. But, the community still had the feeling that no matter what that person had done (barring highly egregious crimes), that person was still a member of that community, would continue to belong to that community, and needed to be dealt with within that community. Shaming the individual in very public ways was the norm and the severity of punishment was less a goal than providing good swift lessons to include restitution and repentance.

Warnings and fines were common penalties. Pillories and stocks and dunking pools were also types of penalties. For serious kinds of crimes, banishment was one of the worst punishments that a person could be afforded. And, death was used in colonial times only when a person who had been banished returned uninvited. The norm, though, except for the egregious offenses, was to deal with the offenders with the recognition that they were to be incorporated back into the community, and that repentance could be something that could return them to community status. The restoration of equilibrium was important as a community goal and as a logical goal. And, they used, what we think is a new phrase, restorative justice frequently.

Seldom was imprisonment used at that point in time as a penalty. The idea of incarceration had not yet been born, and incarceration was used generally as a temporary measure for holding somebody until trial, and trial came swiftly and some other penalty then was imposed. The concept of moving people out of the community to some remote place was a foreign concept at this point in time. And the important thing again was to shame the person in the community. It was thought to be healthy to shame the person, healthy both for the individual as well as the community. The jails and prisons that dominate our correctional systems today were unknown other than possibly to hold a person, again for trial or for debtors (quite interesting). For all of us that have Mastercards and VISAs and things, we probably would not have done so well in those days.

As a society, the United States grew rapidly, and as it did grow, people become migratory and rootless, cities became large and impersonal, and attitudes toward criminal behavior changed. And, instead of blaming the sinful individual, we began to blame the environment, the weakness in our families and the vice-laden cities. A solution for criminals became to remove them from their communities and evil surroundings and put them in, as David Rothman said, "an artificially created and therefore corruption-free environment." Ha! I build those today.

Themes in corrections from the late 1800s evolved as follows: A dungeon was created out of old copper mines in Simsburg, Connecticut, and was renowned for its horrid gloom and forced labor. Any Connecticut folks here? The Philadelphia Walnut Street Institution added solitary confinement cells as a new correctional concept. The Pennsylvania Constitution of 1776 ordered a less sanguine setting for prisoners, setting up a system of visible punishment of long duration, meaning that prisoners should perform hard labor in public view. Now, this backfired because they took the crews out, and the public chastised the crews, and the crews yelled back at the public, so they changed the law. And the law was reversed and the solution became to add unremitted solitude to laborious employment, and to reform as well as to deter. It was further suggested that they should be hidden from the public, wear coarse clothes, eat inferior food, and do work of the hardest and most servile kind. Sounds very much like what is happening today.

The philosophies then generally promoted isolation, silence, and labor. In Massachusetts in the late 1820s, the theme was rejuvenation and uniformity in the name of punishment and reformation. They didn't call them boot camps, but the concept was not far off of that. In the 1830s, one observer who toured the northern prisons suggested of several of those prisons that, "The prisons are barbarous; the goal is not to make the prisoners better, just detain their malice instead; instead of being corrected, they are being rendered brutal." The rage in the mid-1800s was not only to have prisoners work, but to rent them out. They could not only reduce the cost to taxpayers, but make a profit for those so lucky or entrepreneurial [as] to use them. Again, not a concept that's unknown today. By the late

1850s, financial and philosophical concerns drew new innovations. Good time laws proliferated. Indeterminate sentences came into vogue; parole and parole boards came into being and, of course, [so did] probation.

So, skipping ahead and admitting 140 years of changes, what is different today? I am not sure—that may be the end of my speech. First, we remain a highly mobile society that espouses individual freedom, and, indeed, generally allows that freedom. We have become a legalistic society—certainly not a concept that is challengeable on the face of it—which engages in a process that challenges resources and undermines the public confidence that the criminal justice system can respond quickly and appropriately. We have become a society ingrained in the thought that someone else should take care of us. No longer do we join the posse to catch the bank robber; we complain about the ineffectiveness of the police because they did not stop the bank robber in the first place.

Our homogeneity is our success and our challenge. Our country, states, and communities have such diverse populations that homogeneity offers us both strength as a nation and as communities, but also provides major challenges in trying to accommodate. Our personal values conflict with many others, and the process to find common values can be challenging and tedious. We know people are fearful; we know that the media reports of violence exaggerate what may happen to us as Americans; but for those affected, the results are traumatic; and victimization is real, frightening, and clearly must be addressed. However, the political and rhetorical response is a Trojan horse.

I would like to borrow from a national columnist I read in the last couple of weeks. Ellen Goodman, of the *Boston Globe*, said, in talking about this issue of our response to crime in America is, "What are we afraid of? We're afraid of car-jacking, guns in schools, and eleven-year-olds throwing five-year-olds out of the window. And what's the political debate? Building prisons, 'three strikes and you're out' laws, and the death penalty." She asked, "What are we scared of? We're afraid of disintegrating communities and letting our kids roam the streets in a fearful manner." She said, "What is the dialogue? The death penalty and boot camps." And she goes on to say, "In our bewilderment we are looking for easy answers, and they are being provided with cynical abandon. Instead of leading, politicians are following. To even speak of crime prevention is to be labeled as soft." She goes on to say, "But the gap between fear and punishment is real. What will happen when getting tough doesn't make us safe? Will we get tougher? And when that doesn't make us safe? Will candidates run on the promise of implementing the death penalty with their own hands?" This is an interesting thought.

So, although many of the policies of colonial times and subsequent national criminal justice policies remain visible in our system today, the least changing of everything is the politics. Our communities seldom take responsibility for those who break their laws. Our politicians feed on campaign rhetoric, designed by consultants and pollsters to lean on attractive, simple, and inexpensive solutions. We lean heavily on out-of-sight and out-of-mind philosophy. We speak in generalizations, talking of a million inmates in prison, 10,000 new prisoners in this jurisdiction this year and X million dollars for this or that. And, we minimize what we really must do. What we really must do is what so many of you do, and what you have been doing for a long time.

Before I conclude with what I think we must do, I'd like to tell you one story. Not only are the prisons overcrowded, as I understand, but I was advised the other day by the head chaplain in the department of corrections, that heaven is getting a bit crowded too, to the point that St. Peter is personally reviewing each entrance into heaven these days. Recently, three candidates presented themselves to St. Peter for entrance. And he said to the three, "As crowded as we are, I must screen for individuals who are different and truly worthy. Your affiliation and the tasks you perform on Earth will influence my decision." The first candidate said, "Well, I belong to the ABA, and I sued many defendants, some of whom did something wrong." And St. Peter said, "That's not noteworthy. We already have too many attorneys in heaven. You must go down." The second candidate said, "I belong to the AMA, and I operated on many movie stars, and I gave them many of their good looks." And St. Peter said, "That's not worthy. We already have too many plastic surgeons and other doctors here in heaven. You must go down." And the third candidate said, "I belong to IARCA. And I spent twenty-five years trying to site community-based residential facilities." And St. Peter said, "You obviously have spent your time in hell on earth." And he opened the gate and let her in.

Now, here is my opinion on what we must do. In your case, more of the same. You have all resisted the rhetoric, and shown commitment to humanity and pragmatism, and demonstrated repeatedly that things do work. But the rhetoric is alive and well, or should I say persistent, divisive, and destructive. On Wednesday of this week, a group represented by former Attorney General William Barr held a press conference at the National Press Club in Washington, D.C. And here is a summation of their position (You must realize that former Attorney General Barr and I are not such good friends): "Our schools, streets, neighborhoods, and homes are unsafe, and crime is clearly the leading course of America's decaying social fabric. Yet there is an effective solution. Punishment is a proven deterrent of crime. And we need to enact tougher punishment policies which take the profit out of crime. The message here is unequivocal. Leniency is associated with higher crime rates; getting tough brings crime rates down. The bottom line, harsher attitudes towards crime make for a safer nation."

Sadly, this message in my opinion was sort of a, "Hallelujah, we're incarcerating increasingly large numbers of people," and quite honestly, I think we need to be treating the incarceration of millions of people with a great deal of concern, not with a great deal of self-righteousness. And I'm very saddened by that kind of message.

Secondly, I think we need to avoid the generalizations of numbers. The benefit of a successful case can be more powerful than the huge numbers of prisoners and the millions of dollars. We must learn the reverse of the Willie Hortons. We need to promote public knowledge of the many successes rather than the few failures. And I still feel sad and remiss that we keep talking about recidivism rates when we should be talking about success rates. Indeed, this conference with its focus on what works, with specific kinds of offenders is right on target. Instead of touting singular solutions for the crime problem, we must break the issue down into component parts. And by concentrating on what works with special offenders, we can maximize the impact of our interventions and avoid stereotypical solutions.

Thirdly, we need to continue to search for excellence, not only intuitively, but empirically. We must promote research into our actions and our programs. Again, this conference, a research conference, is right on target. It is critically important that we learn more about what we do. Our intuitions may be right, but for our gratification, as well as that of policy makers and the public, the more finite data we can bring to the table, the better. A technological world demands data-driven solutions.

Fourthly, we must educate the public and challenge the policymakers. Political activity is essential, not to win, but to keep our citizens rightfully informed. No matter how we interpret the crime statistics, and people are doing that many different ways these days, what we do know is that the fear of crime and victimization is real. And, as usual, a political recognition of crime is a purient issue to voters and the public, and results in political promises being translated into the law. "Three strikes and you are out" laws, locking up kids sooner and longer, hard time for armed crime, boot camps, no-frill prisons, 100,000 cops, and more death penalty are the results of this trend. Several years ago, a friend of mine who had injured his leg badly was told by a physician that his leg would have to be amputated, and he argued long about having that critical kind of operation. And finally, he reported for surgery, and a few hours after surgery was visited by the surgeon, who said, "I've got some bad news and some good news. The bad news is, we made a mistake and cut off the wrong leg. The good news is, we were able to repair and save the other one." Well, if we're unable to educate the public as to the real issues around crime and violence and incarceration and things that work, we, too, may end up amputating our good leg—the things that actually do work.

Fifthly, we must work to change the policies of our jurisdictions. We must work to give definition to titles like community corrections. Over the last several years, I have been extremely impressed with what law enforcement is doing with articulating in practice the title "community policing," and I think it is about time that we take the title of community corrections and be able to articulate it as concisely to the public and to our communities as we possibly can. It no longer is good enough for a state department of corrections to simply label something community corrections and not be able to articulate that in a way that makes sense to the general public. I think that we know many of the things we do, but do not translate them well, and we do not articulate them well. We must be able to provide the leadership where it is absent and articulate what the title means. We must work to bring our communities back to the point where inclusion of the offender and responsibility for him or her is more important than the physical banishment and exclusion of responsibility.

And finally, we must build upon our best practices and continue to search for new ones. We cannot fall into the trap of choosing between lenient and tough. We must concentrate our policies and our programs on what works best. We must continue to promote humaneness, hope, and compassion, over vindictiveness and rhetoric. IARCA and its members have a long history of putting compassion into practice, promoting humaneness, and dealing with many troubled and disadvantaged people. I enjoin you to put in practice what you have learned at this conference, and I enjoin you to continue to put into practice those things and those values that you have for so long. I consider it an absolute privilege to have been able to spend time with you, I thank you very much, and I thank the leadership of IARCA.

Keynote Speech: Alternatives to Imprisonment in Comparative Perspective

3

Dr. Kurt Neudek, LL.M.
Former Senior Officer
Centre for International Crime Prevention
Office for Drug, Alcohol and Crime Prevention
United Nations Office, Vienna, Austria
on behalf of Dr. Eduardo Vetere, Director of the Centre

As you are aware, the United Nations is, so to speak, a mirror of the world community in general and an attentive observer of the American scene, in particular, as well as its beneficiary. It is fully conscious that this country is a major player in the pioneering and exportation of alternatives to imprisonment. It is good to be speaking in a place where it can be seen that "this works!" and also that "more of this must work!"

The United Nations always has paid special attention to the treatment of offenders, both in and out of prison, starting with the Standard Minimum Rules for the treatment of prisoners, adopted by the First United Nations Crime Congress in 1955. The key document that deals with noncustodial measures is the Tokyo Rules. These are the result of global discussion and exchange of expertise and experience, initiated by the Asia and the Far East Institute for the Prevention of Crime and the Treatment of Offenders, which worked in close cooperation with experts from all parts of the world to develop standard minimum rules based on a common perception of and aspirations for good practice. The Rules were adopted by the Eighth United Nations Crime Congress and the United Nations General Assembly in 1990, recommending them for action at national, regional, and international levels. They are a useful tool to promote noncustodial measures in pursuit of better ways to protect society from crime by treating some offenders differently and to facilitate more effective reintegration of such offenders into society.

Unfortunately, despite efforts to decrease its use, imprisonment still remains the cornerstone of our present penal systems. Apart from the death penalty, it is considered the most severe form of punishment in most contemporary justice systems, and there is broad agreement about what offenses warrant imprisonment, for example, those involving serious danger to life, health, and well-being; large scale illicit drug-trafficking; economic crime, offenses against the environment; and offenses that endanger national security. Imprisonment is also considered to be necessary for certain repeat offenders whose response to alternatives has been demonstrated to be negative and who continue to offend. Yet, the disadvantages of imprisonment, both to the offender and to society, have been well documented. But for less serious offenses and for several special types of offenders, there is considerably less unanimity on whether imprisonment should be imposed. Imprisonment is now clearly seen as a most expensive sanction that has serious negative effects on the great majority of the inmates and their social situation. Additionally, although prison certainly can incapacitate, it does not seem to deter effectively. The problems inherent in the realities of the world faced by ex-offenders overwhelm any good intentions they might have and their ability to act on them.

These factors have led criminal justice agencies, nongovernmental organizations, and the United Nations to search for and promote noncustodial measures. The introduction of alternative sanctions has been one of the most important developments in justice practice in the last decades. It has meant looking at offenders, victims, the community, and sentencing in general in a totally different light. The United Nations policy in this particular field aims at promoting the use of noncustodial measures; involving local communities; balancing the rights of victims, offenders, and the public; and encouraging member states to adopt and use information about these noncustodial measures.

Given the importance of these matters, the Ninth United Nations Congress on the Prevention of Crime and the Treatment of Offenders, which was held in Cairo, Egypt, in April 1995, gave priority attention to noncustodial measures with a view to recommending their further action.

Use and Application of Noncustodial Measures

Noncustodial measures represent an important step in increasing the effectiveness of society's response to crime. They play a significant part in criminal justice in many different cultures and legal systems. Most penal sanctions imposed on convicted offenders are, in fact, noncustodial. One goal of the United Nations, therefore, is to emphasize the importance of noncustodial sanctions and measures themselves as a means of dealing with offenders.

Developing views around the world about the problems of imprisonment have led to increased interest in finding effective ways of helping offenders in the community without resorting to imprisonment. Doubts are increasing about whether imprisonment can rehabilitate offenders. It is often suggested that sending offenders to prison can turn them into worse criminals and that, for that reason, imprisonment should be reserved for the more serious and dangerous offenders. Imprisonment, which is itself a costly undertaking, brings with it other social costs. Prison overcrowding is a problem faced by many countries. In severely overcrowded prisons it can be impossible to train prisoners to lead law-abiding lives following their release.

Against this background, there is a growing belief that noncustodial sanctions and measures may constitute a better way, providing penalties that are proportionate to the offense committed by the offender and that carry greater possibilities for the rehabilitation and constructive reintegration of the offenders into society.

Noncustodial measures do not restrict offenders' liberty as imprisonment. They do not require offenders to leave their families or communities, relinquish their responsibilities or give up any employment they might have had. Nevertheless, offenders undergoing noncustodial measures may be subject to various conditions and requirements. In order to enforce a noncustodial measure, the appropriate authorities must have the power to require offenders to comply with certain conditions and to refrain from certain activities. To exercise this power, the authorities need to collect information on the actions and misbehavior of offenders. The authorities also have the power to modify or revoke the conditions during implementation of the sanctions or measures. Accordingly, the implementation of noncustodial measures to a certain extent is intrusive. Furthermore, noncompliance with the conditions imposed can have serious consequences for offenders, such as imprisonment. Safeguarding respect for human rights and human dignity requires that standards be set for the imposition and implementation of any restrictions and conditions.

There is a great variety in the political, economic, social and cultural conditions in the world; noncustodial measures should be formulated so as to be applicable in a wide range of legal systems and to help those systems in the promotion of fair and equitable use of community sanctions and measures. Noncustodial measures relate closely to life in the community. The potential for developing new ways of keeping offenders in the community is substantial. There is much scope for requiring offenders to make recompense to society in some way for their crimes. At the same time, offenders can undertake some form of rehabilitation that well could reduce the likelihood of their returning to crime.

Noncustodial measures are being used at both pretrial and trial stages (in other words, prior to a potential custodial sentence), and at a later stage (such as during a prison sentence). This is not the place to describe all of them in detail. These comments will focus on the ones most used, especially those which are the most promising, particularly community services. These remarks, however, will not refer to measures that can be applied during a prison sentence.

Courts have a range of alternatives open to them. The decision about which one or ones to use will depend not only on the offender's criminal and social/personal history and circumstances, but on the purpose of the sentence. The noncustodial measures can serve more than one purpose. It is helpful to think of them as a menu of choices from which the court can choose a balanced diet designed to promote health and redress nutritional deficiencies while being easy to prepare and economical to provide. For example, just as cheese provides protein and fat, supervision provides personal attention and restriction of activity.

Noncustodial Measures (pretrial stage)

Ensuring that the suspect returns to court is the purpose of bail. In some jurisdictions, it is understood as release pending trial. In others, it is understood as the posting of property as surety that a released person will appear in court at the appointed time. This is used in many countries (such as Uganda), but not in others (such as Sweden). Its primary drawback is that it can be discriminatory for poor suspects who cannot afford bail, or vice versa: it can give a privilege to the rich, which may give the impression that they can buy justice.

A successful return to court also may be achieved by asking the suspects to promise that they will return at the appointed time, and then releasing them on recognizance.

Noncustodial Measures (trial stage)

The purpose of some measures is to *discount criminal proceedings.* If the offense is not serious and public trial and a formal conviction are not, therefore, required on grounds of special or general prevention, the disposition can be made either by the court or by the prosecution. In the United Nations survey on the use of alternatives, Japan reported that the prosecutor has a considerable degree of discretion and a nonprosecution rate of 34.8 percent in cases concerning nontraffic offenses. Discontinuance of criminal proceedings includes diversion, which is generally used to deal with minor offenses. This provides the administrator of justice with additional means to deal with more serious offenses, thus saving human and financial resources.

Some measures are intended to *mark the offense*, to invest it with significance for both the offender and the public. This is achieved through verbal sanctions or penal warnings, and through declarations of guilt. This happens, for example, in Austria, Germany, the Netherlands, and Portugal.

The suspension of a sentence is another means whereby the offense can be marked. It is known by different legal terms, exists in the legislation of many countries, and is applied in most countries. Usually, it implies conviction and imposition of a sentence whose enforcement is suspended. The suspension is subject to compliance by the offender with certain conditions during a probationary period and to no further offense being committed. Developments in different countries show that suspension of a sentence or of its enforcement is a very effective and socially acceptable way of reducing imprisonment. In many cases, probation, consisting mainly of supervision in the community through casework, is imposed as a condition for a suspended sentence.

A simple and obvious purpose is to *restrict the offenders* in the, hope that restricting them will render them less likely to reoffend. This can be achieved by requiring them to stay within a certain area or premises, probably the place where they live. Violation may lead to detention. Observance generally is enforced through monitoring by the local police or probation service, or can be carried out electronically as far as the available facilities permit.

Restriction also can be achieved by requiring the offenders or suspects to report to the police or another agency at intervals, or a representative of the agency may make random checks to ensure that the persons are where they should be or are not where they should not be.

Electronic monitoring was introduced 1971 as an alternative to placement in a juvenile institution. Although it was presented as a way of reducing psychologically destructive detention and improving social integration, the objectives gradually changed. Currently, the principal objective is to provide a contribution to the solution of prison overcrowding. In addition, it costs less. Finally, it has elements of punishment because it intrudes into the offender's life. In the 1980s there was a real explosion in electronic monitoring projects. In 1990, they were established in all states in the United States, and there were between 10,000 and 20,000 people under daily electronic supervision.

From evaluation research, it is evident that most of the convicted offenders eligible for electronic monitoring have the same characteristics as prisoners, but in about half of the cases, and sometimes more, prison is avoided and overcrowding can be relieved. Electronic monitoring may be used in combination with other measures such as frequent contacts between staff and offender and urine tests to check on the use of drugs. The target group is changing from less serious to more serious offenders.

A very demanding intervention, whose aim is both *supervision and treatment*, is the intensive supervision program (ISP), which consists of a number of punishment and treatment elements carried out under the strict control and supervision of the probation service. This sanction is oriented towards a relatively high-risk category of offenders and has the following objectives: a more efficient use of scarce prison cells—a cheaper alternative to loss of liberty—the reduction of criminal behavior, the recovery from alcohol or drug addiction, and the administering of appropriate (sufficiently severe) sentences.

The supervision and treatment may include urine checks for drug and alcohol abuse and compulsory assistance and/or treatment on the basis of recognized needs and requirements such as counseling on finances, and for individual and/or family problems; victim awareness courses;

therapy in the case of drug, alcohol, or gambling addiction; education and training; and assistance in finding employment.

Conflict resolution, through the use of mediation and conciliation, is another useful alternative applied by the courts. Such measures exist in Canada, the United States, and in many European countries. They started in Ontario, Canada in 1974, and the practice quickly spread to the United States, where more than twenty states have similar projects at the moment, and subsequently, it spread to Europe. Mediation is based on two fundamental elements: a conciliatory meeting between the offender and his or her victim (or an offender and a victim of a different offender), organized by a supervisor from a criminal justice agency such as the probation service, or someone delegated to do so by the court, and some form of restitution. This may be financial, or it may be a contribution of work (such as repair of damage caused by the offender). The principal objectives of mediation are as follows: to value the interests of the victim more effectively through the reparation of damage, to promote a real reconciliation between the offender and the victim, and to make the offender explicitly aware of the consequences of his or her offense.

The court's purpose may be the *imposition of economic sanctions* and monetary penalties, including a range of options such as a fine, compensatory payment, personal reparation, confiscation, and the Islamic *diyya*. Fines are the best known and most widely used form of monetary sanction. They save money and labor, and should be practical to manage and administer, although this is not necessarily the case. They are also humane, since they cause a minimum of social harm. They however, can create inequities by discriminating against the poor, for whom nonpayment often means imprisonment. This disadvantage can be overcome by imposing a day fine related to the offender's financial situation, by granting a postponement of payment, or by allowing the fine to be paid in installments. Day fines are widely used in European countries, where the fine has become the most important alternative for short-term prison sentences (usually a sentence of up to six months).

Compensatory payment as an independent sanction is applied in only a few countries, but the use of confiscation or forfeiture of personal property as an independent sanction appears to be expanding. This trend is encouraged by the 1988 United Nations Convention Against Illicit Traffic in Narcotic Drugs and Psychotropic Substances. Generally, however, confiscation of the property derived from or used in the offense is considered a penal measure, to be applied in addition to a sanction, and not as an independent penal sanction.

Restitution and compensation are included in sentence options in practically all countries. In Canada, about three-quarters of conditional sentences include compensation and/or unpaid work as special conditions. In most countries, restitution is seen as a supplement to another sentence. Mostly, compensation and restitution are handled as civil matters, even if in many jurisdictions they often are imposed by a criminal court.

Courts also can impose revisited military-style measures in their determination to oblige offenders to respect *discipline and conformance* and *to deter*. "Boot camps" are intended to do this. They are used for young adult offenders in the United States (the average length is three months' detention) and are followed by a period of intensive supervision. The first experiments were in the early 1980s; by 1991, there were already 34 boot camp prisons in 23 states containing a total of 4,000 convicted offenders. Their main objectives include deterrence (specific and general) by a shock experience, rehabilitation through a severe regime, and additional therapeutic programs, punishment, and making the prison system less expensive. Although the costs of boot camps are higher than imprisonment, due to the much shorter period of detention, they are cheaper in the end.

Great emphasis also is given to treatment, since up to 95 percent of the participants are drug addicted. Boot camps are the subject of much criticism because the system, based on a strong hierarchy, unquestioning obedience, submissiveness, strict discipline, and the development of an aggressive combative mentality, can be seen as preparing inmates for military operations rather than participation in ordinary society.

A quite different purpose of the court is met through the use of *indigenous practices*. In these, the responsibility for dealing with offenders is given to the indigenous community to which the offender belongs. This is a creative response on the part of the court in its search for something that works, and it can result in effective measures that simultaneously award value to a society that may be marginalized. For example, recently many newspapers worldwide reported a crime committed by two seventeen-year old juveniles in Canada. They had assaulted a pizza serviceman and robbed him of $50. As they were Indians, the court decided to give responsibility for action to their tribe, the Tlingits. The elders of the tribe sentenced the two juveniles to exile on separate islands for eighteen months. Each of them was to be accompanied for the first week by an older man who would teach him how to survive, and they were each to be given a dog for protection against bears. The offenders agreed to this, stating that they preferred this to the three to five year prison sentence that might otherwise have been imposed.

In New Zealand, Maori communities are increasingly involved with Maori offenders, many of whom have become dislocated from their original community, been drawn into the Pakeha (white European) cities, and have become involved with crime. The Maori elders are involved with criminal justice agencies in identifying those who might wish to join Maraes (centers of Maori culture) and in encouraging them to do so.

In many cultures worldwide, there may be many traditional ways of dealing with offenders and, whenever possible and appropriate, they also should be considered when alternatives to imprisonment are discussed.

Community Service: A Most Promising Measure

Community service can be chosen by courts for a variety of reasons. Unlike the sanctions outlined previously, community service combines several purposes. In particular, these can include the *reintegration of the offender into the community, the expenditure of purposeful effort on the part of the offender, close supervision by a supervisor, and the acquisition of work and social skills.*

This form of penal sanction, known for over a century as a substitute for fine-default detention or even earlier as a substitute for imprisonment in traditional societies (as reported by Nigeria for the last United Nations' survey), constitutes a very promising alternative to imprisonment. In its contemporary form, it was started in the United States in 1966 in Alameda County (CA) as a penalty for traffic offenses. This penalty has now spread over the whole of the United States but is mainly used for so-called "white collar" criminals, for juvenile delinquents, and for nonserious crimes. As a result of this, the sanction is used primarily as a supplement to other sentences and only rarely as a sentence in itself. This is unlike Europe where community service is imposed more frequently as an independent sanction.

In a large number of European countries, community service has become a frequently used sentence. Originally, it was introduced nationwide in England and Wales in 1975 and in Scotland in 1978. Since then, a number of countries either have introduced it in their legislation (for example, Germany, France, Ireland, Northern Ireland, and Portugal) or are undertaking experiments with it with a view to introducing it (such as in Finland).

As is well known, its essence lies in the fact that an offender is sentenced to perform a certain number of hours—often between 40 and 240 hours—of unpaid work for the benefit of the community. The results appear to indicate that the imposition of many more hours than the maximum period of 240 hours only leads to more failures. In this connection, if community service is to be used for more serious crimes, this sanction should be in the form of a package of alternatives.

In most countries, community service is intended to be a substitute for imprisonment of up to six months. The sentence, therefore, is used as a punishment for offenses considered to be in the middle range of criminality. The United Nations' survey on the use of alternatives showed that, insofar as noncustodial measures were applicable at all, none of the statutory or experimental regulations excluded particular offenses or offenders, in principle, from community service. In some countries, however, for example, Denmark, provisional reservations were made for certain offenses, such as drunken driving. In France and Switzerland, offenders, such as drug addicts or multiple recidivists, were unlikely to receive a community service sentence. In some countries, such a Denmark, the Netherlands, and Norway, community service only could be imposed for short-term imprisonment.

In a number of countries, community service can be used for fine defaulters. In England and Wales, 16,659 fine defaulters (about 25 percent of those who received that sentence) were received into prison service establishments during 1990 (Home Office 1991); from 1981 to 1986 about 30,000 persons experienced this type of incarceration every year in the (former) Federal Republic of Germany (Heinz, 1989: 208); and in Canada, in the period 1990 to 1991, more than 40,00 persons were incarcerated for nonpayment of fines (Canadian Centre for Justice Statistics, 1993: 104-105). These figures show that large numbers of offenders are implicated when there is an opportunity to serve a community sentence instead of going to prison. The legislative provision for that exists in several American States, in Germany, and in several Canadian provinces.

Evaluation research from such a program in Quebec (Landreville, 1994) shows the positive effect of this provision in terms of justice, equability, and humanity, but points to the fact that financial savings do not match up to expectations. German evaluation research (Jehle, Feuerhelm and Block, 1990), which describes the limits of the use of community sanctions, also underlines their general positive effect. After interviews with procurers, employees of organizations, and fine-defaulters, researchers concluded that the system works.

Community service orders are used in several African countries. With strong support from Penal Reform International, a nongovernmental organization that provides government officials with relevant information and runs training courses, this alternative was introduced in Zimbabwe in 1992, where it can replace a prison sentence of up to twelve months. In South Africa and Swaziland, community service is part of the legal system.

One of the advantages of community service lies in the fact that it gives offenders an opportunity to make amends by working for the well-being of others and simultaneously makes it possible for the community to contribute actively to the integration of those offenders into society. It also provides an opportunity to educate offenders in social relations. That may be a reason that this kind of sentence (either as a principal sentence or as a substitute for short-term imprisonment in the form of a condition attached to a suspended or conditional release) is practiced—according to the last United Nations survey on alternatives—in Australia, Germany, Israel, Kuwait, Luxembourg, the Netherlands, New Zealand, Portugal, Sri Lanka, and the United States. While it has been introduced in recent years in other countries, it is in the experimental stage.

Target Groups of Offenders

Some main objectives must remain clearly in sight; that is, promotion of public safety by treating some offenders differently and the reduction of the prison population, but which offenders should be targeted? And for what reason?

There are several groups that spring to mind. One is those who are unsentenced, forming a large percentage—up to 80 to 90 percent in some places—of the national prison populations. Many of these will not be found guilty, and of those who are, many will not receive custodial sentences. Indeed, by the time of their trial, some of them will have completed what amounts to months of imprisonment even though they never have been sentenced. This is "lost" time, which cannot be recovered. This unsatisfactory and indefensible situation exists mainly because of the bottleneck in court processes and procedures. These people who are waiting do not need alternatives or prison, they need faster access to court.

Another obvious group is the severely mentally disordered offenders. They are usually in prisons (where this type of offender should not be) because beds can be found, with difficulty; but beds cannot be found for them in special hospitals (where they should be). Decisions about where these offenders go depend on where beds are available. No one wants the offender to be in a prison. Providing more beds in special hospitals costs more than providing prison places because of the dual needs for particularly high security and specialist treatment, but that is what is needed.

Another group includes those with long sentences, for it is they who take up the most places for the most time and who experience the most personal damage. Some of those who are locked up are of no danger to the public although they committed a violent offense. For example, few domestic murderers will kill a second time. They never again will be in the situation and relationship that led to the murder—no one else is at risk. Should they be a target group for noncustodial measures, once they have demonstrated some years of steady behavior in custody? Many of them and others with long sentences tend to be more mature and sensible in prison and often have a much more substantial stake in the community than those who repeatedly commit offenses.

But it is usually regular thieves, vandals, and those who commit crimes in pursuit of or under the influence of drugs and alcohol who are at the "in/out" border of the decision-making continuum. Some prosecutors and courts keep them out; others put them in. These are the people whom the criminal justice system finds it hard to agree on, and it is they who are usually the subjects of noncustodial court orders at present and who are the most likely to benefit from the increased and varied range of alternatives that are envisaged.

The factors in decision-making about "in/out," or regarding which of the "out" options to use, must rely on information about the offender (previous offending, personal circumstances such as relationships, employment, home) and circumstances of the present offense(s), considered within the framework of the sentencing guidelines. Most of the necessary information is provided by a team of social workers, probation officers, schools, employers, the police, and doctors. Sophisticated diagnostic measures have been developed and used that chart and interpret data on, for example, the number of convictions as a juvenile/adult, drug use as a juvenile/adult, single/living with a partner, whether employed or not, and so forth. These are helpful to courts now, and would be of increased importance when a wider range of alternatives exists.

Risk and dangerousness are hardest to predict. Information about personal circumstances is an indicator, but it can lead into the controversial and difficult territory of equality, fairness, and consistency. The criminal justice system cannot be blamed for society's prejudices and divisions, but it can contribute to reinforcing them. Obviously, any system that is discriminatory, whether in terms of gender, race, or age, is wrong. It is already the case that minority groups and those who are socially disadvantaged are underrepresented in noncustodial sentences. New measures, therefore, should be carefully designed and researched to prevent this from happening.

The assessment of offenders' needs is an easier task. In many cases, the needs are only too clear. There is often existing documentation and visible evidence of mental illness, social dysfunction, illiteracy, physical disability, and/or drug and alcohol abuse. The extent of these can be measured through existing tests, but measurement is simple compared to the task of providing the means to heal what needs healing and of ensuring that the offender benefits from it. Many offenders have been in and out of drug treatment units, mental hospitals, special schools, and life skills classes already. It is the provision and takeup of continuous treatment that has failed, not the diagnosis. The challenge is to improve access to resources and ensure participation, not to replace what exists now.

In the case of early release from prison, in principle, the same techniques can be applied. However, the prediction of risk is likely to remain problematical, whenever decisions are made about home leaves, parole, and moves to less secure accommodation. It is impossible to make decisions that are 100 percent correct without reducing the eligibility for such privileges to a bare minimum.

Degree and Type of Control

As indicated, existing sanctions can be described as a continuum, with lengthy imprisonment warranted by serious offenses at one end and noncustodial or no attention for minor offenses at the other. The midpoint, or "in/out" divide, should be the result of planned policies, mechanisms, and options that enable it to be less rigid, but still definable and of crucial importance. When this happens, two things may occur: first, some offenders who currently avoid any sanction may find themselves being subject to some sort of attention (net-widening effect). Second, when noncustodial measures increase in quality and quantity, many of those who are subject to them will receive closer supervision than is the case at present. Their failures to conform will be detected quickly, necessitating a response that may or may not lead directly to imprisonment.

There are already offenders who say they prefer going to prison than serving a sentence in the community; or who prefer to complete their sentence in the prison rather than be released on license because they resent any type of control in the community, although they accept it in prison. They would rather have all or nothing. If they are eligible for non-custodial measures, should they be allowed to choose?

The degree of control that noncustodial measures lead to may be wider than that just within prisons and in the community because it reaches more people. Or, the degree of control can be narrower, because fewer people are imprisoned, even though those who avoid prison may experience more and different types of control in the community. Or the control can be looser, because the courts can be flexible in their specifications. Or it can be denser, because the level of supervision increases outside prisons and may exceed that of some prisons. The most important point is that the control afforded by noncustodial measures can be more sophisticated and less clumsy than the all-or-nothing situation it replaces. This is surely desirable.

Staff

The staffing involved in any introduction or expansion of noncustodial measures is one of the key issues. There is considerable impact on at least parts of the workload and responsibilities of existing staff involved in the criminal justice procedure—judges, magistrates, prosecutors, court staff, police officers, probation officers, and social workers. Administrative work increases. For example, there are more decisions to record, more fines to be collected, more agencies to liaise with, and more breaches and appeals with which to deal.

Qualified staff are needed to be responsible for administrating schemes, supervising offenders, and liaising with the courts. In particular, these need to be people with skills and experience not only in the crucial business of motivating and managing offenders, but in developing projects, seeking work, liaising with officers from various agencies and the community, advocating, and managing staff and finances.

The importance of these new staff should not be underestimated. They must be people who can create a balance between fairness and firmness, between care and control—the sort of people we already seek as police, probation, and prison officers. They need to have had or be prepared to undergo formal training in at least negotiation skills, supervisory skills, first aid, the prevention of suicide and self-harm, health and safety at work, race relations, and dealing with aggression.

Where are these people to be found? Where are they now? Are they already qualified and working in the justice or caring professions? The

Toyko Rules recommend using volunteers, and there are countries (notably Japan) where this works well. Volunteers clearly have a major contribution to make, but the time, commitment and energy demanded of them should not be underestimated. The Rules also state that volunteers should not replace professional, paid staff. They need to be screened, supervised, and supported as well as trained, and their motives have to be assessed. The motivation of some of them evaporates when it becomes clear that they have to deal with offenders who are absent or who misbehave and that they may find themselves as witnesses in court giving evidence against a convicted offender who they have come to know well and who lives close by. We must recognize that these staff are expected to handle people who already have committed offenses and/or have been disruptive, possibly on numerous occasions.

Supervisors working directly with offenders in the community become the translators of court policy, and this stretches beyond mere supervision. Supervisors bridge the gap between the court and the offender. On one side, they hold the interests of the court, on the other, the interests of the offender. In principle, both sets of interests are served when the court order is successfully completed. In practice, the situation is more subtle and more complex than this.

Supervisors are gatekeepers to the court. If an offender fails to arrive at his or her appointed workplace, or is often late, or puts in no effort, what is the supervisor to do? Does noncompliance mean an immediate return to court? Or, is there time for investigation, appeal, discussion, warnings, and so on? If so, what happens? Do offenders and the public lose faith in the use of alternatives and consider them to be a soft option? Clear rules and regulations in case of a breach of community order are needed.

The Role of Sentencing

As long as imprisonment remains the "normal" sanction for convicted offenders, and alternatives still are considered as conditions linked to the norm, it may be difficult to make progress. One impediment in changing this attitude is the lack of knowledge and understanding about noncustodial measures. Another is the fact that judges and magistrates feel that they have to give a public explanation as to why they are offering an offender a different option, and this may be met with considerable criticism from the very community that it is designed to benefit. In short, while the thinking behind noncustodial measures is that offenders should be integrated into the community, the people who live in the offender's neighborhood hold an entirely different view. If courts are to use these measures successfully, they need support as well as additional legislative provisions.

A bigger and better range of options open to courts, however, will not necessarily lead to the desired end product of fewer people out of prison and better community integration. Such options could be ignored or circumvented according to precedent, current practice, or even the whim of a prosecutor, judge, or magistrate. Essentially more options and mixtures of options should be available than now. In addition, decisionmakers should pay appropriate attention to the offender's individual situation, the purposes at sentencing, and the purposes of the sentence. The difference between the last two is important. The purpose at sentencing might be, for example, to incapacitate and deter, but the purpose of the sentence might be to provide drug treatment and reunite the offender with his or her family.

Most of the obstacles facing judges when deciding whether to give custodial or noncustodial sentences would disappear if it were clear to them and to those on whose behalf they act that prisons do not, and that noncustodial measures do, have the effect of rendering the offenders less likely to reoffend.

Why are noncustodial measures used rather infrequently by some judges in comparison to imprisonment? Is it that their wide-scale application creates tensions in the criminal justice systems? Do they cause the rank order of sanctions according to severity to become uncertain and diffuse? The use of noncustodial sanctions currently requires additional explanation and justification, thus reducing the court's ability to handle criminal cases routinely, a state of affairs that often is seen as desirable.

Another issue is that because prisons have been in existence for a long time (but only a few hundred years and less in developing countries), people are familiar with what they are and what they are supposed to do. In contrast, few people are yet familiar with what noncustodial sanctions are, not what they are supposed to do. All that is known is that they are noncustodial, in other words, what they are not. Information about them and attitudes towards them are inaccurate and confused in the eyes of many of the general public, including offenders and victims. Courts cannot ignore this fact.

It is evident that without adequate preparation on all fronts, in the courts, public debate, and practical arrangements, there will be a lack of confidence in the practice of noncustodial sanctions, even if there is an acceptance of their principles. It may be that judges are rather reluctant to make extensive use of noncustodial sanctions. Why is this? Is it because their legal training and education, selection process, and lack of specialization mean that, in professional terms, they tend to be conservative rather than innovative? Is it because there is a traditional belief that a correct decision should be reached by the strict application of legal provisions, although it is evident that this does not always result in consistent sentencing patterns? The use of alternative sanctions calls for additional intellectual efforts, since both the gravity of the offense and the personality of the offender must be examined equally in depth.

Judges cannot be blamed, of course, for the fact that noncustodial sanctions are not yet much used. Several important reasons have been discussed, most of which are outside the control of judges. The legislator has to create a legal framework with a clear policy and detailed regulations. There needs to be an optimum number of alternatives. The requirement of "lex certa" (that a law shall be exact, precise, and clear) may be in question if there are too many alternatives with varying levels of intensity of intervention. Effective supervision has to be established.

There certainly needs to be intensive cooperation among judges, prosecutors, and all agencies involved if there is to be an increased use of noncustodial sanctions. Enforcing compliance with the satisfactory completion of noncustodial court orders will have to rely on the skills of those in charge and the realistic expectation that most people, whether they are offenders or not, behave reasonably most of the time. If they do not and if they persist in refusing to do what they are supposed to do, or do what they are not supposed to do, action will have to be taken. The implementation procedures here may be quite specific; the response to breaches of court orders in the community may be immediate imprisonment, or they may allow the court to make a different choice, depending on circumstances. The Toyko Rules recommend that alternatives to imprisonment should be sought in the case of breaches of conditions, rather than automatic and immediate imprisonment.

Promotion

If noncustodial measures are to be used more than they are now, and further developed and used as a resource so that they are established and sustained as a mainstream and significant part of the criminal justice system, rather than remaining an extra that is bolted on at the edge, they must be promoted. But precisely what is to be promoted? To whom? And how?

The fact that noncustodial measures have several purposes does not make them easier to sell. They are not, for example, like a car whose rust-proof bodywork, reliable engine, central locking system, and CD player all can be delivered at the same time in a single product. Noncustodial measures may have a similar range of attractive features: they keep people out of prison; they benefit communities and offer redress to victims; they oblige offenders to do things; and they raise self esteem. But, unlike a car, they cannot do all these things simultaneously. Selling or promoting noncustodial measures to the public and to criminal justice personnel requires defining which measures are to serve which purposes, by which means, and to what end.

The thinking behind promotion has to be clear, and the public's main fears must be acknowledged, that is, if offenders stay out of prison, they may continue to rape, rob, vandalize and kill, and no one would be deterred or punished. Mass media are a tool that can support or damage this process. The level of fear should be reduced to demonstrate that many offenders are not dangerous; to give reassurance that mayhem will not occur; to show that reliable alternatives are already working; that the response to them is good in that court orders are and will be successfully completed; that breaches are not ignored; and that the cost and size of the prison estate is reduced.

At present, people tend to feel safer because offenders are locked away, and one result of the increased use of noncustodial measures will be that offenders become visible. This fact cannot be ignored and must be addressed. While people feel at risk, they will not be interested in potential cost savings. Most people accept the high cost of prisons without question, just as they accept the high cost of motorways and hospitals. The sums involved are too large to make sense of, and even if money is supposedly saved in one area, it is seldom seen to reappear to public advantage in another.

It is difficult to explain how decisions will be made as to who goes to prison and what happens to those who do not until precisely what is to be done, and how it is to be done, have been established. This is a priority. In particular, new legislative options and mechanisms need to be introduced to enable courts to impose different sanctions than the ones available to them at present.

It is useful to think of sanctions as a continuum that ranges from a sentence of life imprisonment at one end to an unconditional discharge at the other. Somewhere in the middle at an indeterminate point is the "in/out" divide, which was referred to earlier. This point is indeterminate because it cannot be justly determined, and it may be subject to the social, economic, and cultural conditions in a country. If a whole range of measures exists, some community-based and some prison-based, they could be applied concurrently or consecutively, depending on the circumstances. These circumstances would be based on the sort of criteria that are used now in sentencing based on the seriousness of the offense, promotion of the respect for law, justness, deterrence, prevention, incapacitation, protection of the public, resocialization, and the need for education and treatment. For example, a sentence might consist of a fine and two months of weekend imprisonment or attendance at a drug rehabilitation unit with an evening curfew.

The introduction of a range of noncustodial measures will not eliminate the differences in judges' decisions. Indeed, the concept of individualized and tailored sentencing increases the likelihood of difference. But legislative measures are the first step in opening up opportunities. Until the law permits and makes clear provision for the imposition of day fines, community service orders, attendance at treatment centers and so on, only limited progress can be made.

What is hoped for is not a tinkering at the edges of criminal justice sanctions, but a significant change. If legislation is needed, which it is, there will—and should be—public debate about what differences are occurring as the growth of alternatives takes effect. Such a debate should be welcomed with confidence, for the majority of the population will support the introduction of alternatives because they appreciate that, in the long run, they themselves will gain. Few of them will notice that money is not being spent on prisons, so noncustodial measures will have to be seen to benefit the community in quite tangible ways such as safer streets, the construction of local amenities, and successful mediation initiatives. Fewer people will support changed legislation that only benefits offenders.

Access to proper and sustained levels of funding is essential. The current expenditure on law and order is enormous. If we wish to promote noncustodial measures, we should be thinking in terms of diverting a substantial part of that enormous sum to alternatives to imprisonment. Discussion of noncustodial sanctions sometimes tends to underestimate the level of funding needed. It may be more useful, in this connection, to take our baseline from what we spend now, rather than from what we might spend if we were to start afresh. A better product then may be obtained for the same price.

For example, if a country were to introduce new forms of alternative sanctions, it would need a number of new staff in courts and new programs to service those who would not be in prison. There would be advertising and recruitment costs, training costs, pensions and sick pay, as well as salaries. Premises would be needed with offices, workshops, rostrums, canteens, equipment, resources, and fire alarm systems. Additionally, insurance policies and vehicles would be needed. It is not possible to guarantee that these would prove cheaper than prisons for the total costs of small-scale intensive care (including hospitalization) for a minority of offenders, a supervisory system for a large group, and comprehensive administration to supervise all those subject to noncustodial measures. Few countries will have explored the real costs involved in keeping large numbers of people out of prison, except in terms of anticipated per capita prison savings. This is an important part of successful preparation that requires attention.

Evaluation and Research

Deciding what to evaluate is one issue; how to do so is another. Put simply, if research showed 100 offenders who were given noncustodial alternatives completed them satisfactorily and were never convicted, what would be proven? One conclusion could be that those offenders had been given the wrong sentence. They may have needed nothing more than a caution. It might have been possible to identify them initially as highly unlikely to reoffend. Another difficulty facing researchers is the impossibility of creating control groups. However, there are several areas that seem ripe for research, and the Toyko Rules strongly promote research as a useful tool for planning and policymaking in this field, especially in regard to obstacles to progress.

Some statistics can be collated and analysed before the introduction of remedial measures, which predict what might happen. Other research can be carried out after alternatives have been introduced, identifying what does happen.

More research is needed about many issues. For example, how does the community respond to having offenders remain in the neighborhood? What do victims and offenders feel about that? Their families? The police? Have crime levels gone up, stayed the same, or gone down? If noncustodial measures were used more, which type of offenders might be affected, with what result? Have court orders been completed successfully? How many breaches occur? Do race and class make a difference in who goes to prison and who does not?

Other central points for research would be the effects alternatives have on the rate of recidivism, the question of who responds best to certain alternatives, and the problem of whether dangerousness can be predicted more accurately. Further, has the prison population gone down? Have plans for new prisons been abandoned? Have wings of prisons been closed down? What about costs? Have the expenditures on prisons gone down? How much have court expenses gone up? What about probation service costs? What is the cost of establishing all the new initiatives? The answer to these and other questions cannot be obtained without conducting scientific research capable of reaching findings that could be of great help in devising appropriate policies in this field.

Conclusion

When, a little more than 200 years ago in 1776, torture was formally abolished in Austria by Empress Maria Theresa, there was a strong negative reaction by the majority of justice officials. They considered a penal process impossible without the use of torture because they were afraid that they never would be able to discover the truth. The reaction may have been similar in Prussia, when Maria's counterpart, Frederic the Great, the old Fritz, did the same. Today, we look at this time with a mixture of consternation and disbelief. Nobody would advocate the reintroduction of torture. On the contrary, it has been outlawed by all countries, and the United Nations has declared it a crime under international law.

How will future generations look at our time, and at how easily we were ready to lock up our fellow human beings. The intention of this author is to stimulate imagination. Nobody realistically would argue for the total and immediate abolition of prisons today. But there is a large group of people in prisons with no real need to be there and who could serve their sentences in the community. Let us be aware that every day passed in prison without necessity is not only a lost day in the life of a human being, but is also a loss to society in terms of lost productivity, the severance of family ties, and the creation of broken homes.

Let us shift from the image of sanctions as a continuum to the image of sanctions as a suit of clothes. For the last few hundred years, metaphorically speaking, we have forced criminals to wear stigmatizing, heavy, constricting clothes to punish, control, prevent movement, and enforce conformity to society's requirements. We have discovered that these clothes are extremely expensive, that more and more people appear to need them, and that they deform those who wear them to such an extent that they usually become permanently damaged.

We now are trying to replace these clothes with better, more useful garments. If these are too light, of poor quality, ill fitting, or frivolous, they will be no better than the previous ones. But if we can make them so that they are reasonably comfortable, suitable for our and the wearer's purposes, and—most importantly—able to "give" a little when stretched, they will do well. The fabric, the thread, the seams and every fastening will be tested. We must expect this and prepare for it.

The United Nations is committed to the promotion of noncustodial measures. They serve the public better by contributing to social peace and treating offenders differently, while not disregarding public safety. This means working with offenders in a way that is less damaging and less expensive and that has the result of reducing the desire to commit crime.

It means creating new programs and projects, sustaining those that are working well, and learning from those that are not. It is clear that systems management and professionalism are the key issues. Getting these right requires the establishment of appropriate policies and procedures, proper funding, high-level multiagency planning and coordinating, as well as monitoring and evaluating.

There are difficulties in introducing and using alternatives to imprisonment. Some of these difficulties may be caused by the fact that our experience with this kind of sanction is rather recent, and we still have much to learn. These difficulties, however, do not argue against alternatives. On the contrary, they argue for intensifying our efforts and our readiness to learn. Other problems may be inherent in the use of alternative sanctions, but these may be less serious than those caused by the negative effects of imprisonment.

Aside from these difficulties and problems, we have good reasons to be optimistic: the considerable number of good experiences with alternative sanctions worldwide is the main reason, although time did not allow mention of all or even a sufficient number of them. Another important reason for optimism is the fact that there have been numerous legislative changes in many countries aimed at introducing alternatives. The last, but not the least, reason for us to keep our optimism is the growing awareness among the public and politicians of the need for alternatives. That optimism should be coupled with the strong commitment from all of you, whether you are professionals, experts, or volunteers, to continue promoting the application of alternatives to imprisonment all over the world, starting in your own community and extending such positive experience to other countries.

References

Bishop, N. 1988. Non-custodial Alternatives in Europe. *BEUNI Publication Series*. No. 14.

Canadian Centre for Justice Statistics. 1993. *Canada Statistics: Adult Correctional Services in Canada*. Ottawa: Canadian Centre for Justice Statistics.

Heinz, W. 1989. The Problems of Imprisonment Including Strategies that Might Be Employed to Minimize the Use of Custody. In R. Hood, ed. *Crime and Criminal Policy in Europe: Proceeding of the Second European Colloquium*. Oxford: Oxford Press.

Home Office. 1991. *Prison Statistics England and Wales*. London.

Jehle, J.; W. Feuerhelm, and P. Block. 1990. Community Service Instead of Imprisonment in Default of Payment of Fine. Summary of a research colloquium. Wiesbaden.

Joutsen, N., ed. 1988. Alternatives to Custodial Sanctions. *BEUNI Publication Series*. No. 15.

Junger-Tas, J. 1994. *Alternatives to Prison Sentences: Experiences and Developments*. Amsterdam-New York: Kugler Publications

Landreville, P. 1994. Compensatory Work Programme, A Way of Limiting Prison Use? The Quebec Experience. *The Howard Journal of Criminal Justice*. Vol. 33, No. 3, August.

Morris, N. and M. Tonry. 1990. *Between Prison and Probation: Intermediate Punishments in a Rational Sentencing System*. New York-Oxford: Oxford University Press.

Report of the Secretary General: Alternatives to Imprisonment and the Reduction of the Prison Population. A/CONF. 144/12. 28 May, 1990.

Section 3: What Works

Keynote Speech: What Works in Community Corrections: Promising Approaches in Reducing Criminal Behavior[1]

4

Paul Gendreau, Ph.D.
Director, Center for Criminal Justice Studies
University of New Brunswick at St. John
New Brunswick, Canada

There are four questions practitioners frequently ask. Let us address them each in order. First, "Is the 'nothing works' credo that Martinson proclaimed in the mid-seventies still alive and well in academia or in general?" Now, maybe this audience does not particularly care whether it is alive and well in academia (sometimes one wonders about academics themselves), but in any case, there has been a signal shift in the literature. In the "old days" it was very difficult to publish anything about the benefits of rehabilitation in the criminological literature; now it is not that

[1]Some of the material contained here was published in Gendreau, P. "The Principles of Effective Intervention with Offenders," in *Choosing Correctional Options That Work*, ed. Harland, pp. 120-129, 1994, by Sage Publications, Inc. Reprinted by Permission of Publisher, Sage Publications, Inc.

uncommon. Nevertheless, there are still some disconcerting signs. In an article in a recent major journal, one of the leading delinquency researchers quoted studies that showed no effect on recidivism and ignored studies that showed reductions in recidivism of 20 to 50 percent.

Is "nothing works" alive and well in the real world? Well, it depends on where you live. Currently, there is a strong belief that something works in this country (the United States). Unfortunately, it is a belief in the effectiveness of punishment. But in other western societies (and this is important to keep in mind when we talk about ethnocentrism later on as a barrier to knowing "what works"), there is still a fairly strong sentiment that rehabilitative programs can be successful and should be a part of the social fabric.

Let us turn to question number two. It is a particularly important question, and one that gets to the guts of the issue: "Are there effective treatments and how well do they work?" In answer to this question, considerable attention must be directed to conducting an appropriate assessment. What are the characteristics of offenders that best predict recidivism? What are the best measures to use in this regard? These are frequently asked questions by practitioners whether they work in prisons, parole, probation, or treatment program settings. When we get to the principles of effective treatment, it will be self-evident why knowledge of the foregoing has tremendous practical implications for designing an effective treatment program.

Recently, Tracy Little, Claire Goggin, and this author conducted a meta-analysis on the prediction of recidivism literature for adult offenders. To answer some of these questions, we collected all of the studies since 1970 that followed up offenders for at least a six-month period and examined what were the best predictors of recidivism. The data are reported in terms of correlations. Some selective comments on the data that is presented are in Table 1 (see p. 61).

First of all, we find, as expected, that static predictors (those predictors that are rooted in an individual's past and cannot be changed) such as criminal history are good predictors of recidivism. Rearing practices in the family, in other words, parents who provide minimal supervision of their children and inconsistently use punishment were also a reasonably strong predictor. The data on IQ is of interest, given the recent publication of *The Bell Curve* and its emphasis on this variable as the major predictor of criminal behavior. We have taken a very close look at intellectual functioning, which turns out to be, at best, a modest predictor of future criminal behavior.

Table 1. Predictors of Adult Offender Recidivism

Static Predictors	
Age	**.15**
Criminal History	
Adult	**.18**
Pre-adult	**.13**
Family Variables	
Criminality	**.12**
Rearing practices	**.15**
Structure	**.10**
Intellectual Functioning	**.07**
Race	**.13**
SES	**.06**
Mean	**.12**
Dynamic Predictors	
Antisocial Personality	**.18**
Companions	**.18**
Criminogenic Needs	**.18**
Interpersonal Conflict	**.15**
Personal Distress	**.05**
Social Achievement	**.15**
Substance Abuse	**.14**
Mean	**.13**

Socioeconomic status is an important variable when it comes to theories of crime. The traditional sociological theories of crime asserted that one's social class (parents' occupation, education) was a powerful predictor of criminal behavior. It is not. It is one of the weakest predictors.

Let us now turn to dynamic predictors. Dynamic factors are aspects of prison that can be changed through intervention. Heretofore, dynamic factors have been ignored in criminology (for the various reasons see Gendreau, Little, Goggin, 1996, p. 576). Antisocial personality is a strong predictor of criminal behavior as are criminal associates and criminogenic needs, which focus on attitudes, beliefs, and values that are supportive of rationalizations towards criminal behavior.

Here is an interesting one: personal distress. It illustrates why it is important to know what the best predictors are. For years, we have had treatment programs for offenders that have been based on treating an individual's anxiety, depression, and self-esteem. Personal distress is a marginal predictor of criminal behavior. Thus, it should come as no surprise that, upon examining treatment programs in the community that target personal distress, one finds minimal effects on recidivism.

Finally, other good predictors of recidivism are social achievements, which contains items on marital status, education, employment, and substance abuse. On average, dynamic predictors, taken as a group, predict criminal behavior as well as static predictors. This result is exceedingly important because we cannot change offenders' behavior unless we know which dynamic factors are predictive of reoffending.

Table 2. Recidivism Assessment Measures

Risk Scales	
Level of Supervision Inventory	**.35**
Salient Factor Scale	**.29**
Wisconsin	**.27**
Other	**.30**
Antisocial Personality	
MMPI Based	**.16**
Psychopathy Checklist	**.28**
Other	**.16**

Obviously, if you are setting up a treatment program, you will ask the question, "What assessment measure can I use?" Table 2 shows a number of measures that are available and the table shows how they compare. The Level of Supervision Inventory, (LSI) developed by Donald Andrews and James Bonta, is a standardized one-on-one interview that takes about forty-five minutes to do. It produces a correlation of .35, on average, with recidivism. The Salient Factor Scale, which has been widely used in parole in the United States, is typical of almost all of the kinds of risk scales that have been used to date. It is based on several items, most of which are static risk measures. It produces a significant correlation with recidivism, which is quite adequate, but not as good a measure as the LSI, which also includes dynamic factors.

Now, the following may be of more interest to psychologists in the audience who frequently assess the offenders using measures of antisocial personality. The MMPI, the most widely used psychological test, produces relatively weak correlations with recidivism. The best measure is the Psychopathy Checklist, developed by Robert Hare. Some claim this test is useful for predicting violent recidivism as psychopaths often are described as heartless, manipulative, narcissistic types who might be prone to such behavior.

Here are several suggestions for assessment. If we wish to get serious about assessing criminal behavior, a comprehensive assessment protocol that contains dynamic predictors is required. Only dynamic predictors are useful for monitoring the progress of offenders over a period of time because the predictors can change. That is, the offenders risk levels will change over time which, in turn, determines what level of supervision is required and how intense treatment services should be. Unfortunately, however, this author has been able to locate just five studies where anybody took the time to measure change in the risk level of an offender. The studies demonstrate that change scores predict offender recidivism very well. Even with brief six-month intervals, changes in recidivism ranged from 20 to 50 percent.

A recommended follow-up period is anything from one-to-three years. We have found, so far, that no one outcome measure is better than another. This author's personal preferences are reconviction or reincarceration. If anyone is interested in advancing knowledge in this field, which is so desperately needed, compare different existing measures, assess new promising measures, and generate data on special subgroups, such as female offenders and minority groups. Then, you really will be advancing the state-of-the-art knowledge.

We now address the third question: "What type of treatment strategies have been shown to reduce recidivism?" This information is based on three sources of knowledge: (1) years of this author's clinical experience and that of other people who have worked in the area, (2) meta-analytic techniques, a quantitative way of reviewing the literature, and (3) traditional narrative reviews.

Principles of Effective Intervention

(1) Intensive services should be behavioral in nature.

(a) Intensive services should occupy 40 to 70 percent of the offenders' time while in a program and be of three-to-nine months duration.

(b) Behavioral strategies are essential to effective service delivery.

Since practitioners often are confused about what is meant by the term "behavioral," what follows is a thumbnail sketch of behavioral program principles. Virtually all offender behavioral programs are based on the principles of operant conditioning. At the core of operant conditioning is the concept of reinforcement, which refers to the strengthening or increasing of a behavior so that it will continue to be performed in the future. The most efficient and ethically defensible way to achieve this goal is to use positive reinforcers (something prosocial the offender considers pleasant or desirable) and to ensure that reinforcers are contingent (contingency management) upon the behavior being enacted. In contrast, punishment, which is used much less frequently by behavioral therapists, attempts to weaken or suppress behavior by proving unpleasant or harmful consequences.

Three types of positive reinforcers are used to strengthen behavior. They may be tangible (money, material goods), or activities as reinforcers (shopping, engaging in sports, playing music, watching TV, socializing), or social reinforcers that consist of attention, praise, and approval. Behavior modifiers usually employ the last two types of reinforcers because they are natural consequences of a person's life. Positive reinforcers fit nicely into a powerful concept called the *Premack Principle*, which simply states that making a high probability behavior contingent upon a lower probability behavior will increase the latter. Social reinforcers are much preferred because they are cost-effective and require little effort to satisfy contingency management practices. Most programs will have a general menu of reinforcers, but also will try to individualize them, where possible.

There are many types of behavioral programs. The three described below are prevalent in the offender behavioral treatment literature. A well-designed program will employ at least two of the following, as each type overlaps to some degree with the other.

> **Token economies**—Reinforcement system for motivating offenders to perform prosocial behaviors. Tokens can be tangible or symbolic, such as points. They are most often used with groups.
>
> **Modeling**—Offenders observe other persons demonstrating a behavior from which they can benefit.
>
> **Cognitive-behavioral**—There are several "schools" of cognitive-behavioral therapy. At their fundamental level, they attempt to change the offenders' cognitions, attitudes, values, and expectations that maintain their antisocial behavior. Problem solving, reasoning, self-control, and self-instructional training are frequently used techniques. Cognitive therapists stress that a good therapeutic relationship (in other words, empathy, openness, and warmth) is necessary for effective cognitive therapy.

(2) Behavioral programs target the criminogenic needs of high-risk offenders.

Treatment is more effective when it is matched with offenders' risk level. Higher-risk offenders are much more likely to benefit from treatment than low-risk offenders. There are two types of risk, static and dynamic, and as we noted previously, dynamic risks must be the targets for intervention as they are changeable in nature.

This principle is founded on the notion that there can be potent interactions between the characteristics of individuals and their settings or situations. Practitioners must avoid the notion that programs should be limited to one treatment modality only, such as using only a token economy and ignoring all other behavioral strategies, and treating all offenders as if they all had identical personality traits, attitudes, and beliefs.

The principle of responsivity simply states that treatment programs should be delivered in a manner that facilitates learning new prosocial skills by the offender. Essentially, the responsivity principle is one of matching treatment x with offender-type x with x counselor style. The three components of responsivity are as follows:

(a) Match the treatment approach with the learning style and personality of the offender. As a case in point, offenders who prefer high degrees of structure or who are impulsive are likely to function better in programs such as graduated token economies, which initially provide considerable external control with concrete rules for appropriate behavior. Another example is that psychiatrically troubled offenders will perform more adequately in low-pressure, sheltered living environments.

(b) Match the characteristics of the offender with those of the therapist. For example, offenders who are more "anxious" respond best to therapists exhibiting higher levels of interpersonal sensitivity.

(c) Match the skills of the therapist with the type of program; for example, therapists who have a concrete conceptual level problem-solving style will function best in a program that is highly structured.

(4) Program contingencies/behavioral strategies are enforced in a firm but fair manner.

(a) Reinforcement contingencies must be under the control of the therapists.

(b) Staff, with meaningful input from offenders, design, maintain, and enforce contingencies.

(c) Positive reinforcers are used more than punishers by at least four to one.

(d) Internal controls, such as drug testing for substance abuse, are judiciously used to detect possible antisocial activities of the clientele.

(5) Therapists relate to offenders in interpersonally sensitive and constructive ways, and are trained and supervised appropriately.

This principle has all but been ignored in the "nothing works" debate. It initially was formulated in 1979 by Bob Ross and this author in the following questions: "To what extent do treatment personnel actually adhere to the principles and employ the techniques of therapy they purport to provide? To what extent are the treatment staff competent? How hard do they work? How much is treatment diluted in the correctional environment so that it becomes treatment in name only?" These ideas are essential components of what is called therapeutic integrity. Most of the exemplary studies noted previously make mention of some of the four criteria described below. Few studies that do not report reductions in recidivism ever comment in this regard.

(a) Therapists are selected on the basis of interpersonal skills that are associated with effective counseling. Some of these factors are clarity in communication, warmth, humor, openness, and the ability to relate affect to behavior and set appropriate limits. With these sorts of skills, counselors can be effective sources of reinforcement and can competently model prosocial skills.

(b) Therapists have at least an undergraduate degree or equivalent with training in the theories of criminal behavior and the prediction and treatment of criminal behavior.

(c) Therapists receive three-to-six months of formal and on-the-job/internship training in the application of behavioral interventions generally and specific to the program.

(d) Therapists are reassessed periodically on the quality of their service delivery.

(e) Therapists monitor offender change on intermediate targets of treatment.

(6) Therapists should design programs and activities.

Program structure and activities should be designed to disrupt the delinquency network by placing offenders in situations (people and places) where prosocial activities predominate.

(7) Relapse prevention in the community is necessary.

Relapse prevention is a strategy that originated in the alcoholism field and has begun to be adapted to offender populations, such as sex offenders. It is essentially an "outpatient" model of service delivery that is applied after the offender has completed the formal phase of a treatment program, be it in a prison (before release) or in a community residential center. The stages of relapse prevention include the following:

(a) Plan and rehearse alternative prosocial responses

(b) Monitor and anticipate problem situations

(c) Practice new prosocial behaviors in increasingly difficult situations and reward improved competencies

(d) Train significant others such as family and friends to provide reinforcement for prosocial behavior

(e) Provide booster sessions to offenders after they have completed the formal phase of treatment.

(8) Provide a high level of advocacy and brokerage as long as the community agency offers appropriate services.

Where possible, it is desirable to refer offenders to community-based services that provide quality services applicable to offenders and their problems. Therefore, it is vital that community services be assessed in this light in as objective a manner as possible using a measure such as the Corrections Program Assessment Inventory (CPAI), which was designed by Donald Andrews and this author. The reality, regrettably, is that many programs are lacking in most of these effective components. As a case in point, a recent survey of 112 offender substance-abuse programs using the CPAI reported that only 10 percent of the programs had programmatic elements that would indicate an effective service was being provided. An identical result, again using the CPAI, was found for a similar number of juvenile offender programs.

Principles of Ineffective Intervention

The first three principles of ineffective interventions are grounded in therapeutic approaches that have little in common with or are antagonistic to behavioral methods.

(1) Traditional "Freudian" psychodynamic and "Rogerian" nondirective or client-centered therapies

Offender treatment programs that have been based on these two approaches have emphasized the following processes:

(a) "Talking" cures

(b) Good relationship with client as the primary goal

(c) Unraveling the unconscious and gaining insight

(d) Fostering positive self-regard

(e) Self-actualization through self-discovery

(f) Externalizing blame to parents, and society

(g) Ventilating anger

(2) "Medical Model" approaches

(a) Change in diet

(b) Plastic surgery

(c) Pharmacological interventions, such as testosterone suppressants

(3) Subcultural and labeling approaches

These approaches stem from the sociological theoretical perspectives of these names. Subcultural theory emphasizes respecting the offenders' culture and "doing good for the disadvantaged" by providing access to legitimate opportunities. Labeling theory operates on the principle that the criminal justice system stigmatizes youth, and, therefore, offenders should be diverted from the system.

Neither approach favors behavioral-style interventions for offenders. If a program must be offered, nondirective therapies are preferred and, in the case of labeling theory, sanctions such as restitution are considered to be worthwhile alternatives.

(4) Programs, including behavioral ones, that target low-risk offenders

(5) Programs, including behavioral ones, that target factors that are weak predictors of criminal behavior, such as anxiety and depression

(6) "Punishing smarter" strategies

The so-called "punishing smarter" strategies became popular in community corrections in the mid-1980s. In one classic quote of the time, an official of the State of Georgia said, "We are in the business of increasing the heat on probationers . . . satisfying the public's demand for just punishment . . . criminals must be punished for their misdeeds" (Cf. Gendreau, et al. 1993, p. 23). The programs that resulted are commonly known as ISPs, or intensive probation supervision. ISPs contain some or all of the following components:

(a) Greatly increasing contact between supervisors and offenders

(b) Home confinement

(c) Frequent drug testing

(d) Restitution

(e) Electronic monitoring

(f) Shock incarceration

(g) Boot camps

Since "punishing smarter" strategies have become so popular in the United States—they are not in other comparable Western societies, which is an interesting question in itself—the following data will be of interest. Tracy Little and this author completed a preliminary meta-analysis of the "punishing smarter" literature. The analysis consisted of 174 comparisons between a "punishment" group and a control group. We found that these programs produced, on average, a slight 2 percent increase in recidivism.

Indeed, of the entire "punishing smarter" literature, only two studies have been found that reported reductions in recidivism of more than 20 percent. Both were in New Jersey; one was evaluated by Frank Pearson and the other was Mario Paparozzi's Bureau of Parole program (cf. Gendreau, Paparozzi, Little, and Goddard, 1993). Their distinguishing feature is that each attempted to provide as much treatment services as possible. The Bureau of Parole evaluation is of particular interest because it used a carefully chosen matched control group. In addition, this program deliberately targeted high-risk offenders, provided significantly more treatment services to the ISP than the regular probation control group, and examined the quality of implementation of the program and probation officer supervision style. Unfortunately, the quality of services provided in either New Jersey program is unknown.

The matter of why punishment and "punishing smarter" programs have been failures can be found in Gendreau (1996a). The information can be located in three separate sets of literature that go back approximately 30 years and contain approximately 25,000 references. They are the animal and human experimental learning literature, the human behavior modification literature, and the social-psychological literature on resistance processes in attitude change and literature on how to influence behavior. How this literature came to be ignored is illustrated later.

The fourth most commonly asked question arises, in part, from exasperated practitioners who ask, "How can you coerce offenders into a program, if they do not want to be there in the first place?" On the one hand, practitioners worry about any kind of coercion. If you are a licensed professional, you must be concerned about how much you can force a person into a program. On the other hand, if a person is a high-risk sexual offender, should you be upset that an offender is coerced into a program before being released into the community? So, this author along with one of his students, Helen Gray, presently is examining those programs that were successful in reducing recidivism, and trying to see if the element of coercion had any role to play. By and large, what we seem to be getting, and the analysis has not been completed, is that coercing an offender into a program has virtually no effect on recidivism.

Please remember that if you have a program that has enough positive reinforcers, the program really involves an offender's time, and is challenging, then you will find that offenders who were initially unwilling can become very highly motivated.

Question number five is actually two questions: "How can we establish some effective programs? What are the types of barriers we have to overcome?" There is some depressing news here. There are no pat solutions. Lately, this author has been trying to identify some of the barriers to an effective rehabilitation agenda. The first is called theoreticism.

What *theoreticism* means is that you reject knowledge on the basis of your personal values and experiences. One example of theoreticism is the 25,000 relevant studies on punishment never quoted in all of the "punishing smarter" literature. This happens through the technique of theoreticism. When you have people parading evidence that supports a "cause," watch out for theoreticism. It occurs time and again. Always ask, "Does the information being presented come from well-controlled experiments and data bases?" Is the entire literature being reviewed?

There are other aspects to this problem of theoreticism. One is paradigm passion. Think about how you have been trained, likely by very few people. The people you associate with in your training program generally all have similar views. Paradigm passion results; you think that your way of looking at a problem is the only way.

Paradigm passion can contribute to ethnocentrism, which is the belief that one's culture, setting, and so forth, is somehow superior to another. What we have is a massive dose of ethnocentrism at the policy-making level in American criminal justice. Yet, if one travels a little bit, reads broadly, and questions one's sociopolitical ideological boundaries, then public policy will be better informed.

The MBA management syndrome is also a very serious problem. What we have witnessed over the years in the criminal justice area is the involvement of a new generation of high-level corrections administrators, who are generalists with little or no training in the helping professions. Certainly, they appear to have little knowledge about the prediction/treatment of criminal behavior. What are the primary qualifications of this new generation of MBA management syndrome correctional administrators? They probably have some experience as administrators. It also does not help if they are political hacks or appointees. Even if you come across a few administrators who are aware of the correctional literature, they often do not stay in their jobs for long. In the old days (it is a problem looking back to the old days, because you look at it through rose-colored glasses), we used to see people who actually were trained in their area and stayed in the job for more than two years. What did you see then? You saw systems that had some degree of continuity, rationality, and integrity.

This whole "nothing works" credo, by the way, has encouraged the development of the MBA management syndrome. If "nothing works," then what is there to know? Minimal training is necessary. I live on the ocean. I consider myself reasonably well-educated. I notice that we have a lot of fin-backed whales and seals near where I live. I think I will approach our

Premier and just say, "Frank, I'm tired of working in corrections; I certainly can tell the difference between a seal and a fin-backed whale (a fin-backed grows up to be 80 feet and weighs 15,000 tons). Could I have a posting as a senior administrator in the fisheries department on a nice island?" That would be a pleasant change of life style.

What is the consequence of all this? We have ended up with some correctional systems that are basically fraudulent, because the leadership is content-free. They are just floating around grasping at any panacea that comes about which is why a lot of faddish ideas occur in the criminal justice area. Think of it this way: Would you like the health care system to operate on the same principles? What is needed is a citizen revolt that says, "Look, we want people who play significant roles in generating corrections policy in our country to be trained and knowledgeable. Is that too much to ask?"

A separate issue is that of technology transfer. This means, can we get the information into the hands of the people who need it? There is substantial literature on technology transfer that points to some very useful principles of "what works." How do we accomplish this? It means endless presentations at conferences like this. It means writing for periodicals that are not in the usual academic stream. It means dealing with the media in a constructive way. It means lobbying with politicians. Now, that is not easy to do; it is time consuming; we all have jobs and lives to lead. But, if you are able to do some of that, you can have a pronounced effect.

The final issue concerns training. Regrettably, there are almost no training programs around. When this author looked at psychology departments in the United States, he could find about four at most that provided training in the treatment and prediction of criminal behavior. Things are a little better in Canada. We have about three or four major programs. Vern Quinsey, one of the speakers at this conference, is one of the leaders in Canada regarding developing this type of venture. However, if you are able to set up a few training venues, some immediate results will occur. In fairly short order, the graduates of these programs will produce a tangible effect on how we think about corrections and how services are delivered.

In summary, this has been a brief outline of the kinds of assessment strategies and treatment programs that work, and some barriers to implementation. Programs that are of high quality, that use most of the principles that were outlined previously, depending on the setting, will reduce recidivism from 10 to 60 percent. Programs that are based on the principles of what does not work are rarely effective.

Now, for a final sobering fact: What percentage of programs out in the real world meet the criteria of high quality? Our surveys, based on the CPAI, indicate about 10 to 20 percent. Does this mean we should just give up, as some criminologists argue? Definitely not! This author always is impressed with the number of hard-working, well-meaning people out there who are trying to provide services for offenders, and the fact that they are desirous of improving their skills. So, even though the quantity of high- quality programs is lacking at the present time, the situation can and will improve.

Selected References

Cullen, F. T., P. Gendreau, G. R. Jarjoura, and J. P. Wright. 1997. Crime and the Bell Curve: Lessons from Intelligent Criminology. *Crime and Delinquency*. 43: 387-411.

Gendreau, P. 1996a. The Principles of Effective Intervention with Offenders. In A. T. Harland, ed. *Choosing Correctional Options that Work: Defining the Demand and Evaluating the Supply*. Thousand Oaks, California: Sage.

———. 1996b. The Rehabilitation of Offenders: What We Know and What Has to Be Done. *Criminal Justice and Behavior*. 23: 144-161.

Gendreau, P. and C. Goggin. 1997. Correctional Treatment: Accomplishments and Realities. In P. Van Voorhis, M. Braswell, and D. Lester, eds. *Correctional Counseling and Rehabilitation*, 3rd edition. Cincinnati, Ohio: Anderson.

Gendreau, P., C. Goggin, and M. Paparozzi. 1996. Principles of Effective Assessment for Community Corrections. *Federal Probation*. 60: 64-70.

Gendreau, P., T. Little, and C. Goggin. 1996. A Meta-analysis of the Predictors of Adult Offender Recidivism: What Works! *Criminology*. 31: 401-433.

Gendreau, P., M. Paparozzi, T. Little, and M. Goddard. 1993. Punishing Smarter: The Effectiveness of the New Generation of Alternative Sanctions. *Forum on Corrections Research*. 5: 31-34.

Community-based Treatment for Substance-abusing Offenders: Principles and Practice of Effective Service Delivery [1]

5

Michael L. Prendergast, Ph.D.

M. Douglas Anglin, Ph.D.

Jean Wellisch, Ph.D.

Drug Abuse Research Center
University of California, Los Angeles
Los Angeles, California

Introduction

It has been twenty years since Robert Martinson wrote regarding the effectiveness of correctional rehabilitation programs: "With few and isolated exceptions, the rehabilitative efforts that have been reported so far have had no appreciable effect on recidivism" (Martinson, 1974, p. 25). This sentence—or its simplified and popularized form of "nothing works"—signaled a retreat from previous efforts to develop a rehabilitation-oriented correctional system and gave support to correctional philosophies and popular attitudes that emphasized deterrence, retribution, and incapacitation.

Although Martinson examined a wide variety of approaches and programs intended to rehabilitate offenders and reduce recidivism, he did not include evaluations of drug and alcohol treatments for offenders in the body of studies on which he based his conclusions. Furthermore, most subsequent syntheses of the literature on correctional treatment also have excluded substance abuse treatment (for example, Andrews et al., 1990; Basta and Davidson, 1988; Garrett, 1985; Whitehead and Lab, 1989; a notable exception is Gendreau and Ross, 1987). Nevertheless, efforts to treat the substance abuse problems of offenders became tarred with the same brush of skepticism that developed around correctional rehabilitation generally.

In recent years, the pendulum has begun to return to a more rehabilitative orientation. In 1979, Martinson himself modified his earlier negative judgment of treatment and concluded more positively: "No treatment program now used in criminal justice is inherently either substantially helpful or harmful. The critical fact seems to be the conditions under which the program is delivered" (Martinson, 1979, p. 254). Subsequent reviews and meta-analyses generally have concluded that correctional treatment programs do produce positive results (see prior references). The movement back toward correctional rehabilitation also has been influenced by the consequences resulting from the policy of deterrence, retribution, and incapacitation—high incarceration rates and high criminal justice costs. (The popularity among the public and politicians for "three-strikes" laws, however, should dampen any overoptimism about the likelihood of the pendulum swinging far in the rehabilitation direction.) At the same time, as will be noted, research studies show the effectiveness of alcohol and drug treatment programs for offenders.

Numerous studies have documented the large number of crimes committed by drug-dependent offenders, particularly those who use drugs daily or near daily. A consistent finding is that as levels of drug use decline, so also does criminal activity (Chaiken, 1986; Chaiken and Chaiken, 1982; Inciardi, 1979; Johnson and Wish, 1986; Nurco, Kinlock, and Hanlon, 1990; Speckart and Anglin, 1986). Not all crimes committed by drug-involved offenders, however, are related directly to their drug use; for these offenders, whose criminal careers generally began before their heavy involvement in drugs, a certain fraction of their crime is independent of their drug use, and even if their drug use is brought under control, their criminal activity will continue, though usually at a reduced level.

Drug users are heavily involved in criminal activity; similarly, criminal offenders have high rates of drug use. In 1992, the National Institute of Justice's Drug Use Forecasting (DUF) program, which is conducted in twenty-four cities, found rates of illicit drug use among booked arrestees (determined by urine tests) ranging from 47 to 78 percent for men and from 44 to 85 percent for women. In virtually all the DUF cities, over half of the arrestees tested positive for a drug, mainly cocaine (National Institute of Justice, 1993). Self-report data from prison and jail inmates indicate similarly high levels of drug use (Beck et al., 1993; Harlow, 1991). Studies of recidivism have shown that one-third of probationers rearrested within a three-year period were arrested for a drug offense (Bureau of Justice Statistics, 1993). Not only do juvenile and adult arrestees have high rates of drug use, but juvenile and adult offenders who use drugs also have higher rates of felony arrests than do those who have not used drugs recently (Anglin and Speckart, 1988; Dembo, Williams, and Schmeidler, 1993). Thus, treating the substance abuse problems of juvenile and adult offenders is an important part of any overall strategy to reduce recidivism among the offender population.

A growing body of research, despite various methodological limitations, indicates that treatment for substance-abusing offenders can reduce substance use, criminal behavior, and recidivism, whether the offender enters treatment voluntarily or under some form of coercion (Anglin and Hser, 1990a, b; Falkin, Lipton, and Wexler, 1992; Leukefeld and Tims, 1992). As will be noted, however, much of the effectiveness of treatment in a specific program is dependent upon whether the treatment activities are implemented as intended and whether the program is well managed and adequately staffed.

Effective treatment for substance-abusing offenders must take into account the nature of alcohol and drug dependence. Dependence can be described as a complex psychological, behavioral, social, and physiological disorder with multiple causes. It is a chronic, relapsing condition embedded within a complex of dysfunctional and maladaptive behaviors and often within a social environment of poverty, violence, and distress (Lowinson, Ruiz, Millman, and Langrod, 1992). In both of the "official" diagnostic classification systems (DSM-IV and ICD-10), the symptoms of dependence include behaviors associated with compulsion, impaired capacity to control drug or alcohol use, a narrowing of attention on drug or alcohol use, and persistence in drug or alcohol use despite adverse consequences; in short, the persons are out of control in terms of their ability to stop or even moderate drug use.[2] There rarely exists a one-time "cure" that frees individuals from the compulsive, problematic use of alcohol or other drugs. Most dependent users cycle through periodic episodes of treatment and relapse. Even when they have stopped using drugs, the desire to use may remain strong, and a variety of both pleasant and adverse life events can trigger relapse (Tims and Leukefeld, 1986).

The chronic nature of substance abuse (and the behaviors associated with it) suggests that outcomes of the all-or-nothing variety (use/no use, rearrest/no rearrest, employed/not employed), which are often used in program evaluation studies, are inappropriate measures of the effectiveness of treatment. Instead, outcomes are more meaningfully and usefully measured in terms of relative reductions in addictive and criminal behaviors and relative improvements in socially productive behaviors and attitudes.

Swartz (1993) has suggested a number of outcomes, beyond rearrest or other recidivism measures alone, that would more adequately reflect the effects of community treatment programs on their clients: treatment retention, the intensity or rate of criminal behavior (by self-report), drug test results, the intensity or rate of drug use (by self-report), the length of time before rearrest, employability, and AIDS risk behaviors. Other measures would include physical and psychological health status, family reunification, educational status, and a stable living situation.

Offenders enter community-based programs in several ways. They may qualify for a diversion program that provides treatment in lieu of prosecution, with charges dropped upon successful completion of treatment. Treatment also may be a condition of probation. In a few states, offenders may enter civil commitment programs that include a brief stay of treatment-based incarceration followed by a lengthy period of community supervision combined with treatment. Some prison-based treatment programs are followed by treatment or aftercare in the community.

Generally, offenders enter community-based treatment under some degree of criminal justice mandate or pressure. Although offenders can and do enter treatment voluntarily, some degree of pressure from the criminal justice system, the child welfare system, or family members is likely to instigate or reinforce the offender's internal motivation. The types of treatment or intervention available for substance abuse range from minimal supervision (random urine testing with sanctions) to various types of education programs, to self-help groups, to outpatient programs of varying levels of intensity, and to residential programs or therapeutic communities.

The following discussion of community-based treatment for substance-abusing offenders first discusses research-based principles of effective treatment, then describes several specific practices or techniques that have been found to be effective, and finally examines issues concerning specific populations (juveniles, women, and racial/ethnic groups). Although the main focus of the discussion is on effective principles and practices within individual programs, a secondary theme is the importance of recognizing and promoting cooperation, linkages, and systems approaches among health care, drug abuse treatment, and criminal justice.

Principles of Effective Treatment

If substance abuse treatment within the criminal justice system is to avoid the "nothing works" mentality, then community-based programs that treat offenders need to adhere to principles that are based on sound research and clinical practice. Although the list is by no means exhaustive, the principles discussed next are those that have particular importance for the treatment and recovery process or that have received insufficient attention from treatment providers and policymakers. (For a discussion of effective strategies to treat substance-abusing offenders generally, see Anglin and Maugh, 1992).

1. Long Duration of Treatment

The chronic, relapsing nature of alcohol and drug dependence suggests that short-term interventions or treatments are likely to have minimal long-lasting effects on truly drug-related behavior. If it is true that drug addicts and alcoholics are never cured but are in a lifelong process of recovery, then various levels of support and (for offenders) supervision are needed over an extended period of time to reduce, and if possible eliminate, relapse.

Length of stay in treatment has been found to be an important factor in producing declines in drug use and criminal behavior across a variety of treatment modalities and settings (Anglin and Hser, 1990b; De Leon, 1991; Hubbard, Marsden, Rachal, et al., 1989; Simpson, Joe, Lehman, and Sells, 1986). Three months is generally thought to be the minimum length of stay required for any positive outcomes, and twelve to twenty-four months is needed to produce substantial and sustained behavioral change.

As the severity of the drug abuse problem increases, the minimum stay to produce positive outcome becomes longer. Although the importance of length of treatment has been consistently found for drug dependence, the results for alcoholism treatment (not specifically from studies of offender populations, however) are less definitive. In a comprehensive review of alcoholism treatment effectiveness studies, Miller and Hester (1986) found that longer terms of outpatient treatment for chronic alcoholics had modest or no advantages over shorter terms of treatment. Differences in the characteristics of alcoholics and drug addicts, in the severity of their addiction, and in their varying degrees of social support may account for the difference in findings regarding treatment length of alcohol and drug programs.

For many clients, treatment of long duration may be more important than intensity of services. Clients often need considerable time to break through denial about their substance abuse problem and to develop the motivation (however ambivalent) to participate actively in program activities that help achieve sobriety and maintain recovery; time is also needed for the initiation and reinforcement of successive iterations of desired change. It is important to emphasize that positive outcomes are not dependent merely on the amount of time that the client spends in treatment. Something must happen during that time that addresses the needs of the client. There is some evidence (McLellan, Arndt, Metzger, Woody, and O'Brien, 1993) that client improvement is dependent on the frequency and variety of services, which have the effect of retaining clients in treatment and addressing the variety of problems they present. The importance of duration should not be thought of merely within the context of a specific program; a person may need to undergo a number of treatment episodes, possibly of different types or different intensities, before achieving a consistent pattern of recovery.

Most publicly funded treatment programs do not provide (or, more precisely, do not receive funding to provide) treatment of sufficient duration to bring about lasting change in the substance use and criminal behavior of those clients with severe substance abuse problems. As long as the focus of treatment services remains at the level of specific programs, it is difficult to provide the types of intervention and supervision needed to deal with the chronic, relapsing nature of substance abuse. If, however, the focus is shifted from the program to the system level, a greater range of options becomes available and a greater likelihood of success becomes possible. This systems approach is developed further under the principles of continuity of care and linkages.

2. Repeated Assessment of Clients and Staged Delivery of Needed Services

A comprehensive treatment strategy requires that a range of approaches and services be provided at appropriate levels of intensity to promote recovery from substance abuse. Careful consideration also needs to be given to the assessment and staged delivery of services so that clients receive appropriate services and are not overwhelmed or not prepared to avail themselves of the services, but rather are able to make use of them when they are ready. Although such a staged approach recognizes the shifting needs of the client over time, it also allows for more cost effective use of services.

A recent nationwide survey of drug treatment programs for women offenders (Wellisch, Prendergast, and Anglin, 1994) found that while most programs did conduct needs assessments of their clients in a variety of areas, few used standardized instruments that had been tested for validity and reliability, relying instead on an intake interview and client observation. Since the survey covered programs that served women only as well as programs for men and women (but had women-specific services), it is likely that the findings apply to drug treatment programs for offenders generally.

A number of instruments are available for assessing the substance abuse and other problems of clients. The most widely used instrument for assessing drug abuse is the Addiction Severity Index, which has been established as a valid instrument for assessing the problems of substance abusers and for matching clients to appropriate treatment (McLellan et al., 1985). It permits trained clinic staff to calculate severity scores in seven areas: medical status, employment/support, alcohol, drug, legal, family/social relationships, and psychiatric status. Although the ASI was originally developed for a general addict population, its creators have established norms for men and women within criminal justice populations. In addition, the ASI has been translated into ten languages.

Another assessment instrument is the Offender Profile Index (OPI), which was developed specifically to match offenders with appropriate treatment in community-based settings (Inciardi, McBride, and Weinman, 1993; McBride and Inciardi, 1993). The initial evaluation of the OPI did not establish significant differences between clients assigned using the OPI and those assigned using other methods of treatment assignment. But interviews with judges and probation officers indicated a high level of acceptance of the OPI; it was viewed as "a reasonable, objective, easy to use initial classification approach based on indicators that were commonly thought to relate to problems and service needs" (Inciardi, McBride, and Weinman, 1993, p. 162). In addition, the OPI has been adopted by several Treatment Alternatives to Street Crimes (TASC) programs and by the State of Delaware as part of a statewide needs assessment survey.

Numerous assessment instruments for substance abuse are available (see Crowe and Reeves, 1994), but most of them have not been specifically developed for, nor tested on, offender populations. The Center for Substance Abuse Treatment has published a Treatment Improvement Protocol (TIP) on screening and assessment of alcohol and other drug abusers in the criminal justice system (Inciardi, 1994). TIPs on three other topics of interest to providers of treatment to offenders are in preparation: treatment planning, alternative sanctions for adults, and alternative sanctions for juveniles.

Screening and assessment instruments are needed to implement effective matching strategies. No single treatment has been found to be effective for all or most drug abusers, but various approaches are available to treat different types of abusers. Clinically, the question is which type of treatment is appropriate for which type of client and in which settings (McLellan and Alterman, 1991; McLellan, Woody, Luborsky, O'Brien, and Druley, 1983). "Type of client" refers both to the drug or drugs with which a person is involved and to the severity of the involvement, which may range from experimentation to long-term addiction. "Type of treatment" refers to a variety of dimensions: residential versus outpatient, type of drug problem (single or polydrug), pharmacotherapy and nonpharmacotherapy, intensity and duration, and specific techniques.

Other considerations in determining appropriate treatment include gender, ethnicity, age, needed services, social support network, language, and level of psychological and cognitive functioning. Finally, differences in individual programs or service agencies (whether in specific services offered, quality of staff, degree of cooperation, and so forth) may or may not mean that a specific program or service is an appropriate referral. Also, matching should not be a one-time event: as the client progresses in treatment, treatment planning should involve additional assessment, evaluation, and referral to new treatment components or new services. Also, program staff need to be responsive to the unexpected, often acute, needs of clients such as pregnancy, arrest, job loss, and death in the family.

A theoretically grounded, clinically usable, and empirically tested technology for matching substance abuse clients to appropriate treatment has yet to be developed, although various research efforts in this area are underway. There is general agreement among researchers and others that, in principle, matching would assist clients in their treatment and recovery and also would make better use of resources. The obstacles facing the implementation of an effective matching system may be more practical than theoretical. To effectively address the multiple needs of substance abusers, matching requires a range of options to which clients can be referred following assessment.

A sophisticated matching system that takes into account multiple factors (client characteristics; type and severity of substance problem; criminal-risk classification; psychological, social, and medical needs; and client preference) requires a well developed, coordinated, and stable system of treatment and service options, a diverse treatment staff, and an efficient communication network (preferably computer based). For the foreseeable future, such a system seems unlikely to emerge. Until it does, however, individual programs or groups of programs within a community at least can develop strategies for assessing client needs, directing clients to services that are appropriate for those needs, monitoring their progress in treatment, and repeating the process as needs changes over the course of treatment.

3. Behavioral Leverage

Individuals involved in the criminal justice system need to have both reinforcing and aversive conditions, or incentives, before they are likely to be amenable and responsive to substance abuse treatment and services. That is, there must be consequences for both negative behavior and positive behavior. At the program level, various forms of contingency contracting (which includes both positive and negative reinforcers) are examples of incentives that may be effective in producing behavioral change (for other behavioral approaches to drug treatment, *see* Onken, Blaine, and Boren, 1993).

Frequent and random biological testing (urine, breath, hair) for alcohol or other drugs is a key element in providing close monitoring of clients' progress in treatment (on testing, *see* Vito, Wilson, and Holmes, 1993; Wish and Gropper, 1990). Positive test results, because they are objective and often can be determined relatively quickly (using onsite, portable equipment), help break through clients' denial and provide useful information on clients' progress for program staff, probation or parole officers, and judges. For less severe users, the knowledge that they will be tested may discourage use; for more severe users, testing enables program staff to adjust the intensity of treatment.

Whether testing with sanctions alone (in the absence of treatment) is effective in reducing drug use and criminal behavior appears to depend upon the stage of the criminal justice system within which it is instituted. For instance, in Washington, D.C., offenders on pretrial release have been tested regularly since the early 1980s, and results of the program indicate reduced rates of rearrest on both drug charges and other charges (Carver, 1993); but Britt, Gottfredson, and Goldkamp (1992) found drug monitoring to have no significant effect on pretrial misconduct. By contrast, evaluations of intensive supervision programs that included drug testing, but not drug treatment, reported no significant reductions in drug use and rearrest (Petersilia, Turner, and Deschenes, 1992). The difference in outcomes may be due to the lower severity of drug problems of the offenders on pretrial release compared with high-risk offenders who usually are admitted to intensive supervision programs.

The California Civil Addict Program (CAP), established by the California legislature in 1961, provides an example of a treatment system that used behavioral leverage effectively. CAP was a compulsory drug treatment program for offenders dependent on drugs (primarily heroin). CAP consisted of an inpatient phase followed by a supervised community aftercare phase. Participants could be returned for further inpatient stays if there was evidence of relapse (as determined by positive tests) or other behaviors that violated the conditions of supervision; they also could receive early release from supervision for avoidance of drug use and criminal activity.

CAP included a variety of leverage points for influencing behavior: short dry-out periods under custody, quick return to the community, urine testing, and sanctions for violations. An evaluation of CAP conducted in 1974-75 (McGlothlin, Anglin, and Wilson, 1977) found that CAP produced significant reductions in drug use and related criminal behavior among the studied sample. Despite these favorable findings, budgetary pressures in the late 1970s led not only to a reduction in the number of offenders enrolled in the program, but also to cutbacks in, or elimination of, some of the more effective elements of the program, including training of personnel, time spent in the program, and close monitoring of clients.

4. Continuity of Care

The importance of aftercare in the treatment of substance abuse was recognized as early as 1979 (Brown, 1979), but the number of substance abuse clients who are discharged from a treatment program and continue to receive support in a less intensive form of treatment or during the difficult transition to community reintegration continues to be small. Aftercare services remain few. Even with the skills learned in relapse prevention training (discussed next), once the person leaves a program, additional support usually is needed to maintain the gains made in treatment, reinforce prosocial behaviors, and discourage relapse. Such support can include self-help groups, alumni groups, monitoring by the person's counselor or case manager, and other mechanisms for formal and informal monitoring of the person's recovery. The various 12-step fellowship groups are helpful in providing a source of support for recovery since they are widely available and easily accessible.

Since relapse is a likely occurrence, an effective system of continuing care would allow the person to reenter a treatment program quickly and easily on a voluntary basis. For those still under supervision, mechanisms should be in place (such as urine testing and identification of potential relapse triggers) so that the person can be returned to a higher level of treatment, such as increased urine testing, outpatient, or even residential treatment.

5. Treatment Integrity

The survival and success of programs may depend as much on how they are developed, implemented, and managed as on their content (Petersilia, 1990). Successful operation of a treatment program involves the selection of a theoretically based, empirically tested treatment model, delivered by a staff trained in its use. A treatment model may be based upon self-empowerment, social learning, cognitive functioning, or other behavioral theories, but to be effective, the model must be implemented and sustained over time with adequate resources and by a management and staff that have appropriate experience and training, participate in ongoing staff development, receive technical assistance as needed, and continually monitor the expected performance of clients.

This may be difficult to maintain in the real-world environment in which community-based programs operate. The degree to which the underlying treatment model can be maintained depends on a variety of factors, including the background and experience of staff, the degree to which management and staff understand and "buy into" the treatment model, the degree to which substance abuse services and other services are integrated and coordinated, the supervision provided to counselors, the degree to which staff rather than clients are in control of program activities, the degree to which program services and activities are documented, and the degree to which clients perceive the program as relevant and sensitive to their needs.

Self-monitoring is needed through staff meetings, regular review of client records, formal MIS systems, and program evaluation. For its survival, a program may need to be able to provide evidence of its accountability and effectiveness. Despite the large body of literature supporting the effectiveness of drug treatment generally and treatment for offenders specifically, policymakers and agency personnel need to be convinced that this program is effective. In addition, the characteristics and problems of substance-abusing offenders change over time (witness the emergence of crack cocaine and AIDS), and traditional approaches no longer may be adequate to address the new needs and problems. Monitoring and evaluation are part of a continuing process of maintaining the integrity of programs.

6. Linkages with Other Services

Substance-abusing offenders tend to have a variety of problems and deficits in addition to their problems with alcohol or drugs. These include medical problems, psychological and emotional problems, limited education, poor job skills, lack of safe and adequate housing, and transportation problems. In addition to these, women offenders often have to contend with other problems, including legacies of physical and sexual abuse, need for gynecological and pregnancy care, and need for child care. Growing numbers of offenders need assistance with the physical, emotional, and financial problems associated with being HIV positive or having AIDS. The relationship of substance abuse to all these problems is complex and varies from one problem or person to another.

For example, treatment clients who use drugs or alcohol as a form of self-medication are likely to have difficulty remaining abstinent during and after treatment if their mental or physical problems are not addressed with appropriate medication or other means. People who cannot find steady employment because they are illiterate or lack the skills and attitudes needed to find and keep a job will likely have difficulty staying away from drugs once they leave treatment. Substance abuse programs represent an opportunity to identify and address problems or situations that have important public health or social implications. It is important to stress that most of these problems, even though they are related to substance abuse, are not necessarily caused by substance abuse, and thus they need to be addressed directly, rather than assuming that they will disappear spontaneously as the person enters recovery (McLellan, Luborsky, Woody, O'Brien, and Kron, 1981).

Of course, few substance abuse programs for offenders have the resources or expertise to address the full range of problems that their clients may have. Although the idea of setting up substance abuse programs as "one-stop shopping" centers—where people can have all their needs met—is attractive in principle, the establishment of such centers faces numerous obstacles that are not likely to be overcome soon. In the meantime, programs that do wish to deal with selected problems of their clients can do so through various methods of linkage and coordination with other programs, agencies, and services. Several models for such coordination are available, including Treatment Alternatives to Street Crime (TASC) and case management, both of which are briefly discussed next.

TASC, which originated in the early 1970s, is the oldest and best developed model of the linkage between the criminal justice system and the treatment system (Inciardi and McBride, 1991; Swartz, 1993; Wellisch, Prendergast, and Anglin, 1993a). Unlike other programs within criminal justice, TASC explicitly and formally addresses the drugs-crime link through referring clients to drug treatment and monitoring of their progress in treatment. Although TASC was originally viewed as a bridge between criminal justice and drug treatment, whereby treating drug addiction (primarily to heroin) was expected to reduce criminal behavior, the bridge metaphor is giving way to a network metaphor to reflect the fact that drug use and crime are associated with multiple problems of drug-abusing offenders. Increasingly, TASC projects assess the multiple needs of their clients and manage the coordination of treatment or attention to these needs through a variety of programs and agencies. Where once TASC provided a bridge between criminal justice and drug treatment, it now is being extended in many directions to serve its clients by providing links among a variety of agencies, programs, and services.

Coordinating the various activities, programs, and agencies involved in delivering services to multiproblem substance-abusing offenders is a difficult task, but a necessary one if treatment is to be effective. Increasingly, this coordinating function is being carried out through case management (Ashery, 1992). Case management is a key element in a coordinated service system in which the case managers help clients obtain the services they need, follow-up on the delivery of the services, and monitor the clients' progress during treatment.

To be successful, case management depends upon small caseloads so that sufficient time and attention can be given to seeing that the needs of clients are met within the substance abuse programs and at the various other service agencies to which clients are referred. Also, case managers usually require a higher level of training and experience than the typical counselor in substance abuse treatment programs, and a considerable amount of their time is spent brokering services with other agencies and organizations. Because of the small case loads, case management tends to be more expensive than counselor-based treatment models, and, if it cannot be implemented for all clients, it at least should be considered for clients who are most in need of coordinated services and least able to access services themselves, such as dually diagnosed clients.

One model of case management that has been developed in Delaware for parolees with substance-abuse problems is the Assertive Community Treatment (ACT) program (Martin and Inciardi, 1993a, 1993b; Martin and Scarpitti, 1993). Under the treatment model followed by ACT, substance abuse is regarded as a biopsychosocial disease or condition that requires multimodal, holistic methods of assessment and treatment. The purpose of ACT is to provide a comprehensive network of continuing support in the community for parolees with substance abuse histories in order to support the clients' efforts at staying clean and establishing a stable and productive life in the community.

After clients receive a comprehensive assessment of their problems and needs and a detailed treatment plan is developed, they pass through the four phases of the ACT protocol: (a) intensive drug treatment (six weeks), including individual and group counseling, drug and AIDS education, family therapy, and special issue groups; (b) moderately intensive treatment (six weeks), including less frequent group and individual counseling, relapse prevention, family therapy as needed, and continuing AIDS education and discussions; (c) relapse prevention (six weeks), including concentrated focus on relapse education, practice, and support in group and individual sessions; and (d) case management (twelve weeks), including vocational training, placing individuals in jobs, providing additional services, and monitoring of drug and alcohol use. After clients are discharged from the program into the community, case managers follow up with clients on a regular basis for twelve months. A major problem encountered in the implementation of ACT is its voluntary nature, which has resulted in high dropout rates of eligible clients who originally agreed to enter the program. This, of course, is a problem in any voluntary program.

Practices

Many different approaches to the treatment of substance dependence are in use, but not all have been found to be equally effective. In an exhaustive review of the research literature on the effectiveness of alcoholism treatments, Miller and Hester (1986) arrived at two lists: one list consisted of treatment methods whose effectiveness was supported by controlled outcome research; the other list included methods that were commonly used in alcoholism treatment programs in the United States. What is remarkable is that there was no overlap between the two lists. In other words, those treatment methods that clinical and field research show to be effective are not the treatments that are generally used to treat alcoholism (although this may be less true today than when the review was published).[3]

According to Miller and Hester, alcoholism treatment approaches with adequate scientific support for their effectiveness are aversion therapies, behavioral self-control training, the community reinforcement approach, marital and family therapy, social-skills training, and stress management. By contrast, those treatment approaches commonly used in alcohol treatment programs in the United States are Alcoholics Anonymous, alcohol education, confrontation, disulfiram, group therapy, and individual counseling. The general implication of Miller and Hester's findings is that greater effectiveness in producing abstinence or reducing heavy alcohol use is to be expected from behavioral approaches to treatment rather than (or in addition to) those in common use.

Regarding treatment for dependence on illicit drugs, evaluation studies generally have concluded that no one treatment modality (of those commonly studied: methadone, therapeutic community/residential, and outpatient drug free) is clearly superior to any other for all clients, although differential effectiveness has been found for users of different drugs and for different subpopulations (Anglin and Hser, 1990b; Gerstein and Harwood, 1990; Prendergast et al., in press). A number of specific approaches to substance abuse treatment that have reasonably strong research support are discussed next.

Cognitive and Behavioral-based Treatments

A growing body of research and clinical literature has focused on the effectiveness of cognitive and behavioral approaches to treating substance abuse problems. This includes cognitive-skills training, relapse-prevention training, and contingency contracting.

Cognitive Skills

In evaluations of rehabilitation programs for offenders, including programs for substance abusers, those that have been shown to be more effective include programs that attempt to improve the cognitive skills of offenders. A considerable body of research literature supports the effectiveness of correctional interventions that include a cognitive skills component (for example, Gendreau and Andrews, 1990; Izzo and Ross, 1990; Ross and Fabiano, 1985). Although much of this research has been based on incarcerated populations, it is reasonable to assume that cognitive approaches would show similar positive outcomes in community-based settings.

Cognitive-skills treatment is a general term that covers several related approaches: problem solving, social skills training, and relapse prevention training (Husband and Platt, 1993). The problem-solving approach to treatment starts from the assumption that successful functioning requires the ability to make effective use of various problem-solving skills, and that deficiencies in these skills lead to various types of dysfunctional behavior, including crime and substance abuse. A second assumption is that it is possible to actively intervene with substance abusers to remedy these cognitive deficits and thus to help them learn more socially acceptable and productive ways to lead their lives. While training in problem solving focuses on how to think, social skills training is concerned more with specific social or behavioral skills. Again, the assumption is that teaching social skills will help the person learn more adaptive ways of functioning and relating to others. The elements of social skills programs include modeling appropriate behavior, role playing, rehearsing of target behaviors, instructing and coaching in the target behaviors, and providing feedback.

A number of theoretically grounded and empirically tested models of cognitive skills training have been developed and implemented in a variety of settings (Interpersonal Cognitive Problem Solving [Platt, Prout, and Metzger, 1986], Problem Solving Therapy [D'Zurilla, 1986], Time to Think

[Ross and Fabiano, 1985], and Moral Reconation Therapy [Little, Robinson, and Burnette, 1993]).

Relapse Prevention

High relapse rates have been a common finding in substance abuse treatment programs and in the criminal justice system, and efforts to develop methods and approaches to reduce relapse rates have been a major focus of treatment research. At the program level, probably the leading method has been various forms of relapse-prevention training (Gorski, Kelley, Havens, and Peters, 1993; Marlatt and Gordon, 1985; Rawson, Obert, McCann, and Marinelli-Casey, 1993). These programs are based on theoretically and empirically based models of recovery and relapse, embody specific cognitive and behavioral principles and procedures, and use manual-driven protocols. They also have been adapted to a variety of criminal justice settings (for examples of relapse prevention programs in criminal justice settings, *see* Gorski, Kelley, Havens, and Peters, 1993).

Relapse-prevention approaches have been found to be effective with a variety of substance-abusing populations, including incarcerated inmates; while published evaluations of relapse prevention approaches in community-based programs are lacking, there is no reason to believe that they would not be effective with offenders under community supervision, although a particular model may need to be adapted to local circumstances. Also, the principles and procedures of relapse prevention are not confined to the treatment of alcoholics and drug addicts, but have been adapted to other behaviors characterized by problems with impulse control such as smoking, gambling, committing sexual offenses, and behaving violently. Presumably, effective relapse prevention techniques in these other areas also might prove useful in substance abuse treatment.

Contingency Contracting

Another behavioral approach to substance abuse treatment is contingency contracting, in which contracts signed by counselors and clients spell out specific consequences for specific behaviors. Although contracts often focus on negative consequences (sanctions) for noncompliance, such contracts can and should also include positive reinforcement (rewards) for appropriate behavior or for achieving specific treatment goals (Anker and Crowley, 1982; Stitzer, Iguchi, Kidorf, and Bigelow, 1993).

Examples of the use of contingency contracting and other behavioral approaches are found in the drug courts that have been established in recent years. In the Oakland drug court, contingency contracts specify the expectations for clients and the responsibilities of treatment staff, define success and failure, indicate rewards for positive behaviors and penalties for negative behaviors, and provide a clear structure for judicial decisions regarding clients. This behavioral approach to treatment and supervision in the Oakland drug court has enabled the county to rent jail space to surrounding counties (Tauber, 1994).

The drug court in Washington, D.C., includes a "graduated sanctions" track in its treatment program, which consists of a prescribed set of progressively more stringent sanctions in response to negative results of clients' weekly drug tests. The sanction for the first positive test is three days in the jury box observing the proceedings against other defendants; the second positive test results in one day in jail; the third, six days in a jail-based detoxification program; the fourth, twelve days in jail; and the fifth, twenty-four days in jail. Preliminary results suggest that this combination of drug testing and sanctions is having a positive effect on clients' drug use ("Positive effects," 1994).

Pharmacotherapy

Treating specific forms of substance dependence with pharmacological agents, while not without controversy, nonetheless, has become a well-established practice, evidenced in particular by the use of methadone and LAAM for opiate addiction and disulfiram for alcoholism. Although a number of medications to treat cocaine/crack dependence are under study, none has been established as generally effective.

Disulfiram

A recent review (Heather, 1993) of research on disulfiram (trade name Antabuse) reported that well-designed studies of disulfiram have shown that although unsupervised taking of disulfiram is no more effective than a control condition in promoting abstinence at one-year follow-up, the medication was effective in delaying the time to relapse and in reducing the frequency of drinking. Higher rates of effectiveness (usually measured by abstinence) have been found in studies in which disulfiram was taken under various types and degrees of supervision.

Various reinforcement contingencies also have been found to increase compliance and improve effectiveness. In addition to supervision, the effectiveness of disulfiram depends on individualizing the dose, which may range from the typical dose of about 250 mg up to 500 mg. (Patients who do not tolerate disulfiram may be given calcium carbimide.)

An important finding of a recent study (Azrin, 1993) is that alcoholics whose disulfiram taking is closely monitored by a family member (particularly a spouse) achieve high rates of sobriety (along with other positive behaviors) without the need for additional psychological counseling; but for alcoholics with no close family ties, supervised disulfiram ingestion, to be effective, needs to be accompanied by behavioral psychological treatment. The finding highlights the fact that clients, depending on their situations, may need different types or intensities of service, and that providing such differential treatment requires careful and thorough assess-ment at admission and reassessment over the course of treatment.

As regards treatment for offenders with alcohol problems, a number of studies (beginning in 1966) have found that if such offenders "can be persuaded to take disulfiram, then even marginal, unskilled, isolated, and brain-damaged alcoholics will generally stop drinking" (Brewer, 1993b, p. 38). These studies support the view that disulfiram, combined with the authority of the court, can be a useful intervention to help alcoholic offenders reduce or even end alcohol abuse.

Methadone

A large body of literature supports the effectiveness of methadone treatment in reducing opiate use and criminal activity, in improving psychosocial functioning, and in reducing HIV-risk behaviors, particularly injection drug use (Ball and Ross, 1991; Cooper, Altman, Brown, and Czechowicz, 1983; Senay, 1985).[4] For instance, researchers at University of California-Los Angles (Anglin and McGlothlin, 1984, 1985; Hser, Anglin, and Chou, 1988) have shown that the percentage of nonincarcerated time engaged in daily opiate use decreased from about 70 percent (averaging across several studies) when not in maintenance methadone treatment to about 12 percent when in methadone maintenance.

Likewise, property crime involvement decreased from about 18 percent when not in methadone maintenance to about 11 percent when in methadone maintenance. Even when addicts are discharged from treatment, sustained improvement is still observable, although to a lesser degree when compared with in-treatment effects.

Other studies also support the effectiveness of methadone maintenance treatment in reducing crime. Maddux and Desmond (1979) studied the association between community crime rates and the rates of institutional and methadone maintenance treatment in the San Antonio area. As treatment rates increased, community crime rates decreased, but when cutbacks forced the premature discharge of methadone maintenance patients, community crime rates increased. Ball, Corty, Bond, and Tommasello (1988), in a study of six methadone maintenance programs in three eastern cities, found that methadone maintenance was effective in reducing illicit drug use and crime during treatment for the 671 subjects studied. The reduction in criminality was dramatic: the average number of crime days per person, per year, decreased from 307 during the addiction period just before treatment to 20 after 6 months of treatment.

Despite repeated admissions to treatment programs by people with chronic drug dependence, only limited research has focused on the cumulative behavioral effects over time of multiple treatment episodes. In an examination of the possibility of incremental gains from one up to five episodes of methadone maintenance treatment, Powers and Anglin (1993) reported the following notable findings: (a) a dramatic reduction in daily narcotics use was achieved during each treatment episode; (b) the level of daily use between periods of treatment remained less than the level observed before initial treatment; and (c) many addicts returned for additional episodes of treatment despite failure to maintain gains after discharge. Despite such findings as these, methadone treatment is seldom one of the options when criminal justice personnel refer opiate addicts to treatment, although the reasons seem to be based less on evidence of effectiveness than on ideology and community opposition to methadone programs.[5]

LAAM

LAAM is a long-acting form of methadone, which is taken three times a week rather than every day as with methadone. LAAM was approved by the Food and Drug Administration in the summer of 1993 for use in the treatment of opiate addiction. Given the time it takes for states to give their approval, for clinics to apply for and receive a license to use LAAM, and for staff to be trained in its use, it will be some time before LAAM is available generally. Once it is, it will provide an alternative to opiate-addicted clients who do not do well on methadone, who prefer not taking methadone, or who would benefit from less frequent attendance at the clinic.

Naltrexone

Naltrexone (Trexan) is an opiate antagonist[6] approved by the Food and Drug Administration for use in the treatment of opiate addiction. A single 50 mg dose of naltrexone blocks the euphoric effects of a 25 mg dose of heroin for up to 24 hours, and 150 mg is effective for up to 3 days. Naltrexone does not produce euphoria, is not addictive, has minimal side effects for most people, and is not subject to abuse.

Naltrexone administration can begin only after the patient has been completely detoxified from all opiates, including methadone. A period of five to seven days of abstinence from opiates following heroin withdrawal and ten to fourteen days from methadone withdrawal must pass before naltrexone is administered; otherwise, the patient will suffer withdrawal symptoms. Once on naltrexone, patients cease to crave and use opiates as a result of naltrexone's blockade of opiate euphoria. A disadvantage of naltrexone is the low rate of patient acceptance and compliance, especially by street addicts. It has had more success with recovering physicians and other professionals and with people of higher socioeconomic status. As with disulfiram, treatment with naltrexone is likely to be more effective if it is administered under some type of close monitoring system (Brahen and Brewer, 1993; Brewer, 1993a; Kosten and Kleber, 1984; Rawson and Tennant, 1984).

Cocaine Treatments

Because of the relative recency of the cocaine/crack epidemic, efforts to develop treatments specifically designed for cocaine dependence have lagged behind treatments for opiate and alcohol dependence, and these efforts have tended to be modeled on treatment regimens developed for other types of substance abuse. Findings from studies evaluating the effectiveness of cocaine treatment have begun to appear in the scientific literature only in the last few years, and few of these evaluations focus on cocaine-abusing offenders in community-based programs. Still, the principles and practices previously discussed apply to cocaine treatments, except for pharmacotherapy, where research still continues for a medication to treat cocaine addiction. A number of recent evaluation studies of cocaine treatment are briefly summarized next (for a convenient summary of various approaches, *see* Tims and Leukefeld, 1993).

Khalsa, Anglin, and Paredes (1992) assessed the relative effectiveness of the common treatment modalities for cocaine abuse (inpatient, outpatient, self-help groups), separately and in various combinations, as provided to 300 cocaine users at a Veterans Affairs medical center. The two most disparate groups in terms of outcome were those patients whose treatment consisted of an initial twenty-one-day inpatient period, an outpatient follow-up regimen (individual and group counseling), and continued involvement in self-help groups throughout most of the follow-up period, and those patients whose treatment consisted solely of a single twenty-one-day inpatient treatment episode. Of the inpatient-only group, 45 percent relapsed to severe cocaine use within a year, whereas only 12 percent of the group receiving more and longer treatment exposure did so. The latter group also showed more favorable outcomes in terms of total time abstinent from cocaine, lesser use of alcohol and other drugs, and decreases in drug dealing and other criminal activities. The findings confirm the importance of providing long-term treatment and continuity of care to bring about long-term positive outcomes.

Programs using behavioral approaches have shown potential in treating cocaine abuse. One promising approach includes behavioral modification procedures in a multicomponent treatment program originally developed to treat alcoholics. Called the "community reinforcement approach," it is based on the concept that reinforcement for positive behaviors begins in the treatment clinic and must then be transferred to the client's community environment. The program consists of tangible reinforcers purchased through funds earned for cocaine-free urines and participation in family, behavioral, employment, and recreational counseling. In an evaluation of this program (Higgins et al., 1991), the outcomes of thirteen clients treated with this approach were compared with the outcomes from fifteen clients attending a 12-step group. Eleven of the behavioral subjects and five of the 12-step subjects were retained for three months. In the behavioral program, 23 percent of the clients achieved three months of continuous abstinence, compared with none of those in the 12-step group. These results were replicated in a random-assignment study (Higgins et al., 1993).

Rawson and associates have developed a neurobehavioral model of cocaine treatment. This treatment approach is intended to address the types of problems (behavioral, cognitive, emotional, relationship) that cocaine users have at entrance to treatment and during the course of treatment within the context of a structured, behaviorally oriented protocol. A pilot study (Rawson, Obert, McCann, and Mann, 1986) compared outcomes among subjects who self-selected into one of three groups: (a) no formal treatment (participation in 12-step groups), (b) twenty-eight-day hospital treatment, and (c) a six-month outpatient program using the neurobehavioral model. At a follow-up telephone interview (an average of eight months after the initial interview), subjects in the neurobehavioral program reported significantly lower rates of cocaine use than either of the other two groups. In addition, subjects in the outpatient program expressed greater satisfaction with treatment than those in the other types of treatment.

In an open trial of the neurobehavioral model at two clinics (Rawson, Obert, McCann, and Ling, 1993), data were collected on 486 clients during 6 months of intensive treatment. Of those clients who completed six months of intensive treatment, no cocaine use was detected in similar proportions of clients at both clinics. Since there was no comparison group and no long-term follow-up, the findings of this study are largely descriptive rather than evaluative, but a controlled, random-assignment evaluation study of the neurobehavioral model is currently being conducted. The model also is being adapted to alcoholism treatment.

These findings indicate the limited extent of our knowledge about cocaine treatment, but they do provide some support for the effectiveness of existing treatment programs for cocaine dependence. Cocaine treatment programs appear to be able to engage and retain cocaine abusers in treatment, reduce cocaine use during treatment, and maintain some of the during-treatment gains after discharge. The results from better controlled studies currently in progress to evaluate the efficacy of various approaches to cocaine treatment will determine whether these initial findings are confirmed; they also will enable clinicians to refine their protocols based on empirically based data.

Acupuncture

Acupuncture as an adjunct to treating cocaine and heroin abusers has been gaining increased acceptance in criminal justice treatment programs. In particular, many of the recently established drug courts include acupuncture in their treatment protocols, usually on a voluntary basis. Although programs that use acupuncture report success, particularly as an aid in detoxification, the overall research evidence of the effectiveness of acupuncture has been mixed. A review of controlled research on acupuncture as a detoxification treatment by researchers at Lincoln Medical and Mental Health Center, which pioneered the use of acupuncture in treating addictions, concluded that, "Research findings from several areas have provided converging evidence supporting the role of acupuncture as an aid in the treatment of substance abusers" (Brewington, Smith, and Lipton, 1994, p. 305).

The National Institute on Drug Abuse convened a technical review panel to examine research findings on acupuncture over the past two decades and to arrive at a conclusion regarding its efficacy. The panel concluded that the research on acupuncture has serious methodological weaknesses, that the findings of its effectiveness are inconclusive, and that "there is no compelling evidence for the efficacy of acupuncture in the treatment of either opiate or cocaine dependence" (McLellan, Grossman, Blaine, and Haverkos, 1993, p. 575). Most research has focused on the effectiveness of acupuncture in alleviating withdrawal symptoms during detoxification; its long-term effects in maintaining abstinence have not been studied.

Despite these findings, there is a relatively common clinical belief that acupuncture is effective, or at least helpful, for some clients in their efforts to detoxify from drug use. Programs do need to consider whether the cost of providing acupuncture is justified given the limited research support on its effectiveness with clients in general. Future research will be needed to determine whether acupuncture is effective with certain types of clients or during certain stages of drug dependence. For instance, one study of the use of acupuncture in heroin detoxification found the procedure to be more helpful for patients with less severe drug problems (Washburn et al., 1993).

Special Populations

These principles and practices generally apply across all categories of substance-abusing offenders. But the principles and practices may not have equal salience for particular offender groups such as juveniles, women, and members of racial/ethnic groups. This section discusses some of the issues, based on limited available research data, that need to be considered in providing substance abuse treatment to these groups.

Juveniles

Treatment programs for juvenile offenders often have been designed using treatment models for adults, but what works with adults does not necessarily work with youthful offenders. As with adults, several treatment approaches have been found to be effective, but no one approach is equally effective for all youths with different drug problems and those from different sociodemographic groups (for reviews and meta-analyses of juvenile correctional treatment, *see* Basta and Davidson, 1988; Gordon and Arbuthnot, 1987; Gottschalk, Davidson, Gensheimer, and Mayer, 1987; Lab and Whitehead, 1988; Wright and Dixon, 1977).

Also, as with adults, substance abuse problems among young offenders exist within the context of a variety of psychological and social problems, though the problems are often different from those of adults. In fact, the substance abuse problems of delinquent youth (which are less likely than those of adults to have progressed to addiction) may be less serious than their other problems. Dembo, Williams, and Schmeidler (1993, p. 115) list a number of differences that have been found between adolescents and adults in residential treatment. These differences also may be applicable to clients in outpatient treatment:

> Compared to adults, adolescents (1) use drugs at an earlier age, (2) have less involvement with opiates, shorter abuse histories, and more involvement in alcohol, marijuana, and multiple drug use, (3) have a greater incidence of family deviance and experience of past psychological treatment, (4) tend to be more fascinated with the drug-related lifestyle and less fatigued with failure and the negative social consequences of their drug use, (5) have an unrealistic sense of their invulnerability, and (6) require a greater emphasis on addressing educational needs and parental/family support in the treatment process.

These problems—which may include physical and sexual abuse, family problems, emotional and psychological disorders, low educational achievement, and gang involvement, together with the environmental deprivation and strong peer influences that they may face—place them at high risk for drug use, delinquency, and criminal behavior (Dembo, Williams, and Schmeidler, 1993). Although the principles of effective treatment discussed here apply to treatment for both juveniles and adults, their implementation as specific programs, procedures, and activities will need to be adapted to the characteristics, problems, and situations of youthful offenders.

Regarding relapse prevention for juvenile offenders, one review (Catalano, Wells, Jenson, and Hawkins, 1989) found that post-treatment experiences were more important than pre-treatment or during-treatment factors in accounting for relapse after treatment. The following post-treatment factors have been found to be especially associated with relapse: thoughts and feelings about drugs and drug cravings, lack of involvement in productive activities (school or work), and few or less satisfactory leisure activities (Dembo, Williams, and Schmeidler, 1993). Aftercare services for juvenile offenders should provide a comprehensive range of services, make use of graduated sanctions, and emphasize incentives and positive reinforcements to encourage prosocial behaviors (Altschuler and Armstrong, 1991).

Women

In the past, most programs that included women were developed with little or no reference to the needs and characteristics of women; they were designed by and for men. Fortunately, this situation is changing, as more programs specifically designed for women are currently in operation or are being developed (Wellisch, Prendergast, and Anglin, 1994). Few independent evaluations of treatment programs for women offenders in the community are available, but a number of observations can be made on the basis of the available literature and site visits to programs for women offenders (Falkin et al., 1994; Wellisch, Prendergast, and Anglin, 1993c).

Women offenders with substance abuse problems face a number of unique issues: domestic violence, single motherhood, history of physical and sexual abuse, and limited, low-wage job skills. Women in substance abuse treatment have been found to have lower levels of psychological functioning than men, particularly in the areas of depression and anxiety. Most women offenders are mothers, and most are the sole support of minor children. As many as one-half of the parole revocations for women offenders are for drug-related violations (American Correctional Association, 1990; Benishek et al., 1992; Robinson, 1992; Wallen, 1992; Wellisch, Prendergast, and Anglin, 1993b).

Particular needs of substance-abusing women offenders include gynecological and obstetrical health care, psychological and psychiatric support, counseling, and groups to deal with sexual and physical abuse, housing (particularly if they are in an abusive relationship), transportation, child care, and parenting skills (these latter are important for men also, but women who are single mothers usually are responsible for child rearing). Housing and transportation are less a problem in residential programs, but lack of child care discourages women from entering such treatment and may lead to their leaving early if they do enter. Education, pre-vocational training, and job training (preferably in nongender-specific jobs) are also important to improve the economic self-sufficiency of women offenders, which in turn should have an impact on their drug use (and criminal behavior), although the condition of the local job market will be an important factor in the success of job skills and vocational training programs.

Racial/Ethnic Groups

As with treatment programs for women, models of addiction and recovery and models of appropriate intervention and treatment largely have been based on studies of white men and thus may not be optimally suited to men or women who are of African-American, Hispanic, or of other racial/ethnic backgrounds. Generally, researchers have found that drug abusers of different ethnic groups tend to have different drug use patterns and different kinds of problems associated with their drug use and, consequently, require different approaches to treating their problems (Anglin, Booth, Ryan, and Hser, 1988; Anglin, Ryan, Booth, and Hser, 1988; Kosten, Rounsaville, and Kleber, 1985).

A study of arrestees in Los Angles found that among daily drug users, the perceived need for treatment was lower among African-Americans and Hispanics than among whites; in addition, both of the former groups had more negative attitudes toward treatment than did whites (Longshore, Hsieh, and Anglin, 1993). These attitudes may reflect cultural attitudes that are skeptical of treating personal problems outside of the family or group, but they also may be accurate perceptions of a treatment system that fails to respect the cultures of African-Americans and Hispanics and fails to address their specific needs.

To engage clients in treatment and discourage their dropping out, programs can establish referral, intake, and treatment activities that are culturally congruent with the racial/ethnic groups they serve. An obvious effort here would be to ensure that some staff members are bilingual to accommodate the language preferences of their clients. Providing different treatment approaches that are adapted to the learning styles of client groups also may promote positive outcomes.

In an evaluation of a program for cocaine and crack abuse, Perez-Arce, Carr, and Sorensen (1993) found that African-American men, and to a lesser extent Hispanic men, benefited from a confrontational approach that also emphasized interdependence and emotional support. African-American women, by contrast, did less well in a confrontational approach; instead, they responded better to a treatment protocol that focused on family and social networks, strong women as role models, and training in assertive behavior and adaptive coping mechanisms. While solid research conclusions are lacking to provide clear guidance to offender treatment programs in addressing the needs of different racial/ethnic groups and in promoting cultural competence among program staff, a number of sources do discuss issues of cultural competence in interventions for the general substance-abusing population (*see* De la Rosa and Recio Adrados, 1993; Orlandi, 1992; Oyemade and Brandon-Monye, 1990).

Brown, Joe, and Thompson (1985), in a study of over 500 clinics nationwide, found that whenever a particular ethnic group made up more than 75 percent of the clientele within outpatient drug-free programs, members of that group remained in treatment longer than did members of other ethnic groups. Interestingly, this effect of minority/majority status was not found in methadone maintenance programs or in residential programs. The findings of this study suggest the importance, at least in outpatient drug-free programs, either of avoiding an extreme imbalance in the ethnic composition of programs or of ensuring that the ethnic composition of the staff roughly reflects that of the clients.

Finally, just as programs need to directly address their women clients' negative stereotypes and experiences of sexual and physical abuse, they also need to deal with the social and emotional problems of their clients associated with experiences of racism and discrimination. Programs that are based on the 12-step model may need to adapt the model to the needs and culture of their clients. For instance, programs that serve African-American clients have been able to reduce resistance to participation in 12-step groups by redefining the first step regarding powerlessness since African-Americans have a social legacy of being powerless in dealing with racism, discrimination, and poverty (Smith, Buxton, Bilal, and Seymour, 1993). Taylor and Jackson (1990), in testing a model for predicting alcohol consumption among black women, found that internalized racism (black internalization of white stereotypes about blacks) had a significant direct effect (second only to life events) on alcohol consumption, leading the authors to recommend the importance of efforts to strengthen black cultural identity as a way to curtail alcohol problems.

Conclusion

Research on substance-abuse treatment among general and offender populations has resulted in a sufficient body of knowledge to provide community correctional providers with a set of principles and practices that have proven effective with many, if not all, offenders with substance abuse problems. We have passed the time when a strategy of "try anything to *see* what works" is defensible scientifically, clinically, or financially. The principles outlined in this chapter provide the basis for assessing whether a treatment approach, at the program level or the system level, is likely to be effective and at a reasonable cost. Evaluation research on treatment for substance abuse has progressed to the point where it is no longer necessary to ask, "Is substance abuse treatment effective?" Researchers and clinicians have come to realize that the appropriate question about substance abuse treatment is not "What works?", but rather "What works most cost effectively for which types of offender, under which conditions, and in which settings?"

For offenders with serious drug or alcohol problems, it is treatment, not merely supervision, however intensive, that is needed. Supervision alone, whether in jail or prison, in a shock incarceration program, or under probation or parole, is seldom sufficient to have an impact on the substance abuse problems of most offenders (Petersilia, Turner, and Deschenes, 1992; Shaw and Mackenzie, 1992). For offenders with severe dependence ("hard-core users"), low-intensity treatment or intervention efforts alone, such as educational programs or 12-step groups, or intermediate sanctions such as community service, day fines, or electronic monitoring, also are unlikely to have much impact, although they may be important elements of a comprehensive program. Treatment for hard-core users needs to be intensive, long-term, and comprehensive.

The treatment of substance abuse, particularly of high-severity or hard-core abuse, has some similarities to interventions used by the mental health delivery system in treating the chronically mentally ill. While a "cure" is not a generally expected goal of treatment, reasonable goals for substance abuse treatment are to minimize the number of individuals who enter higher restriction supervision or higher intensity treatment, to minimize the need for the more serious and costly options of long-term incarceration or residential treatment, and to maximize the time in the community with acceptable behaviors. For many substance-abusing offenders, this process may be accomplished in a few months or years; for others, long-term intervention, with constant support and monitoring, may be necessary (Anglin and Hser, 1990a).

Although individual programs can implement principles and practices to improve outcomes for their clients, significant gains in the overall effectiveness of substance abuse treatment within the criminal justice system will require closer cooperation between criminal justice agencies and drug treatment providers, along with the participation of other service agencies (Baker, 1993; Crowe and Reeves, 1994; "Forging links," 1993; Wellisch, Prendergast, and Anglin, 1993a). What is needed is an approach to treating offenders that is more systems oriented—that includes recognizing the importance of ongoing communication among drug treatment and criminal justice agencies, the need for planning together, providing services jointly where appropriate and feasible, and generally, supporting efforts to offer the range and continuity of services needed for this population. TASC and drug courts are examples of this coordinated approach, and other examples can be found at the state and county levels throughout the country. But it is a trend that needs support from policymakers, providers, and researchers if it is to succeed in improving the delivery of services to substance-abusing offenders.

Notes

[1] Comments of panel members at the IARCA conference and a review of an earlier draft by Gregory Falkin improved the final version of this paper.

[2] "Abuse" and "dependence" are not the same clinical condition, each requires a somewhat different approach, but they both fall under the broader category of "problems" that may result from alcohol and drug use and that require some type of intervention. In this chapter, they are used interchangeably for variety of expression. For the same reason, "drug" is often used to include alcohol, as well as illicit drugs.

[3] A somewhat distressing commentary on the influence of research on practice is the findings of a study (Holder, Longabaugh, Miller, and Rubonis, 1991) that alcoholism treatment approaches with insufficient evidence of their effectiveness tend to be those that are most expensive.

[4] It must be emphasized that methadone is pharmacologically effective only with opiates, although methadone treatment may have some indirect effects on the use of other drugs (for example, use of cocaine when taken with heroin in the form of "speedballs").

[5] Some of the opposition to methadone programs results from a Federal policy of requiring all clients receiving methadone to attend stand-alone clinics, which encourages the loitering, illegal parking, dealing, and other problems about which neighbors complain. These occasions for complaint could be reduced, if not eliminated, through

changes in Federal regulations and policy that would allow for greater flexibility in providing methadone treatment, such as methadone buses, hospital-based methadone clinics, and physician dispensing to long-term, well-functioning clients (medical maintenance) (Brady, 1993; Novick and Joseph, 1991).

[6] An opiate antagonist is a drug that nullifies the effects of opiates by binding to receptor sites in the brain, thereby blocking access to the receptor for opiates.

References

Altschuler, D. M. and T. L. Armstrong. 1991. Intensive Community-based Aftercare Prototype: Policies and Procedures. Report submitted to the Office of Juvenile Justice and Delinquency Prevention, U.S. Department of Justice.

American Correctional Association. 1990. *The Female Offender: What Does the Future Hold?* Laurel, Maryland: American Correctional Association.

Andrews, D. A., I. Zinger, R. D. Hoge, J. Bonta, P. Gendreau, and F. T. Cullen. 1990. Does Correctional Treatment Work? A Clinically Relevant and Psychologically Informed Meta- Analysis. *Criminology*. 28(3), 369-404.

Anglin, M. D., M. W. Booth, T. M. Ryan, and Y-I Hser. 1988. Ethnic Differences in Narcotics Addiction. Part II. Chicano and Anglo Addiction Career Patterns. *International Journal of the Addictions*. 23(10), 1011-1027.

Anglin, M. D. and Y-I Hser. 1990a. Legal Coercion and Drug Abuse Treatment: Research Findings and Social Policy Implications. In J.A. Inciardi, ed. *Handbook of Drug Control in the United States* (pp. 151-176). Westport, Connecticut: Greenwood Press.

———. 1990b. Treatment of Drug Abuse. In M. Tonry and J. Q. Wilson, ed. *Crime and Justice: An Annual Review of Research, Vol. 13: Drugs and Crime* (pp. 393-460). Chicago: University of Chicago Press.

Anglin, M. D., and W. H. McGlothlin. 1984. Outcome of Narcotic Addict Treatment in California. In F. Tims and J. Ludford, eds. *Drug Abuse Treatment Evaluation: Strategies, Progress, and Prospects* (NIDA Research Monograph 51, pp. 106-128). Rockville, Maryland: National Institute on Drug Abuse.

———. 1985. Methadone Maintenance in California: A Decade's Experience. In L. Brill and C. Winick. Eds. *The Yearbook of Substance Use and Abuse*. 3: 219-280.

Anglin, M. D. and T. H. Maugh. 1992. Ensuring Success in Interventions with Drug-using Offenders. *Annals of the American Academy of Political and Social Sciences*. 521: 66-90.

Anglin, M. D., T. M. Ryan, M. W. Booth, and Y-I Hser. 1988. Ethnic Differences in Narcotics Addiction. Part I. Characteristics of Chicano and Anglo Methadone Maintenance Clients. *International Journal of the Addictions*. 23(2), 125-149.

Anglin, M. D., and G. Speckart. 1988. Narcotics Use and Crime: A Multisample, Multimethod Analysis. *Criminology*. 26, 197-233.

Anker, A. L. and T. J. Crowley. 1982. Use of Contingency Contracts in Specialty Clinics for Cocaine Abuse. In L. S. Harris, ed. *Problems of Drug Dependence* (NIDA Research Monograph 41, pp. 452-459). Rockville, Maryland: National Institute on Drug Abuse.

Ashery, R. S., ed. 1992. *Progress and Issues in Case Management* (NIDA Research Series 127). Rockville, Maryland: National Institute on Drug Abuse.

Azrin, N. H. 1993. Disulfiram and Behavior Therapy: A Social-biological Model of Alcohol Abuse and Treatment. In C. Brewer, ed. *Treatment Options in Addiction: Medical Management of Alcohol and Opiate Abuse*. London: Gaskell.

Baker, F. 1993. Coordination of Alcohol, Drug Abuse, and Mental Health Services (Technical Assistance Publication Series 4). Rockville, Maryland: Center for Substance Abuse Treatment.

Ball, J. C. and A. Ross. 1991. The Effectiveness of Methadone Maintenance Treatment. New York: Springer-Verlag.

Ball, J. C., E. Corty, H. R. Bond, and A. Tommasello. 1988. The Reduction of Intravenous Heroin Use, Non-opiate Abuse and Crime During Methadone Maintenance Treatment: Further Findings. In L. S. Harris, ed. *Problems of Drug Dependence* (NIDA Research Monograph 81, pp. 224-230). Rockville, Maryland: National Institute on Drug Abuse.

Basta, J. M. and W. S. Davidson. 1988. Treatment of Juveniles: Study Outcomes Since 1980. *Behavioral Sciences and the Law*. 6(3), 355-384.

Beck, A., et al. 1993. Survey of State Prison Inmates (NCJ-136949). Washington, D.C.: U.S. Department of Justice, Bureau of Justice Statistics.

Benishek, L. A., K. J. Bieschke, B. E. Stoffelmayr, B. E. Mavis, and K. A. Humphrey. 1992. Gender Difference in Depression and Anxiety Among Alcoholics. *Journal of Substance Abuse*. 4, 235-245.

Brady, J. 1993. Enhancing Drug Abuse Treatment by Mobile Health Service. In J. Inciardi, F. M. Tims, and B. Fletcher, eds. *Innovative Strategies in the Treatment of Drug Abuse: Vol. I. Program Models and Strategies* (pp. 35-42). Westport, Connecticut: Greenwood Press.

Brahen, L. S. and C. Brewer. 1993. Naltrexone in the Criminal Justice System. In C. Brewer, ed. *Treatment Options in Addiction: Medical Management of Alcohol and Opiate Abuse* (pp. 46-53). London: Gaskell.

Brewer, C. 1993a. Naltrexone in the Prevention of Relapse and Opiate Detoxification. In C. Brewer, ed. *Treatment Options in Addiction: Medical Management of Alcohol and Opiate Abuse* (pp. 54-62). London: Gaskell.

———. 1993b. Probation-linked Treatment with Disulfiram: Dosage and the Alcohol-disulfiram Challenge. In C. Brewer, ed. *Treatment Options in Addiction: Medical Management of Alcohol and Opiate Abuse* (pp. 38-45). London: Gaskell.

Brewington, V., M. Smith, and D. Lipton. 1994. Acupuncture as a Detoxification Treatment: an Analysis of Controlled Research. *Journal of Substance Abuse Treatment.* 11(4), 289- 307.

Britt, C. L., M. R. Gottfredson, and J. S. Goldkamp. 1992. Drug Testing and Pretrial Misconduct: an Experiment on the Specific Deterrent Effects of Drug Monitoring Defendants on Pretrial Release. *Journal of Research on Crime and Delinquency.* 29(1), 62-78.

Brown, B. S., ed. 1979. *Addicts and Aftercare: Community Integration of the Former Drug Abuser.* Beverly Hills: Sage Publications.

Brown, B. S., G. W. Joe, and P. Thompson. 1995. Minority Group Status and Treatment Retention. *International Journal of the Addictions.* 20(2), 319-335.

Bureau of Justice Statistics. 1993. *Drug and Crime Facts, 1992* (NCJ-139651). Washington, D.C.: U.S. Department of Justice.

Carver, J. A. 1993. Using Drug Testing to Reduce Detention. *Federal Probation.* 57(1), 42-47.

Catalano, R. F., E. A. Wells, J. M. Jenson, and J. D. Hawkins. 1989. Aftercare Services for Drug-using Institutionalized Delinquents. *Social Service Review.* 63(4), 553-577.

Chaiken, J. M., and M. R. Chaiken. *Varieties of Criminal Behavior.* Santa Monica, California: RAND Corporation, 1982.

Chaiken, M. R. 1986. Crime Rates and Substance Abuse among Types of Offenders. In B. D. Johnson and E. Wish, eds. *Crime Rates among Drug-abusing Offenders* (Final Report to the National Institute of Justice). New York: Narcotic and Drug Research, Inc.

Cooper, J. R., F. Altman, B. S. Brown, and D. Czechowicz, eds. 1983. *Research on the Treatment of Narcotics Addiction: State of the Art (NIDA Treatment Research Monograph)*. Rockville, Maryland: National Institute on Drug Abuse.

Crowe, A. H., and R. Reeves. 1994. *Treatment for Alcohol and Other Drug Abuse: Opportunities for Coordination* (Technical Assistance Publication Series 11). Rockville, Maryland: Center for Substance Abuse Treatment.

D'Zurilla, T. J. 1986. *Problem-solving Therapy: A Social Competence Approach to Clinical Intervention.* New York: Springer-Verlag.

De La Rosa, M., and J-L. Recio Adrados, eds. 1993. *Drug Abuse among Minority Youth: Methodological Issues and Recent Advances.* (NIDA Research Monograph 130). Rockville, Maryland: National Institute on Drug Abuse.

De Leon, G. 1991. Retention in Drug-free Therapeutic Communities. In R. W. Pickens, C.G. Leukefeld, and C. R. Schuster, eds. *Improving Drug Abuse Treatment* (NIDA Research Monograph 106). Rockville, Maryland: National Institute on Drug Abuse.

Dembo, R., L. Williams, and J. Schmeidler. 1993. Addressing the Problems of Substance Abuse in Juvenile Corrections. In J. A. Inciardi, ed. *Drug Treatment and Criminal Justice* (pp. 97-126). Newbury Park, California: Sage Publications.

Falkin, G. P., D. S. Lipton, and H. K. Wexler. 1992. Drug Treatment in State Prisons. In D. R. Gerstein and H. J. Harwood, eds. *Treating Drug Problems* (Vol. 2, pp. 89-131). Washington, D.C.: National Academy Press.

Falkin, G., J. Wellisch, M. Prendergast, T. Kilian, J. Hawke, M. Natarajan, M. Kowalewski, and B. Owen. 1994. *Drug Treatment for Women Offenders: a Systems Perspective* (Project Report, National Institute of Justice Grant No. 92-IJ-CX-K018). Los Angeles: UCLA Drug Abuse Research Center; New York: National Development and Research Institutes, Inc.

"Forging Links to Treatment of the Substance-abusing Offender." 1993. Spring. TIE Communiqué: A Memo to the Field from the Center for Substance Abuse Treatment (Special Issue).

Garrett, C. J. 1985. Effects of Residential Treatment on Adjudicated Delinquents: A Meta-analysis. *Journal of Research in Crime and Delinquency.* 22(4), 287-308.

Gendreau, P., and D. A. Andrews. 1990. Tertiary Prevention: What the Meta-analysis of the Offender Treatment Literature Tells Us about "What Works." *Canadian Journal of Criminology.* 32, 173-184.

Gendreau, P., and R. R. Ross. 1987. Revivification of Rehabilitation: Evidence from the 1980s. *Justice Quarterly.* 4(3), 349-407.

Gerstein, D. R. and H. J. Harwood, eds. 1990. Treating Drug Problems: Vol. 1: A Study of the Evolution, Effectiveness, and Financing of Public and Private Drug Treatment Systems. Washington, D.C.: National Academy Press.

Gordon, D. A., and J. Arbuthnot. 1987. Individual, Group, and Family Interventions. In H. C. Quay, ed. *Handbook of Juvenile Delinquency* (pp. 290-324). New York: Wiley and Sons.

Gorski, T. T., J. M. Kelley, L. Havens, and R. H. Peters. 1993. *Relapse Prevention and the Substance-abusing Criminal Offenders* (Technical Assistance Publication Series 8). Rockville, Maryland: Center for Substance Abuse Treatment.

Gottschalk, R., W. S. Davidson, L. K. Gensheimer, and J. P. Mayer. 1987. Community-based Interventions. In H. C. Quay, ed. *Handbook of Juvenile Delinquency* (pp. 266-289). New York: Wiley and Sons.

Harlow, C. W. 1991. *Drugs and Jail Inmates, 1989* (NCJ-130836). Washington, D.C.: U.S. Department of Justice, Bureau of Justice Statistics.

Heather, N. 1993. Disulfiram Treatment for Alcohol Problems: Is it Effective and, If So, Why? In C. Brewer, ed. *Treatment Options in Addiction: Medical Management of Alcohol and Opiate Abuse* (pp. 1-18). London: Gaskell.

Higgins, S. T., A. J. Budney, W. K. Bickel, J. R. Hughes, F. Foerg, and G. Badger. 1993. Achieving Cocaine Abstinence with a Behavioral Approach. *American Journal of Psychiatry*. 150(5), 763-769.

Higgins, S. T., D. D. Delaney, A. J. Budney, W. K. Bickel, J. R. Hughes, F. Foerg, and J. W. Fenwick. 1991. A Behavioral Approach to Achieving Initial Cocaine Abstinence. *American Journal of Psychiatry*. 148(9), 1216-1224.

Holder, H., R. Longabaugh, W. R. Miller, and A. V. Rubonis. 1991. The Cost Effectiveness of Treatment for Alcoholism: A First Approximation. *Journal of Studies on Alcoholism*. 52(6), 517- 540.

Hser, Y-I., M. D. Anglin, and C. P. Chou. 1988. Evaluation of Drug Abuse Treatment: A Repeated Measures Design Assessing Methadone Maintenance. *Evaluation Review*. 12(5), 547-570.

Hubbard, R. L., M. E. Marsden, J. V. Rachal, H. J. Harwood, E. R. Cavanaugh, and H. M. Ginzburg. 1989. *Drug Abuse Treatment: A National Study of Effectiveness*. Chapel Hill: University of North Carolina Press.

Husband, S. D. and J. J. Platt. 1993. The Cognitive Skills Component in Substance Abuse Treatment in Correctional Settings: A Brief Review. *Journal of Drug Issues*. 23(1), 31- 42.

Inciardi, J. A. 1979. Heroin Use and Street Crime. *Crime and Delinquency*. 25(3), 335-346.

———. 1994. Screening and Assessment of Alcohol and Other Drug Abusers in the Criminal Justice System (Treatment Improvement Protocol 7). Rockville, Maryland: Center for Substance Abuse Treatment.

Inciardi, J. A. and D. C. McBride. 1991. Treatment Alternatives to Street Crime (TASC): History, Experiences, and Issues (DHHS Pub. No. (ADM) 91-1749). Rockville, Maryland: National Institute on Drug Abuse.

Inciardi, J. A., D. C. McBride, and B. A. Weinman. 1993. The Assessment and Referral of Criminal Justice Clients: Examining the Focused Offender Disposition Program. In J. Inciardi, ed. *Drug Treatment and Criminal Justice* (pp. 149-193). Newbury Park, California: Sage Publications. (Includes the Offender Profile Index, with instructions.)

Izzo, R. L., and R. R. Ross. 1990. Meta-analysis of Rehabilitation Programs for Juvenile Delinquents: A Brief Report. *Criminal Justice and Behavior.* 17(1), 134-142.

Johnson, B. and E. Wish, eds. 1986. *Crime Rates among Drug-abusing Offenders: Final Report to the National Institute of Justice.* New York: Narcotic and Drug Research, Inc.

Khalsa, H., M. D. Anglin, and A. Paredes. 1992. Cocaine Abuse: Outcomes of Therapeutic Interventions. *Substance Abuse.* 13(4),165-179.

Kosten, T. R. and H. D. Kleber. 1984. Strategies to Improve Compliance with Narcotic Antagonists. *American Journal of Drug and Alcohol Abuse.* 10(2), 249-266.

Kosten, T. R., B. J. Rounsaville, and H. D. Kleber. 1985. Ethnic and Gender Differences among Opiate Addicts. *International Journal of the Addictions.* 20(8), 1143-1162.

Lab, S. P., and J. T. Whitehead. 1988. An Analysis of Juvenile Correctional Treatment. *Crime and Delinquency.* 34(1), 60-83.

Leukefeld, C. G. and F. M. Tims. 1992. Drug Abuse Treatment in Prisons and Jails (NIDA Research Monograph 118). Rockville, Maryland: National Institute on Drug Abuse.

Little, G. L., K. D. Robinson, and K. D. Burnette. 1993. Cognitive Behavioral Treatment of Felony Drug Offenders: A Five-year Recidivism Report. *Psychological Reports.* 73, 1089-1090.

Longshore, D., S. Hsieh, M. D. Anglin. 1993. Ethnic and Gender Differences in Drug Users' Perceived Need for Treatment. *International Journal of the Addictions.* 28(6), 539-558.

Lowinson, J. H., P. Ruiz, R. B. Millman, and J. G. Langrod, eds. 1992. *Substance Abuse: a Comprehensive Textbook* (2nd ed.). Baltimore, Maryland: Williams and Wilkins.

Maddux, J. F. and D. P. Desmond. 1979. Crime and Drug Use Behavior: an Areal Analysis. *Criminology.* 19, 281-302.

Marlatt, G. A. and J. R. Gordon. 1985. *Relapse Prevention: Maintenance Strategies in the Treatment of Addictive Behaviors*. New York: Guilford.

Martin, S. S., and J. A. Inciardi. 1993a. Case Management Approaches for Criminal Justice Clients. In J. A. Inciardi, ed. *Drug Treatment and Criminal Justice* (pp. 81-96). Newbury Park, California: Sage Publications.

———. 1993b. A Case Management Treatment Program for Drug-involved Prison Releasees. *Prison Journal*. 73(3-4), 319-331.

Martin, S. S., and F. R. Scarpitti. 1993. An Intensive Case Management Approach for Paroled IV Drug Users. *Journal of Drug Issues*. 23(1), 43-59.

Martinson, R. 1974. What Works? Questions and Answers about Prison Reform. *Public Interest*. 35, 22-54.

———. 1979. New Findings, New Views: A Note of Caution Regarding Sentencing Reform. *Hofstra Law Review*. 7(2), 243-258.

McBride, D. C., and J. A. Inciardi. 1993. The Focused Offender Disposition Program: Philosophy, Procedures, and Preliminary Findings. *Journal of Drug Issues*. 23(1), 143-160.

McGlothlin, W. H., M. D. Anglin, and B. D. Wilson. 1977. *An Evaluation of the California Civil Addict Program* (NIDA Services Research Monograph Series, DHEW Publication No. (ADM) 78-558). Rockville, Maryland: National Institute on Drug Abuse.

McLellan, A. T. and A. I. Alterman. 1991. Patient Treatment Matching: A Conceptual and Methodological Review with Suggestions for Further Research. In W. R. Pickens, C. G. Leukefeld, and R. C. Schuster, eds. *Improving Drug Treatment* (NIDA Research Monograph 106). Rockville, Maryland: National Institute on Drug Abuse.

McLellan, A. T., I. O. Arndt, D. S. Metzger, G. E. Woody, and C. P. O'Brien. 1993. The Effects of Psychosocial Services in Substance Abuse Treatment. *Journal of the American Medical Association*. 269(15), 1953-1959.

McLellan, A. T., D. S. Grossman, J. D. Blaine, and H. W. Haverkos. 1993. Acupuncture Treatment for Drug Abuse: A Technical Review. *Journal of Substance Abuse Treatment*. 10(6), 569-576.

McLellan, A. T., L. Luborsky, J. Cacciola, J. Griffith, J. McGahan, and C. P. O'Brien. 1985. *Guide to the Addiction Severity Index: Background, Administration, and Field Testing Results* (DHHS Pub. No. (ADM) 85-1419). Rockville, Maryland: National Institute on Drug Abuse.

McLellan, A. T., L. Luborsky, G. E. Woody, C. P. O'Brien, and R. Kron. 1981. Are the "Addict-related" Problems of Substance Abusers Really Related? *Journal of Nervous and Mental Disease*. 169, 232-239.

McLellan, A. T., G. E. Woody, L. Luborsky, C. P. O'Brien, and K. A. Druley. 1983. Increased Effectiveness of Substance Abuse Treatment: A Prospective Study of Patient Treatment and Matching. *Journal of Nervous and Mental Disease*. 83, 597- 605.

Miller, W. R. and R. K. Hester. 1986. Treating the problem drinker: Modern Approaches. In W. R. Miller, ed. *The Addictive Behaviors: Treatment of Alcoholism, Drug Abuse, Smoking, and Obesity* (pp. 11-141). Oxford: Pergamon Press.

National Institute of Justice. 1993. Drug Use Forecasting: 1992 *Annual Report: Drugs and Crime in America's Cities*. Washington, D.C.: National Institute of Justice.

Novick, D. M. and H. Joseph. 1991. Medical Maintenance: the Treatment of Chronic Opiate Dependence in General Medical Practice. *Journal of Substance Abuse Treatment*. 8, 233-239.

Nurco, D. N., T. W. Kinlock, and T. E. Hanlon. 1990. The Drugs-Crime Connection. In J. A. Inciardi, ed. *Handbook of Drug Control in the United States* (pp. 71-90). Westport, Connecticut: Greenwood Press.

Onken, L. S., J. D. Blaine, and J. J. Boren, eds. 1993. *Behavioral Treatments for Drug Abuse and Dependence* (NIDA Research Monograph 137). Rockville, Maryland: National Institute on Drug Abuse.

Orlandi, M. A., ed. 1992. *Cultural Competence for Evaluators: a Guide for Alcohol and Other Drug Abuse Prevention Practitioners Working with Ethnic/racial Communities* (OSAP Cultural Competence Series 1). Rockville, Maryland: Office for Substance Abuse Prevention.

Oyemade, U. J., and D. Brandon-Monye, eds. 1990. *Ecology of Alcohol and Other Drug Use: Helping Black High-risk Youth* (OSAP Prevention Monograph 7). Rockville, Maryland: Office for Substance Abuse Prevention.

Perez-Arce, P., K. D. Carr, and J. L. Sorensen. 1993. Cultural Issues in an Outpatient Program for Stimulant Abusers. *Journal of Psychoactive Drugs*. 25(1), 35-44.

Petersilia, J. 1990. Conditions that Permit Intensive Supervision Programs to Survive. *Crime and Delinquency*. 36(1), 126-145.

Petersilia, J., S. Turner, and E. Deschenes. 1992. Intensive Supervision Programs for Drug Offenders. In J. M. Byrne, A. J. Lurigio, and J. Petersilia, eds. *Smart Sentencing: The Emergence of Intermediate Sanctions* (pp. 18-37). Newbury Park, California: Sage Publications.

Platt, J. J., M. F. Prout, and D. S. Metzger. 1986. Interpersonal Cognitive Problem-solving Therapy. In W. Dryden and N. Gordon, eds. *Cognitive-behavioral Approaches to Psychotherapy* (pp. 261-289). London: Pergamon.

Positive Effects Are Seen in D.C. Court Project. 1994, June. *CJN Newsletter*. 2(12).

Powers, K. I. and Anglin, M. D. 1993. Cumulative Versus Stabilizing Effects of Methadone Maintenance: a Quasi-experimental Study Using Longitudinal Self-report Data. *Evaluation Review*. 17(3), 243-270.

Prendergast, M., M. D. Anglin, T. Maugh, and Y. Hser. (In press). *The Effectiveness of Treatment for Drug Abuse*. Rockville, Maryland: National Institute on Drug Abuse.

Rawson, R. A., J. L. Obert, M. J. McCann, and W. Ling, W. 1993. Neurobehavioral Treatment for Cocaine Dependency: A Preliminary Evaluation. In F. M. Tims and C. G. Leukefeld. *Cocaine Treatment: Research and Clinical Perspectives* (NIDA Research Monograph 135, pp. 92-115). Rockville, Maryland: National Institute on Drug Abuse.

Rawson, R. A., J. L. Obert, M. J. McCann, and A. J. Mann. 1986. Cocaine Treatment Outcome: Cocaine Use Following Inpatient, Outpatient, and No Treatment. In L. S. Harris, ed. *Problems of Drug Dependence, 1985* (NIDA Research Monograph 67, pp. 271-277). Rockville, Maryland: National Institute on Drug Abuse.

Rawson, R. A., J. L. Obert, M. J. McCann, and P. Marinelli-Casey. 1993. Relapse Prevention Models for Substance Abuse Treatment. *Psychotherapy*. 30(2), 284-298.

Rawson, R. A., and F. S. Tennant, Jr. 1984. Five-year Follow-up of Opiate Addicts with Naltrexone and Behavior Therapy. In L. S. Harris, ed. *Problems of Drug Dependence, 1983: Proceedings of the 45th Annual Scientific Meeting, The Committee on Problems of Drug Dependence, Inc.* (NIDA Research Monograph 49, pp. 289-295). Rockville, Maryland: National Institute on Drug Abuse.

Robinson, R. A. 1992. Intermediate Sanctions and the Female Offender. In J. M. Byrne, A. J. Lurigio, and J. Petersilia, eds. *Smart Sentencing: The Emergence of Intermediate Sanctions* (pp. 245-260). Newbury Park, California: Sage Publications.

Ross, R. R. and E. A. Fabiano. 1985. *Time to Think: a Model of Delinquency Prevention and Offender Rehabilitation*. Johnson City, Tennessee: Institute of Social Sciences and Arts, Inc.

Senay, E. C. 1985. Methadone Maintenance Treatment. *International Journal of the Addictions*. 20(6-7), 803-821.

Shaw, J. W. and D. L. Mackenzie. 1992. The One-year Community Supervision Performance of Drug Offenders and Louisiana DOC-identified Substance Abusers Graduating from Shock Incarceration. *Journal of Criminal Justice*. 20, 501-516.

Simpson, D. D., G. W. Joe, W. E. K. Lehman, and S. B. Sells. 1986. Addiction Careers: Etiology, Treatment, and 12-year Follow-up Procedures. *Journal of Drug Issues*. 16(1), 107-121.

Smith, D. E., M. E. Buxton, R. Bilal, and R. Seymour. 1993. Cultural Points of Resistance to the 12-step Recovery Process. *Journal of Psychoactive Drugs*. 25(1), 97-108.

Speckart, G. R. and M. D. Anglin. 1986. Narcotics and Crime: A Causal Modeling Approach. *Journal of Quantitative Criminology*. 2, 3-28.

Stitzer, M. L., M. Y. Iguchi, M. Kidorf, and G. E. Bigelow. 1993. Contingency Management in Methadone Treatment: The Case for Positive Incentives. In L. S. Onken, J. D. Blaine, and J. J. Boren, eds. *Behavioral Treatments for Drug Abuse and Dependence* (NIDA Research Monograph 137, pp. 19-36). Rockville, Maryland: National Institute on Drug Abuse.

Swartz, J. 1993. TASC—The Next 20 Years: Extending, Refining, and Assessing the Model. In J. A. Inciardi, ed. *Drug Treatment and Criminal Justice* (pp. 127-148). Newbury Park, California: Sage Publications.

Tauber, J. S. 1994, Summer. Drug Courts: A Judicial Manual. *CJER Journal* (Special Issue).

Taylor, J. and B. Jackson. 1990. Factors Affecting Alcohol Consumption in Black Women: Parts I and II. *International Journal of the Addictions*. 25 (11, 12), 1287-1300, 1415-1427.

Tims, F. M. and C. G. Leukefeld, eds. 1986. *Relapse and Recovery in Drug Abuse* (NIDA Research Monograph 72). Rockville, Maryland: National Institute on Drug Abuse.

———. 1993. *Cocaine Treatment: Research and Clinical Perspectives* (NIDA Research Monograph 135). Rockville, Maryland: National Institute on Drug Abuse.

Vito, G. F., Wilson, D. G., and Holmes, S. T. 1993. Drug Testing in Community Corrections: Results from a Four-year Program. *Prison Journal*. 73(3-4), 343-354.

Wallen, J. 1992. A Comparison of Male and Female Clients in Substance Abuse Treatment. *Journal of Substance Abuse Treatment*. 9, 243-248.

Washburn, A. M., R. E. Fullilove, M. T. Fullilove, P. A. Keenan, B. McGee, K. A. Morris, J. L. Sorensen, and W. W. Clark. 1993. Acupuncture Heroin Detoxification: a Single-blind Clinical Trial. *Journal of Substance Abuse Treatment*, 10(4), 345-351.

Wellisch, J., M. Prendergast, and M. D. Anglin. 1993a. Criminal Justice and Drug Treatment Systems Linkage: Federal Promotion of Interagency Collaboration in the 1970s. *Contemporary Drug Problems*. 20(4), 611-650.

———. 1993b. Numbers and Characteristics of Drug-using Women in the Criminal Justice System: Implications for Treatment. *Journal of Drug Issues*. 23(1), 7-30.

———. 1993c. Treatment Strategies for Women Offenders. In J. Inciardi, ed. *Drug Treatment and Criminal Justice* (pp. 5-29). Newbury Park, California: Sage Publications.

———. 1994. *Drug-abusing Women Offenders: Results of a National Survey* (NCJ 149261). Washington, D.C.: National Institute of Justice.

Whitehead, J. T. and S. P. Lab. 1989. A Meta-analysis of Juvenile Correctional Treatment. *Journal of Research in Crime and Delinquency*. 26(3), 276-295.

Wish, E. and B. Gropper. 1990. Drug Testing by the Criminal Justice System: Methods and Applications. In M. Tonry and J. Wilson, eds. *Drugs and Crime* (pp. 321-391). Chicago: University of Chicago Press.

Wright, W. E. and M. C. Dixon. 1977. Community Prevention and Treatment of Juvenile Delinquency: A Review of Evaluation Studies. *Journal of Research in Crime and Delinquency*. 14(1), 35-67.

TREATMENT AND REINTEGRATION OF VIOLENT OFFENDERS

6

Jeffrey Fagan, Ph.D.
School of Criminal Justice
Rutgers University
Newark, New Jersey

Introduction

Violence has become an obsession of American society. Since the 1960s, when three national task forces addressed its root causes, violence has been the bellwether of crime control policy and sentencing practices. Beginning in 1980, a succession of national commissions and task forces has addressed the causes and cures of interpersonal violence. Collectively, these efforts identify a set of recurring themes: (1) there are a wide range of violent behaviors that cause injury, (2) there are identifiable risk factors that suggest a social and spatial concentration of violence and injury, (3) violence has multiple and complex causes, (4) violence is difficult to predict, (5) the problem cannot be controlled exclusively by increasing the severity or certainty of punishment, (6) evaluations of prevention and intervention programs have mixed results,

(7) programs should be conceptually grounded in theories about how violence starts and stops, and (8) significant investment is needed in intervention experiments and rigorous evaluation.

Despite this consensus, violence has persisted since the early 1970s at rates far higher than any prior decade (Reiss and Roth, 1993). The historical difficulty of finding effective controls for violence once again has raised social concern about violent crime. Today, the long and rancorous debate on correctional effectiveness is focused on violent offenders. Law and policy reflect skepticism about the efficacy of programs that attempt to rehabilitate offenders. Among policymakers, the ideals of individualized treatment collapsed in the 1970s, giving way to sentencing practices underwritten by deterrence and incapacitation theories (Cullen and Gilbert, 1982). The public agenda also was driven by promises of high returns to public safety from sentencing algorithms based on identification and incapacitation of "career criminals" who are responsible for a disproportionate share of violent and other serious crimes (Blumstein, Cohen, and Nagin, 1979; Greenwood and Abrahamse, 1982). For retributive as well as protective purposes, sentencing practices and parole policies shifted dramatically starting in the 1970s, relying increasingly on longer sentences, more certain incarceration terms, and greater difficulty in obtaining release on parole.

The result was an unprecedented increase in prison populations over the past two decades. Incarceration rates rose steadily beginning in the mid-1970s, reaching record levels in many states by the 1990s (Cohen and Canela-Cacho, 1994; Tonry, 1995). Total adjusted prison population rates grew by 146 percent from 1975 to 1989 (Cohen and Canela-Cacho, 1994: 298). Detailed analyses in six states show that incarceration rates for robbery, murder, and aggravated assault rose during this time at about the same rate (Cohen and Canela-Cacho, 1994: 303), and the amount of time served per violent offense nearly tripled in that time (Cohen and Canela-Cacho, 1994: 314). The adult index crime rates also grew (Cohen and Canela-Cacho, 1994: 310).

But, these increases in prison populations are not easily attributed to a rise in the indexed (serious) crime rate, especially after controlling for changes in the age and racial composition of the population during this time (Cohen and Canela-Cacho, 1994). In fact, violent crime rates for 1979 and 1985 adjusted by age and race remained stable (Cohen and Canala-Cacho, 1994). Accordingly, one would have expected that a near tripling of both the prison population and the average sentence would have yielded significant reductions in violent crime rates. There were none. The

National Academy of Science's violence panel concluded that there were no marginal returns in deterrence or incapacitation from expanding the prison populations, and that further expansion of prison capacity would be necessary to begin to realize reductions in violent crime rates (Reiss and Roth, 1993: 292-4). These authors suggested that policies to control violent crime look elsewhere.

The failure of this mass social experiment to reduce violence suggests the importance of searching for alternatives to incarceration and alternative uses of incarceration in a broader conceptualization of intervention. The absence of significant effects of treatment interventions in part reflects the narrow range of sanctions that accompany most substantive interventions (Weisburd, 1993). That is, there is little reason to expect criminal sanctions to have crime-control effects except when mediated through interventions that interact with offender characteristics and sanctions (Andrews et al., 1990). Accordingly, the integration of treatment and punishment has implications for correctional policy in three ways: (1) in the structuring of punishments to incorporate elements of effective interventions, (2) in the design of substantive interventions that respond to the individual characteristics of violent offenders, and (3) in the design of punishment-intervention combinations that are rationally allocated to the various types of violent offenders.

In this chapter, the prospects for treatment interventions for violent offenders are examined within the context of legal sanctions. Contemporary law and policy dictates that treatment interventions for violent offenders will take place in a correctional context, and that part of it is likely to involve a nontrivial deprivation of liberty. However, we may substitute for the retributive vision of the past twenty years, a new vision of correctional intervention as a transformative process. Instead of a correctional experience that reproduces crime, we assess the prospects for correctional services that maximize the gains from rehabilitation for a high stakes, politically salient population where tolerances for failure are quite narrow.

The discussion begins with a review of empirical knowledge of violent offenders that will serve as a basis for consideration of appropriate intervention services. Next, the effectiveness of correctional interventions is reviewed, including services for both violent and other offenders. Their applicability for violent offenders is discussed. The next section then proposes a set of design principles and substantive considerations for correctional interventions. A research agenda and policy directions conclude the chapter.

Understanding Violence and Violent Offenders

One source of variation in correctional outcomes is the interaction between programs and characteristics of individuals (Andrews et al., 1990; Lipsey, 1992; Palmer, 1994). Interventions should be differentiated by individual characteristics and appropriate interventions provided according to risk and need. Accordingly, understanding the heterogeneity of violent offenders is a basic step in assigning individuals to treatments. We begin therefore with a review of the characteristics of violent offenders and an assessment of causal mechanisms that appear to underlie violent behaviors. The several commissions that have examined violence in the past decade have generated a massive body of empirical knowledge about violent offenders, information that is timely and useful in considering the design of correctional interventions. This information is summarized here.

Types of Violent Behavior

We begin by defining the types of behaviors and offenses that have become the focus of the public debate on violence. Compared to aggression, which includes threats of physical injury or acts that cause psychological harm, the term *violence* specifies behaviors that inflict physical injury (Gelles and Straus, 1979). In this chapter, we focus on interpersonal violence, not aggression. Violence evokes a social and legal response, and is the behavior that is codified in penal code and delinquency statutes. While threats of violence are legally proscribed, they represent a dimension of harm different from physical injury.

Violent sexual behavior is included because it includes the threat or actual use of force to gain sexual compliance. The chapter also is concerned with violence by individuals, rather than small groups or collectivities. Although small groups are important, they are considered contexts for violence. It is the *individual* within the group who commits the violent act, responding to contingencies within the group. Also, the law punishes individuals, and it is individuals who populate prisons and correctional programs. Finally, the majority of social and behavioral science literature focuses on individuals, and it is from this literature that the principles for intervention are derived. Behaviors that result in self-directed and unintentional injuries are excluded, as they do not incur a legal sanction.

Interpersonal violence includes several types of interactions that differ in their contexts and motivations. The differences are important for understanding the opportunities and foci for intervention. There also may be different segments of the population who engage in the various forms of violence, again suggesting the possibility of different social, therapeutic, and legal responses. For example, Felson (1993) distinguishes between dispute-related and predatory violence. Megargee (1982) differentiates between expressive and instrumental violence. Some violence is difficult to explain in any of these terms, and even possibly is gratuitous (Katz, 1988). Tolan and Guerra (1994) identify four types of violence: situational, relationship, predatory, and psychopathological. Goldstein (1985) shows that drug-related violence involves three patterns: economic compulsive violence (to supply money or drugs to satisfy addictions), systemic violence (associated with the drug trade), and psychopharmacological violence (where violence results from altered physiological or emotional states after drugs are consumed). Fagan and Wexler (1988) distinguish adolescents who engage in sexual violence from other types of violent adolescents by showing the differences in family and social risk factors in these two groups.

Whatever the taxonomy, there is consistent recognition that there are meaningful distinctions among different types of violent transactions. Common to these taxonomies are several factors with implications for intervention. Because some individuals are only violent in specific contexts, such as bar fights or toward intimates, the social context of violence is an important risk factor. Some people become violent only after becoming intoxicated or after exposure to some other form of stress. This, too, suggests specific directions for interventions.

Still others may suffer from a mental disorder or unprovoked expressions of uncontrolled rage, conditions that Lewis et al. (1979; 1984) show are related to severe psychological trauma or neural system damage from physical trauma to the head. Predatory violence involves violence as a form of coercion to gain material goods or compliance, while other violence is motivated by drives for domination and degradation. Expressive violence involves violence as an exaggerated display of manhood, or as the result of a social "script" where some perpetrators may perceive no other behavioral choice (Oliver, 1994). Still other violence is defensive or preemptive toward a person who is perceived of as threatening.

While it is useful to consider these taxonomies in understanding violence and determining appropriate interventions, it also is important to remember the heuristic nature of such taxonomies. The types they suggest do not themselves have specific causal mechanisms, but instead are descriptive categories that may change as more information becomes known. They also are not likely to be exclusive. Fagan and Chin (1990) offer the following example: a drug user who sells small quantities to finance his drug use, in robbing a would-be buyer, is engaging in violence that is *both* systemic and economically compulsive.

The various types of violence are likely to vary in their prevalence, stability, causes, and appropriate interventions. Most programs do not focus on violence, with the exception of programs for sex offenders. Among those that do, few distinguish among types of violence. But we reasonably may assume that interventions for one type may not apply to the next, and that interventions are not generalizable across the different types of violence. The types of violence (and appropriate interventions) also may vary by developmental stage, with some types disappearing over the life course. For example, expressive violence may be quite prevalent during adolescence, but may transform over time toward other forms, such as situational or instrumental violence. There is much to be learned about careers of violence, and effective interventions should anticipate this broad range of behaviors in the larger domain of violence.

Individual and Neighborhood Characteristics

Despite the errors and omissions in both official arrest records and offender surveys, several characteristics of violent offenders are well known. Males have higher base rates of violence than females, for most types of violence. In 1991, men comprised 89 percent of all arrestees for violent crimes. Women accounted for only 10 percent of homicide arrests, 8 percent of robbery arrests, and 1 percent of arrests for forcible rape. However, female arrest rates are changing quickly. The prevalence of arrests for women generally is increasing, and the increases are greater for African-American and Latino women compared to whites (Sommers and Baskin, 1992). For violent offenses involving intimates, self-report data suggest that the gender gap persists but is narrower than for stranger crimes (Straus and Gelles, 1990; but also *see* Fagan and Browne, 1994). However, women more often tend to use violence against spouses defensively, and more often suffer physical injury from an assault by an intimate (Browne and Williams, 1993).

Among both males and females, arrest rates for murder, robbery, aggravated assault, and manslaughter have been highest among persons ages fifteen to twenty-four for several years. Arrests for forcible rape were highest for males ages twenty to twenty-nine. Adolescent males fifteen to nineteen had the highest robbery arrest rates, while males twenty to twenty-four had the highest aggravated assault arrest rates. Rates for females are about 10 percent of the rates for males for all age groups through age forty-four.

African-Americans are disproportionately represented in arrests for violent crimes, including homicide, aggravated assaults, and robberies. In 1991, for example, their arrest rates were nearly six times greater than whites (Reiss and Roth, 1993). Their rates are slightly higher than white and Hispanic youths in the National Youth Survey (Elliott, Huizinga, and Menard, 1989). The narrower gap by race in the National Youth Survey is important since the National Youth Survey cohorts are younger and closer to the peak age for violent offending.

Nearly three in four violent crimes are committed by single offenders. The presence of multiple offenders is associated with multiple victimizations. While there is significant overlap between victim and offender characteristics, and many offenders also are victims, there are important differences in the characteristics of victims of violence and violent offenders (Sampson and Lauritsen, 1994).

Violent offenders consistently come from neighborhoods characterized by some measure of poverty or social deprivation (Sampson and Lauritsen, 1994). This trend is especially true for homicide (Land et al., 1990). The effects of neighborhood change are especially strong: communities that are rapidly becoming poorer or gentrified are more vulnerable to violence than stable but poor communities (Taylor and Covington, 1988).

High rates of family disruption, population density, joblessness and social mobility—that is, high rates of population turnover in a community—also are tied to higher violence rates (Sampson, 1987). Fagan (1993b) showed that risks of spouse assault were highest in neighborhoods with high rates of unmarried adults and high population turnover, trends he attributed to the low premium assigned to intimate relationships and weak social controls among neighbors. Because the predictors of area-wide violence rates are similar for African-Americans and whites, Sampson (1987) concluded that the effects of joblessness and family disruption on violence rates were independent of any cultural factors associated with specific ethnic or racial groups. Another characteristic of these areas is their weak or attenuated networks for supervision of adolescents, a factor of critical importance in the design of interventions with violent delinquents. Because of their social disorganization and weak social control, these also tend to be areas where gangs are active and formal institutions are weak (Bursik and Grasmick, 1993).

Risk Factors and Causal Paths

The causes of violence involve biological, psychological, situational, and social factors. Violence often arises from the interactions of these factors, in many cases beginning with complex developmental processes during early childhood (Reiss and Roth, 1993: 105 and Appendix A). There also appear to be protective factors such as shy temperament, high IQ, and stable family life that help defeat the influence of other risk factors (Huesmann, 1988; Moffitt, 1990). Recent theoretical work suggests that explanations of violence are shareable with the etiology of other forms of deviance and can be traced to poor socialization and low self-control (Gottfredson and Hirschi, 1990). The several commissions who reported in the early 1990s on the antecedents of violence disagree with this perspective, and claim that there are multiple causes and pathways to violence.

Risk factors and causal mechanisms are likely to vary according to the type of violence, and many causal relationships are likely to be contingent. That is, the antecedents of chronic fighting or robbery may vary from the factors underlying violent sexual behavior or homicide. Many factors may be disproportionately present among violent offenders, but they may be only weak predictors when viewed longitudinally among a cohort who share the risk. For example, sexual abuse in childhood has a very strong and well known causal relationship to subsequent violent sexual behavior. Yet, most sexually abused children do not grow up to become child molesters (Prentky, 1990). Whether this risk factor becomes a causal factor depends on many contingencies: the child's relationship to the adult, his or her reaction to the childhood event, and the reactions of important adults.

Similar conclusions can be reached for such early childhood risk factors of violence generally, such as perinatal complications prior to birth, genetic influences, family disruption, embedment as a child in a violent family or neighborhood, or learning disabilities. Moffitt (1990) shows that biological risks of antisocial behavior among adolescents often interact with social processes in the occurrence of violence. Overall, risk factors and causal mechanisms either can be aggravated or mitigated by later social processes and contexts. These contexts point to loci for intervention that may be more influential due to their proximity to the behaviors rather than the distal influences of early childhood socialization.

Other risk factors include concurrent behavioral problems that result from a common set of underlying risks and deficits. Elliott, Huizinga, and Menard (1989) view a wide range of "problem behaviors" in late adolescence as the outcome of the same antecedents in adolescent and early childhood development that are implicated in violence. These concurrent or related behaviors include teenage pregnancy, emotional symptomology, substance abuse, and school dropout. Epidemiologists consider these as factors of "comorbidity," and weigh them as risk factors for other behaviors that tend to occur in clusters. But risk factors are not necessarily causally implicated, and resolving one risk factor may not lead to a cessation of comorbid behaviors. Although comorbidity is helpful in assessing the risks of violence, violence still may persist even after comorbid behaviors cease.

The salience of causal factors in correctional intervention is likely to vary by age. Intervention on risk factors and antecedents is likely to have a higher payoff for younger offenders, but may be less influential for older individuals who have progressed through several developmental stages and life roles. For younger offenders, the continuing presence of risk factors, their temporal proximity to causal mechanisms, and the developmental context of adolescence present opportunities for specific interventions that focus on redirecting socialization.

For example, socially learned aggression, reinforced by peer groups, suggest that interventions should address learned responses to violence or the facilitating role of peer interactions. But for older violent offenders, interventions may be more effective by concentrating on hastening the natural processes of career termination or desistance. They are some time from the developmental stages where violence began, and interventions on those risk factors no longer may influence learned and practiced behaviors. Involvement in violence also may truncate their social networks in later life, making it difficult for developmentally focused interventions to be effective. For example, older offenders who are more motivated to leave violence may be more responsive than adolescents or young adults to job opportunities and material incentives that enable them to occupy new social roles (Sampson and Laub, 1993).

Situational Contexts of Violence

Violence is concentrated in specific locations and social contexts (Fagan, 1993a, 1993b). The dynamics of interpersonal transactions in these milieus often contribute directly to violence. Individuals who are violent in no other setting may engage in routine and serious acts of physical violence in specific milieus. Because individuals function in social units—families, bars, gangs, markets, workplaces, prisons, schools—there are processes within those social contexts that create conflict or establish norms for using violence to settle conflicts. There is variation among these social units in their rates of violent incidents, after controlling for the composition of the people in those places. That variation is explained by the specific rules, norms, and the social dynamics of those places.

For example, fights are more common in bars with low lighting, impersonal styles of selling alcohol, frequent alcohol sales, and groups of individuals unknown to each other (Gibbs, 1986). Gangs vary in the frequency and severity of violence among their members (Fagan, 1989), and young people are more likely to engage in violence during their tenure in the gang than either before joining or after leaving (Thornberry, Farnworth, and Krohn, 1993). Drug markets also are places with high violence rates (Goldstein, 1985; Fagan and Chin, 1990). Robberies (for cash or drugs) and homicides often occur in the course of drug transactions since these are unregulated illegal businesses that are not subject to the usual means of settling disputes (Goldstein et al., 1989). Some schools have high rates of violence between students. Gottfredson (1986) shows how neighborhood factors interact with the school context to influence rates of violence in schools. Families are fertile grounds for assaults due to the shield of privacy, the frequent contact between assailants and victims, the cultural imperatives that men may invoke to control women, and conflicts between partners over sharing resources and tasks (Fagan and Browne, 1994).

In all these situations, violence results from the interaction of individual characteristics with the contingencies of the setting and the aggregate characteristics of people in those settings. In situations where alcohol is present, for example, the effects of intoxication on cognition may result in perceived threats or conflicts where none is intended, leading to a fight (Fagan, 1990c).

When weapons are present, these fights may readily escalate to lethal violence as calculations of risk and threat are skewed by the combination of intoxication and strategic decisions fueled by fear. In inner cities, social imperatives and behavioral "codes" may leave people little choice but to engage in violence to preserve their sense of self or to protect their immediate physical space (Oliver, 1994; Anderson, 1994).

Accordingly, situations contribute to violence in several ways: by shaping behavioral norms that support the use of violence in disputes, by compromising social controls that may otherwise defuse or prohibit violence, and by providing a social milieu that produces a range of triggering events. These events may lead to arousal of fear or physiological arousal, or altered emotional states such as paranoia or hostility, or launch a social script that leaves disputants few options other than physical violence to settle conflict. Other contexts simply may remove restraints on behavior or furnish a supply of opportunities and victims for motivated offenders to rob or assault.

Implications for Policy and Program Design

These risk factors and causal mechanisms are related to violence in complex ways. Some are direct influences, while others lead to violence only under certain contingencies or in specific interactions. The complexity and range of risk factors or causal pathways point to the importance of appropriate treatment for specific needs. Correctional programs for violent offenders must have a strong diagnostic capability and anticipate a flexible range of specific interventions within a single program umbrella. Mechanisms to allocate interventions according to need then can influence program effectiveness in controlling violent behavior.

How this information is applied in planning interventions is a matter of program philosophy. Some programs may elect to focus on specific causal dynamics—for example, socially learned behaviors—and fashion interventions to address these dynamics. Thus, we can envision therapeutic services that attempt specific types of behavior change. Others may elect to address a wider range of identified risk factors, both "underlying" problems such as personality factors and comorbid behaviors such as substance abuse, through case management models that emphasize matching individuals to appropriate treatments. All are necessary given the multiple causal paths to violence. Programs working with violent offenders can anticipate this range and plan for addressing the psychological, physical health, and human capital (education and work skills) needs of participants, as well as addressing a range of concurrent problem behaviors.

Whatever the content and structure of interventions, two factors point toward community and neighborhood as critical factors in controlling violence: (a) the social concentration of violent offenders and violent events in poor and socially disorganized communities, and (b) the highly contextualized nature of violent behavior within groups and social domains. When offenders complete programs, they return to neighborhoods and communities where they are likely to encounter the same contingencies and contexts that they left.

In these contexts, there is a continuing supply of triggering mechanisms for violence, a reinforcement of the antecedent mechanisms and motivations for violence, and a compromised social control structure to restrain violent events or acts. There also may be, depending on the community, few economic or social motivations for avoiding violence. For example, socially disorganized neighborhoods provide few means of achieving social status through conventional social roles such as a worker or a neighbor. Instead, the premium placed on violence to enhance one's standing—one's "respect" in the community—is unchecked in social areas with concentrations of joblessness and weak conventional institutions.

Just as violence is highly contextualized in communities, interventions, too, must be contextualized. This means including in interventions a range of cognitive developmental skills in settling disputes, managing one's "presentation of self," (Campbell, 1986; Felson, 1993), and anticipating the behavioral contingencies in social situations. Disputes in the workplace are likely, especially in the first few months of employment, and skills will be needed to deal with conflicts with workers and supervisors (Mincy, 1994). Accordingly, the range of interventions also must be appropriate for the range of concrete circumstances where behavioral skills will be applied.

Effective Correctional Interventions for Violent Offenders

Since the 1980s, the debate on the effectiveness of correctional interventions has been informed by a series of meta-analyses, reviews of evaluation literature, and new findings from treatment experiments. Rejecting the "nothing works" dogma of an earlier era, a series of publications revived analytic thinking about the possibilities of behavioral change and reductions in recidivism among criminal offenders. The new information was neither pessimistic nor naive. Instead, it focused in new ways on the issues of program theory, therapeutic integrity, intervention design, and offender-treatment interactions that shaped recidivism rates.

However, sorting out the implications of the new information on correctional effectiveness for *violent* offenders is a task complicated by several factors. First, comparisons of treatment effectiveness across types of settings was complicated by selection of artifacts. That is, violent offenders are not well represented in settings other than institutions. Second, because treatment effects may reflect interactions of offenders with interventions and settings, it is difficult to isolate the effects of any one of these factors. Third, the reviews took varying approaches to classifying programs. Some focused on the nature of the interventions, while others examined the setting in which interventions occurred. Fourth, the literature concentrates heavily on juvenile offenders, and research on life course perspectives on offending suggests that significant changes occur in the risks and contingencies of offending in the transition from adolescence to adulthood. Fifth, definitions of violence and eligibility of different types of violent offenders vary. Finally, the confounding of treatment with punishment further complicates efforts to tease out treatment effects.

In this section, we focus on the *results* of the meta-analyses, literature reviews, and evaluations of specific programs. Because programs for violent offenders are rare, we build from the lessons of programs generally to design programs for violent offenders. We focus most closely on the types of treatment interventions, but examine also the structural features of programs. These include their organizational auspice, the point of intervention in the justice system, and other design features. The results are discussed according to these dimensions of program design.

Intervention Approaches

There is consistent evidence that approaches based on "cognitive-behavioral" and "life skills" theories are generally effective across crime types, and that shock therapies and psychotherapeutic programs are not. Garrett (1985) reviewed 111 experimental studies from 1960 to 1983 focusing on residential programs for adjudicated delinquents. These programs were mostly private, and parole and probation programs were not included. Comparison groups usually were institutional programs. The residential programs were more successful in achieving in-program changes, but also had consistently significant effects on recidivism. The most powerful approaches were "cognitive-behavioral," family-centered interventions, and "life skills." However, there were few programs in the Garrett sample that focused on violent offenders, and the mix of violent offenders in the program populations was unknown.

Lipsey (1992) reached similar conclusions based on analyses of 400 published and unpublished experimental studies of juvenile delinquents. Although his terminology differed from Garrett's, the conclusion was much the same: approaches rooted in behavioral conditioning and "skill-oriented" approaches had the strongest impacts among the range of intervention approaches. Palmer (1994) characterizes the Lipsey review as "the broadest and most systematic to date." Davidson et al. (1984) analyzed over ninety studies published prior to 1983. They included quasi-experiments as well as experiments, and both community and institutional programs. They, too, found that "behavioral" interventions yielded better results than did group therapy or vocationally based programs.

Andrews et al. (1990) reanalyzed forty-five of the fifty studies reported by Whitehead and Lab (1989), and added thirty-five others. Breaking down the studies to form comparisons of adults and juveniles as well as different levels of treatment, they constructed 154 treatment-recidivism comparisons using the phi coefficient that Lab and Whitehead (1988) and Whitehead and Lab (1989) had used to reject the efficacy of treatment. Whitehead and Lab (1989) had used extremely conservative criteria to conclude that 24 percent of the juvenile offender treatment programs were effective in reducing recidivism. Using a disaggregated approach, Andrews et al. (1990) found that over two-in-three comparisons yielded successful reductions in recidivism, and over 30 percent were significant. They avoided classification of treatments, opting instead for a typology that focused on "appropriate" treatments versus others. This dimension emphasized whether programs provided interventions according to a rational and need-based allocation of services. Not only were "appropriate" services more effective than others, but the type of service was more important than other dimensions of program design in recidivism reduction.

Gendreau and Ross (1987) reviewed over 150 studies, building on their previous review (1979) of studies published after 1973. Their later review included both experiments, quasi-experiments, and studies with no control groups; they did not use meta-analytic procedures. With this wider range of programs and therapeutic approaches, but with less statistical rigor, they also cited "behavioral-cognitive" approaches as more effective than others. Their study was notable for examining programs for violent offenders, but they found no controlled studies to make sound comparisons. Citing other reviews, Gendreau and Ross (1987) noted that most studies of aggressive adolescents focused on intraprogram changes in psychosocial risk factors and dodged the question of recidivism reductions.

Palmer's (1994) comprehensive review of treatment approaches also notes the limited data on violent offenders. There is a notable list of ineffective or undistinguished interventions: confrontation models (such as

Scared Straight), physical challenge (for example, Vision Quest), restitution, group counseling, or therapy (such as milieu therapy), and individual counseling. Palmer also classifies several approaches as showing limited results: results that are either mixed or where there is evidence of recidivism reductions but in a small sample of programs. This includes family interventions, vocational training, and employment.

According to Palmer, approaches with more promising results include educational training, behavioral approaches, cognitive-behavioral change, and life skills models. Behavioral change programs emphasized operant-conditioning principles: token economies, and contingency contracting. Life skills approaches may be better termed as investments in human capital, or the skills necessary to function effectively in an economic world. Some of these programs also focus on "interpersonal" life skills developed through completion of shared tasks in outdoor programs. However, the development of marketable educational and work skills was the core of these efforts. Conceptually, these programs address the strain that offenders may experience when they are ill-equipped to compete in the labor market.

Few if any of these programs focused on violent offenders. Tolan and Guerra (1994) reviewed dozens of intervention evaluations for adolescent *violence*. The programs were not necessarily aimed at violent *offenders*, but at individuals who have engaged in violent behaviors. Accordingly, these programs often focused on intraprogram changes such as the reduction of risk factors, or the reduction of violent behavior while within the program, but many did not report recidivism outcomes. They did specify minimal design criteria: the inclusion of control groups or multiple baseline comparisons.

Like the other reviews, Tolan and Guerra found that psychotherapeutic programs were not effective. They reported limited effectiveness of behavioral modification programs, and qualified effectiveness of cognitive-behavioral interventions. While effective in controlling antisocial behavior generally, these programs had more limited success in reducing violence. Multiple-component programs had better results than single-component programs. Programs focusing on impulsivity were ineffective, but better results were evident for social problem-solving and social-perceptive skills programs. These interventions train participants to follow a sequence of discrete steps in solving problems that occur in social arenas; in other words, understanding the dynamics of conflict. Tolan and Guerra attribute the success of these efforts to their comprehensive approach that involves several affective and cognitive components: anger management, perspective taking, and self-control. However, missing in these studies is systematic evidence of their effects on post-program behaviors, especially violence. Other approaches, especially social casework models with individual counseling based on vague models of attitudinal change, were either noneffective or negatively effective.

Both program evaluations and literature reviews report positive effects of family interventions for violent adolescents. Although family interventions vary according to their theoretical assumptions, each type shows positive effects in controlling violent adolescents. The approach of Patterson and colleagues (for example, Patterson, Reid, and Dishion, 1992) focuses on interventions with parents to reduce their reliance on coercion.

The second approach, developed initially for drug users and expanded to youths who have other forms of antisocial behavior, focuses on family organization and family emotional cohesion. Based on the work of Minuchin (1974), these interventions focus on the emotional bonds and shared beliefs among family members. Positive intervention outcomes were noted by Tolan et al. (1989), but they also caution that these approaches need to be disaggregated by culture and ethnicity.

The third effective model includes the elements of the first two family-centered approaches, but also includes a component that addresses family skills in managing and resolving external demands. For example, Henglerr et al. (1993) reported that delinquents with at least one arrest for violence had lower rearrest rates after this type of intervention compared to defendants receiving only regular probation supervision. The costs were about 20 percent of the costs of one year of incarceration.

Peer-group interventions have weak results overall with violent adolescents. In recent years, peer-mediation programs have replaced peer-group models such as milieu therapies, recognizing the important triggering mechanisms of seemingly petty disputes. Some programs attempt to shift peer-group dynamics and norms, others attempt to redirect youths from one peer group to the next. Peer mediation or conflict reduction models remain unproven. Although intuitively appealing, these curricula are limited in several ways. First, they seem to disregard the powerful contextual influences of onlookers and peer status dynamics in attempting to get youths to "just say no" to dispute-related violence. Second, they address a narrow range of potential disputes, and overlay a logic to them that seems unrelated to the reality of many dispute-related assaults (see, for example, Oliver, 1994; Anderson, 1994; Felson, 1993). Third, they rely on cognitive skills that may be neutralized or negated by physiological and emotional arousal during potentially violent conflicts (see, for example, Bernard, 1990).

Residential Programs

Residential programs for violent offenders offer a therapeutic milieu in a closed setting. A small number of programs work with mentally ill youths who have committed violent crimes. The Bronx Court-related Unit provided treatment to violent, mentally ill youths in New York City between 1976 and 1979. It was jointly funded by the Division for Youth, the state juvenile corrections agency, and the state department of mental health. The long-term program provided intensive psychotherapeutic interventions to twenty youths who stayed approximately eighteen months in residential care. Treated youths had slightly lower recidivism rates than a comparison group, but overall rates for both groups were high: nearly 70 percent were rearrested within two years (Hartstone and Cocozza, 1983).

Most programs, however, do not work with emotionally disturbed or mentally ill youths. These programs emphasize behavioral conditioning and learning approaches. The most well known was developed by Bakal (Bakal and Polsky, 1979) as part of the reform of the Massachusetts juvenile justice system (*see also* Feld, 1977; McEwen, 1978). However, research on this program did not include control groups. Agee (1979) directed the Closed Adolescent Treatment Center (CATC) in Colorado, a program that relied heavily on token economies and behavioral reinforcement to increase adolescent motivation and resolve underlying psychological problems that were thought to lead to violence. CATC included several therapeutic modalities and was staff-intensive. Evaluation data suggest modest gains in recidivism compared to matched controls who were sent to mainstream juvenile corrections settings. Agee (1979) did not report on reductions in violence either in-program or post-program, a glaring omission considering the explicit entry criterion for violence (*see also* Agee and McWilliams, 1984).

The conceptual framework and program model for the CATC was tested a decade later in the Paint Creek program (Greenwood and Turner, 1993). Like CATC, Paint Creek worked with chronic as well as "serious" offenders who had committed "index" felonies, including violent offenses. The experimental design found small gains among experimental youths in recidivism reduction. But like many other studies, statistical power was not reported, effect sizes generally were small, and there was no analysis of offender subgroups including violent offenders.

Achievement Place also is one of the most carefully evaluated residential programs. Based on behavioral modification principles, modest reductions in minor delinquency and in-program behavioral infractions were reported by Levitt, Young, and Pappenfort (1979) and Ramp, Braukmann, and Wolf (1979). However, post-program effects decayed quickly. Tolan and Guerra (1994), reviewing the results of Achievement Place, show that its effects were far more substantial when programs were disaggregated by the degree of implementation. Program effectiveness varied according to therapeutic integrity and implementation, in the predicted direction. The Achievement Place program has not been fully applied to violent adolescents, and to the extent that violent delinquents were included, they had very limited violence histories.

Summary of Intervention Approaches

Information on effective intervention approaches for violent offenders is limited in several ways. The most commonly used approaches often are not the frequently evaluated programs (Tolan and Guerra, 1994). Many programs only have limited experience with violent offenders, and most of these focus on juveniles. Other than sex offender treatment and programs for mentally disordered offenders, there is virtually no evaluation information on adult violent offenders. Evaluations sometimes focus broadly on antisocial behaviors, not addressing violence specifically. This is especially important because effects on antisocial behavior generally may not transfer to violence. Because violent individuals are not randomly allocated to interventions, the information on offender-intervention interactions is somewhat biased. This is particularly important when the principle of "appropriateness" is considered in program design (*see* Andrews et al., 1990). Randomized or clinical trials of treatment interventions still are the exception, so there are limitations on the strength of the evaluation literature. And even in clinical trials, sample and effect sizes are often low and, in turn, so too is statistical power.

Even with these caveats, there are consistencies across meta-analyses and program evaluations that suggest specific directions for the substantive components of interventions for violent offenders. There is consistent support for behavioral modification and behavioral-cognitive approaches. These programs emphasize general problem-solving skills (skills to resolve interpersonal disputes) and other social-cognitive skills (perspective taking and moral reasoning). When combined in a multidimensional program, their effectiveness is compounded. An extension of this intervention approach involves life-skills training and behavior-modification in real-life situations (Tolan and Guerra, 1994). The highly contextualized nature of violence suggests that interventions focused on situational contingencies will be more effective than those developed for artifactual and artificial program settings. Family skills are also a promising intervention approach. Given developmental and career concerns, the applications of these interventions should be disaggregated by life stage and social role.

There is less consistent support for education and (employment) training interventions that do not focus on building human capital. The crime-unemployment literature distinguishes the positive effects for younger offenders of employment programs with concrete payoffs from the negative effects of training programs that offer skill development but no job placement (See, for example, Fagan, 1994). When focused on instrumental goals for getting jobs, these approaches seem to have some promise. Timing is important, however; allocating individuals to jobs before motivations for work are well developed easily could backfire. Neither peer group nor psychotherapeutic interventions show consistent promise of working with violent offenders.

Criminal Justice Sanctions and Correctional Supervision

In this literature, the effects of specific interventions often are confounded with the context of judicial disposition or criminal sanction. What most people recognize as a two-way interaction—individuals classified by treatments—in fact may be a three-way interaction, with the type of legal sanction as an additional dimension. Andrews et al. (1990, p.372) suggest that ". . . there is little reason to expect that variation among settings or sanctions will have an impact on recidivism except in interaction with offender characteristics and through the mediators of intervention process . . ."

However, the coercive function of interventions that are linked to criminal justice sanctions may facilitate treatment that otherwise would not occur (Royo, 1994). Interventions are delivered through a wide range of criminal sanctions, from diversion programs through prison-based treatment for drug users or sex offenders. Sorting out the effects of the sanction from the intervention is a difficult task, confounded by the skew toward more serious sanctions for violent offenders. Nevertheless, the meta-analyses cited in this review tend to conclude that, after controlling for treatment intervention, the main effects of criminal sanctions are quite weak.

We already have examined therapeutic interventions delivered in residential or institutional settings. In this section, we review the effects of the small number of noninstitutional correctional supervision programs for violent offenders.

Intensive Supervision Programs

Intensive supervision programs may involve either parole or probation supervision. They may function as alternatives to incarceration or as an adjunct to institutional services. The "intensive" element usually involves reduced caseloads with frequent contacts. There are two distinct potential effects of these programs, depending on how they are structured. In one type, generally termed *aftercare programs*, the combination of the deterrent effects of supervision coupled with whatever interventions are provided, will reduce propensities for offending. In the second type, increased surveillance through frequent contact (and ancillary contacts) provides a kind of early warning system that allows supervising officers to initiate some systemic response to ward off reoffending (Sontheimer and Goodstein, 1993).

There have been few tests of intensive probation supervision for violent offenders (Armstrong, 1991; Byrne, Lurigio, and Baird, 1989). One reason is the general tendency toward incarceration of violent offenders, especially among adults (Cohen and Canela-Cacho, 1994). Three experiments involving juveniles suggest that intensive supervision can be at least equally effective with correctional interventions. One experiment involved only violent offenders. Fagan and Reinarman (1991) compared youths adjudicated for violence in regular supervision units with randomly assigned youths in four types of intensive supervision in suburban Contra Costa County (California). The type of intervention varied according to the neighborhood context where the caseload resided. African-American youths in poor neighborhoods were supervised under a system-response model (surveillance), while white and Hispanic youths in the three working-class and middle-class "bedroom" communities received different types of interventions in conjunction with intensive contact. One officer emphasized family therapy, another conducted long jogging sessions with his caseload, while a third used an "eclectic" approach. Recidivism prevalence was no different in the four groups compared to controls, but rearrest charges were more serious in the surveillance caseload. Using self-reports, there were no differences among the four groups and between experimental and control probationers.

Sontheimer and Goodstein (1993) compared "treatment" and "surveillance" intensive supervision caseloads in Philadelphia. Over 25 percent of the sample were charged with violent offenses, and nearly three-in-four had a prior charge for either robbery or a "serious person offense." The probationers came primarily from the city's poorer neighborhoods. There were significant reductions in recidivism for youths in the system response (surveillance) program compared to regular supervision based on an "aftercare" model. The range of proactive responses by the officers in the experimental group tended to combine deterrence and rehabilitative components, although they leaned heavily toward deterrence. What distinguished the two groups was the intensity of the supervision, not the extent or content of the other interventions. Accordingly, Sontheimer and Goodstein conclude that intensive supervision made the officers' interventions more effective, regardless of what they were. Unfortunately, the study did not look at offender-supervision interactions, and conclusions about violent offenders cannot be made.

The "Willie M" program was an intensive casework program for violent youths who were identified in the North Carolina mental health system. The program was named after a youth who sued the state for failing to provide services to youths in juvenile corrections and mental health systems. It used an intensive casework approach to match offenders to treatments, including inpatient and outpatient psychotherapy, family therapy, supervised living, and vocational placements. The program did not use a reintegration model, focusing instead on maximizing in-program treatment gains. When participants were compared with other "Willie M" youths who received less intensive or no services, there were no significant differences in later arrests (Weisz et al., 1990).

The Violent Juvenile Offender Program

One experiment that combined treatment, reintegration, and sanctions for violent offenders was the Violent Juvenile Offender (VJO) Program (Fagan, 1990a, 1990b; Fagan and Forst, in press). The theoretical base addressed the multiple causal paths for violent behavior, integrating strain, control, and learning theories. The integrated theory was based on earlier integrations of theory (cf. Elliott et al., 1979; Weis and Sederstrom, 1981; Hawkins and Weis, 1980; Fagan and Jones, 1984) that stressed the development of prosocial bonds and "unlearning" delinquent bonds, while developing skills applicable to the community setting. The structural design combined residential treatment with intensive supervision, focusing on the transition and reintegration of program youths into the community following institutional intervention. An experimental design was used to compare the impacts on the recidivism and social outcomes of the Violent Juvenile Offender youths with youths in "mainstream" juvenile corrections programs.

The intervention translated the theoretical base into four principles that informed program design by providing practical applications of theory. Therapeutic integrity was addressed by creating "performance measures," or operational definitions of each element, to create a bridge from theory to practice. Implementation was measured to determine the strength and integrity of treatment (Sechrest et al., 1979). Briefly, the four underlying principles included:

- **Social Networking**—the strengthening of personal bonds (attitudes, commitment, and beliefs) through positive experiences with family members, schools, the workplace, or nondelinquent peers
- **Opportunities Structures**—the strengthening of social bonds (attachments and involvement) through achievement and successful participation in school, workplace, and family activities
- **Social Learning**—the process by which personal and social bonds are strengthened and reinforced. Strategies include rewards and sanctions for attainment of goals or contingent behaviors
- **Behavior Specificity**—the linkage of specific behaviors to each client's needs and abilities, including problem behaviors and special intervention needs (such as substance abuse treatment and mental health services)

The structural elements were designed to maximize the implementation of the principles. The program was a multiple-phase residential program, which included an institutional stay, a transitional residence, and a reintegration phase. This ensured that project youths received the maximum amount of treatment in the least-restrictive environment, providing a graduated reentry into community living. Movement to less restrictive phases was contingent on achieving treatment goals. Case management was used to allocate individuals to specific interventions according to a diagnostic evaluation. It also was designed to provide continuity from institutional placement through intensive supervision, and to set consistent goals and expectations across placements.

Reintegration was the primary goal of the intervention—that is, interventions were contextualized to be appropriate for the neighborhood conditions where youths eventually would return. A simple rule-of-thumb was followed: projects should spend as many dollars on youths when they are in the community as they do in earlier phases, through supervision and purchase of services. Reintegration was designed to sustain new behaviors and skills learned during treatment, and to reinforce them during transition to family and community life on the streets and in the workplace.

The results showed that adolescents in experimental programs with strong implementation of the program design had lower recidivism and reincarceration rates, and delayed rearrest longer compared to youths in mainstream juvenile corrections (Fagan, 1990a). In one site, there was negative implementation: youths in the control programs actually received higher levels of the experimental treatment than did the youths in the experimental group. In that site, the controls had significantly lower recidivism rates than did the experimentals. In addition to validation of the theoretical model and its structural implementation, the experiment showed the important role of therapeutic integrity and implementation in explaining program outcomes. It also illustrated the possibilities for enriching the role of supervision officers to include case management with low caseloads. Rather than deliver interventions, the case managers were responsible for allocating appropriate treatments pursuant to a thorough and theoretically informed diagnostic procedure.

Implementation was influenced by a series of organizational factors, and these proved critical to explaining program outcomes at the individual level (Fagan and Forst, in press). Programs had to struggle to achieve a degree of autonomy to implement a flexible program. Flexibility was central to the program design. The target population was a high-visibility offender group that posed two types of risks of failure: programmatic risk, since a weak intervention could lead to a loss of control over an aggressive population, and political risk that could undermine the program should a failure result in a fatality. The ability to implement an effective program required both risk taking and political strength. The determining influence of violence on crime control policy suggests that these lessons will persist for some time.

Implications for Interventions and Policy

Few correctional programs focus specifically on interventions for violence, and few of the meta-analyses or literature reviews look separately at violent offenders. There have been far more efforts for violent juvenile offenders compared to adults. This bias is important given developmental changes over the life course in the likelihood and severity of criminal violence. It also suggests that effective interventions for adolescents may not be effective for adults, while adults may benefit from interventions that require a level of maturity that most adolescents have not yet reached.

Because of the risks associated with violence, a narrower range of interventions has been tested, and most are skewed toward institutional treatment. Controlled studies are rare for violent offenders, and measures focus more often than not on intraprogram changes rather than subsequent violence (Gendreau and Ross, 1987). Accordingly, no strong assertions about program effectiveness can be made. All this complicates efforts to develop a coherent view of whether treatments work for violent offenders, in what settings, and for which types of offenders. Yet, there are useful lessons in the literature reviews and a few experimental programs for violent offenders. We also learn important lessons from the meta-analyses and literature reviews that address intervention programs generally. Together, this information suggests specific directions for further program development and testing.

The Unique Context of Violent Crime and Violent Offenders

Compared to other types of crime, violence poses different challenges politically and programmatically. Although violence often is part of a diverse pattern of offenses in a criminal career, there are unique causal paths to violence that differ from other patterns of offending (Reiss and Roth, 1993). Moreover, effective programs for other types of antisocial behavior may not transfer to violent behavior. If the causes of violence differ from other crimes, the group on which other interventions has proven effective may be quite different from a population of violent offenders. Programs must be specific about violence in their conceptual framework and intervention design. Knowledge about the processes and contexts of violence in a population must inform the design of interventions. Knowledge about the risk factors for violence also must be included in the design of programs. Variation within the domain of violent offenses suggests a range of interventions may be needed for populations sentenced under assault versus robbery statutes, for sex offenders, or for homicidally aggressive youths.

Politically, the risks of violence are different from the risks of drug selling or auto theft, and the price of failure in a noninstitutional program differs from other types of risk. Injury or fatality carry salience that can drive legislation and funding. These political implications and risks have shaped programs and sentencing reforms. Public safety concerns dictate sentencing policies that minimize those risks, and these ensure that interventions for violent offenders are more likely to take place within closed settings, if not institutions.

Because punishment and incapacitation are part of legislative intent in sentencing for violent offenders in many states, programs are likely to begin in institutional settings. This may complicate efforts to reintegrate offenders. If there are diminishing returns from longer periods of incarceration (Cohen and Cacho-Canela, 1994), this will further burden and challenge programs that attempt to reintegrate violent offenders who have served long periods in institutions.

The risks of failure are considerable, too. There are few proven treatments for violence that are effective. Some actually do more harm than good, leading to a worsening of behaviors (see, for example, Sherman, 1992). Some approaches are worth avoiding, no matter how intuitively appealing and no matter how effective they may be for nonviolent offenders. Andrews et al. (1990) suggest that higher risk cases be assigned higher levels of service. The lessons for violent offenders are obvious.

The Principle of Need: A Range of Treatment Interventions

The complexity of violence suggests that a range of treatment interventions will be needed for violent offenders. The Violent Juvenile Offender program was based explicitly on this assumption. The need for a range of services is suggested as well by the principle of appropriate intervention (Andrews et al., 1990). Need was one principle of effective interventions in the review by Andrews et al. of correctional effectiveness. A corollary principle is responsivity, or matching offenders with needs. This addresses the interaction of individual characteristics with services.

In the Violent Juvenile Offender program, this was accomplished by a careful diagnostic process and matching of offenders to services.

Matching offender needs to services requires active case management. Case management principles are an effective method of achieving the principle of the need for a range of services. Learning styles of offenders are likely to vary, depending on their developmental stage as well as the varieties of their behaviors. The principles of need and responsivity also suggest that criminal sanctions should not be confounded with intervention. Punishment without intervention is not intervention, and generally is ineffective. At the same type, the meta-analyses are consistent with program evaluation data in identifying the weakness of legal sanctions or legal interventions without treatment content.

Therapeutic Integrity

There are two dimensions to the issue of therapeutic integrity. First, effective programs tend to have a sound theoretical basis. More often than not, effective programs are behaviorally centered or are based on learning principles. Behavioral, cognitive-behavioral, and life skills, or skill-oriented interventions were more effective compared to other approaches, in part because of their correspondence to developmental pathways into and out of violence. Tolan and Guerra (1994) advance similar arguments for family-centered interventions, while the Lipsey (1992) meta-analysis suggests that human capital development (employment and skill-oriented programs) are critical. The Violent Juvenile Offender program suggests that learning principles tied to movement through program phases toward release to the community is effective in motivating participation in treatments (Fagan, 1990a).

Second, therapeutic integrity addresses the question of implementation. Programs may fail because of faulty theory, or they also may fail because good theory was poorly implemented (Rezmovic, 1984; Scheirer and Rezmovic, 1983). Some argue that this is a "dosage" question, but it also may be conceptualized as a "purity" argument. The strength of treatment and its integrity are separate dimensions, but both are concerns of effective interventions (Sechrest et al., 1979). Dosage addresses the amount and intensity of treatment, while purity addresses the implementation of theory. Both are important.

This is a long way of saying that program quality counts. Where therapeutic integrity is high, interventions are far more likely to be effective. In the Lipsey meta-analysis, dosage was well correlated with effect size

(.24), exceeded only by the correlation for "treatment philosophy." In the Violent Juvenile Offender program, implementation outcomes determined the recidivism outcomes. Independent of experimental and control conditions, the groups which had the strongest implementation of theory were those that had the lower recidivism rates. Programs should devote considerable attention to the translation of theory into practice, the establishment of performance measures that operationalize standards, and the measurement of implementation based on the extent to which performance measures have been attained.

Reintegration and the Role of Exogenous Factors

Just as neighborhood and community are risk factors for violence, program effectiveness is mediated by exogenous factors, such as regional labor markets or neighborhood cohesion. If reintegration is a critical step in intervention, its effects can be compromised by conditions in communities to which offenders return. Guns, gangs, drug trafficking, racial discrimination, adverse housing and basic services, and other obstacles offer a constant stream of negative arousal and illegal opportunity. Programs based on behavioral models must anticipate these contingencies of violence that are likely to be unchanged from those that contributed to earlier patterns of violence. Programs based on family interventions must anticipate family stresses and problems that reflect the demands of everyday life in difficult conditions.

Programs based on investments in human capital that make ex-offenders salient in the labor market must anticipate difficulty in obtaining work for their participants. Programs placing youths in jobs must recognize their considerable social and psychological distance from the world of work, and the likelihood of workplace conflicts with coworkers and supervisors. On-the-job supervision of newly placed workers may be needed to smooth over the transition to work (Mincy, 1994).

For example, several factors in communities and labor markets may complicate the efforts of ex-offenders in gaining jobs that offer family-sustaining wages. First, there is no incentive for employers to hire ex-offenders in a loose labor market for unskilled or semi-skilled labor. Second, since job quality appears to be an important part of job stability, the availability of job and wage ladders is central to avoiding crime for ex-offenders in the workplace (Fagan, 1994). Third, legal sanctions are ineffective unless complemented by informal social controls within the social contexts of everyday life.

But violence is clustered in precisely those communities that are socially disorganized and where informal social controls are weak (Sampson and Lauritsen, 1994). And the high rates of joblessness in these communities socially devalues success in school or in the workplace, making the transition to work a difficult social journey (Anderson, 1994). The challenge is straightforward for sustaining the gains of correctional intervention once program participation ends.

The effectiveness of correctional intervention depends on a process where social control first moves from a formal-legal domain to the informal structures of the community, and ultimately is internalized within the individual. Treatment plays an obvious role in initiating this process. It teaches behaviors and establishes bonds that reinforce the dictates of the law. The continuity of these behaviors in the community depends in part on its opportunity structure, and also on the availability of social networks that continue to regulate and reinforce positive behaviors. Legal supervision is part of this process, but supervision ends one day. Ultimately, the dimensions of crime or legal opportunity, motivation for crime or conformity, and the structures of control will mediate the effects of correctional intervention. Programs must anticipate and address these imposing tasks.

Implications for Research

Few correctional treatment programs have focused specifically on violent offenders, and few evaluations or experiments have isolated the effects of specific interventions on the reduction of violence. The trend in policy toward incapacitation and punishment for violent offenders in part reflects the limited knowledge about correctional programs for this population, and, in part, reflects the limitations and failures of past intervention efforts. Considering the weight accorded to violent offenders in crime control policy and sentencing reforms, the lack of information is a contradiction that needs to be addressed. This requires systematic efforts in three domains.

First, basic research on violent offenders must become routinized within intervention programs and correctional agencies. The need for basic research on violent offenders and violence is evident. Three major commissions agree that advances in the control of violence will require new research and the creation of a diversified base of empirical knowledge (American Psychological Association, 1993; Reiss and Roth, 1993; Centers for Disease Control, 1991, 1992). Yet, many programs, whether private or public, see basic research on the causes and correlates of crime as a task for others. Some see research as a burden, others see it as a distraction from their mission, and still others see it as exploiting their clients. Even when there is recognition of its importance, knowledge generated from research often is assigned a lesser value than folk knowledge gained from anecdotes and the reflections of staff and administrators. Programs must realize the opportunities for knowledge development from their interactions with violent offenders. There is critical information from research that can inform both theory and practice in interventions. Research is needed in several areas.

(1) Empirical information is needed on the situations and contexts of violence to better understand the variety of types of violence, and to determine if there are different predictors of each type of violence. Understanding the context and dynamics of violent events, apart from their participants, has implications for prevention as well as interventions. An event-analysis framework can look at specific provocations, the process of the dynamics of violent events, circumstances such as intoxication or the presence of guns, and the outcomes of violent transactions. Research should examine the unfolding of patterns of violence over time, including selection of targets and the contexts in which violence occurs. The use of life history methods (Frazier, 1978) is a valuable tool to examine events over different life stages, but also to examine the specific developmental contexts in which they occur.

(2) Research can examine the proximal causes of violence. Using epidemiological methods, including case control designs, researchers can compare individuals with similarly situated but nonviolent controls to determine the contributions of theoretically derived factors or modifiable risk factors. This may include comorbid behaviors, the social contexts of everyday life, and psychological variables. More distal causes are difficult to address with retrospective accounts, but maybe some information can be obtained using thorough searches of archival records.

(3) Research is needed on the cessation of violence to determine how desistance begins and how it may be integrated into program interventions. Using case control designs with individuals who have desisted from violence, researchers can compare the situational and background factors that sustain violent acts with those that seem to promote cessation of violence. This information can assist in modifying program designs to incorporate interventions to hasten processes of desistance, or to create the circumstances that seem to promote it.

There are many other research questions and theory tests that should be pursued using the opportunities created through program interventions with violent offenders. Readers are encouraged to review the research agendas of the three recent commissions.

Second, experimentation and evaluation must be routinized within intervention programs. There are many programs in action that are well-intentioned but not evaluated. This poses risks to the public and to the participants, for the literature is rife with examples of programs that have been ineffective if not having worsened (escalated) violence. Evaluation is needed to avoid such failure, to increase the potential for cost-effective interventions that avoid cost-intensive periods of incarceration, and to create a body of empirical evidence that can influence legislation and policy. Tolan and Guerra (1994) predict that the failure to routinize evaluation and to develop a cumulative base of evaluation data will result in a recurring cycle of reviews like this one that call for more evaluation.

To accomplish these goals, evaluation must be institutionalized within intervention programs and clinical trials incorporated within program designs. Comparison groups are obviously critical, and random assignment should not be avoided. Ethical concerns about withholding interventions can be balanced against the concerns of subjecting participants to interventions of unproven and possibly negative value. Randomization also may include yoked designs where random subjects are randomly allocated to different combinations of interventions, thereby avoiding withholding treatments. A variety of alternative design options are available for constructing control groups. One design may include case controls from other programs or from a group receiving a competing intervention. Multiple baseline comparisons, prior program cohorts, and other alternatives to random assignment can produce results with high internal validity (Toothaker, 1993; Rothman, 1986).

Other dimensions of evaluation should include careful measurement of treatment implementation and therapeutic integrity at the program level, as well as dosage to individuals within the program. Baseline and post-program measurement of violence should be specific. Results should be disaggregated, if sample sizes permit, to examine offender-intervention interactions. This ultimately will contribute to knowledge about responsivity of treatment. The limitations of official records suggest that multiple measures of post-program violence should be recorded. Followup periods should be sufficiently lengthy to determine the decay rates of treatment and the factors that bear on post-program failure.

Statistical significance and effect size (Cohen, 1988) must be measured and reported.

Evaluation should be made a requirement for support. Ongoing assessment of programs is good management, and control of risks and improvement in effectiveness are two dimensions of that assessment. While programs rightfully may fear the withdrawal of funds when programs are ineffective, there are two reasons to take that risk. First, ethical standards mandate that programs ensure they are not doing harm, and the costs of harm in a violence intervention are quite high. Second, poor results should be a cue for refinement of program design, not a sign to abandon efforts at improvement. Funders must be educated so that they understand that political risks are necessary for the evolution of successful and effective programs.

Third, research and evaluation must be supported externally and at appropriate funding levels as part of funding for program operations. Programs should not be confronted with choices between services and research. Part of the institutionalization of research and evaluation should be the creation of a stable funding stream independent from funding for services. This will support an uninterrupted research agenda that is funded at a level needed to create valid information. Independence of researchers from programs is necessary to ensure that programs receive an impartial assessment. The principle of risk-responsivity (Andrews et al., 1990) should apply as well to funding: the higher levels of funding should be allocated to the programs that deal with the highest level of risk or threat (*see also* Tolan and Guerra, 1994). The production of valid and generalizable research knowledge is not cheap, and may cost as much if not more than interventions. Political "shyness" over this reality must be set aside.

This requires careful consideration of the infrastructure for funding both programs and research on interventions for violent offenders. Funds for research, like program funding, tends to be driven by streams tied to specific agencies or problem definitions. Correctional agencies rarely allocate evaluation funding for their interventions, but an agency or foundation concerned with the psychophysiology of violence, for example, may offer funds to evaluate specific interventions. In communities with serious violence problems and extensive service networks, a more rational and need-driven basis for supporting evaluations should be constructed. Accordingly, a "superfund" for evaluation could be constructed, with contributions from specific government entities (that support services), private foundations concerned with developing effective violence interventions, and research agencies concerned with developing basic knowledge or evaluation data on violence. Evaluation block grants from the Bureau of Justice Assistance could provide a Federal share for local or state evaluation "superfunds." Funders of services, programs themselves, or researchers could request evaluation support from the fund.

Finally, collaboration should be encouraged between universities and intervention programs, whether they be community supervision or residential treatment. For example, doctoral programs that emphasize research can establish field placements or internships with intervention agencies to initiate either basic or evaluation research agendas. Violence is a complex phenomenon, not well explained by the traditionally separate disciplines of the behavioral and health sciences. Because it involves theoretical knowledge from several disciplines, the creation of internships within programs can foster interdisciplinary research and the advancement of knowledge beyond the limitations of single disciplines.

The proliferation of commissions and legislative actions suggests that the control of violence has become a national priority. Funding for basic research, evaluation, and intervention programs should reflect that priority. One reason for the inadequate knowledge base about violence or its interventions has been the traditionally low level of funding for violence research (Reiss and Roth, 1993; American Psychological Association, 1993). Reductions in violence, like progress in the fight of disease and technological advancement, will begin when there are investments in knowledge development commensurate with the urgency of the problem. Reliance on secure institutions for the preponderance of correctional interventions is a sign of the failure of current approaches to develop an adequate knowledge base to manage risks and transform people. The shift in priorities and funding that is needed to change this will be relatively small compared to the costs and the tragedy of violence.

Notes:

[1] The National Commission on Law Enforcement and Criminal Justice issued a report of several volumes in 1967 that made recommendations for the improvement of criminal justice administration in response to increasingly serious crime. The Kerner Commission analyzed the causes of the urban unrest that swept American inner cities in 1967-68. The Eisenhower Commission issued its report also in 1968, also focusing on

problems of violence. *see* Curtis (1975) and Currie (1985) for reviews of the activities of these commissions.

[2] The President's Commission on Violent Crime (1982) was convened by President Reagan to address the problems of interpersonal violence as a part of the "war on crime." The (U.S.) Attorney General's Task Force on Family Violence (1984) was convened by Attorney General Edwin Meese as part of the administration's efforts to raise public awareness about child abuse and spouse assault, and to promote law and policy criminalizing these acts. In 1988, the National Research Council began a five-year effort to study violence, identify research needs, and recommend preventive efforts (Reiss and Roth, 1993). Public health officials responded to the consequences of interpersonal violence in a series of reports. The Committee on Trauma Research (1985) issued a report on injuries resulting from interpersonal violence. The Centers for Disease Control and Prevention included interpersonal injury as a central part of its blueprint for improving the nation's physical health, *Healthy People 2000* (CDCP, 1990). The Centers for Disease Control and Prevention also convened a national commission on injury prevention (1993) that focused on injuries resulting from interpersonal and self-inflicted violence. The American Psychological Association Commission on Youth Violence (1994) identified risk factors associated with violence and highlighted "promising" program approaches. Among foundations, the Carnegie Council has funded a Center for the Study and Prevention of Violence, issued a series of recurring reports on violence prevention efforts, and supported a network of twenty-one community-based violence prevention programs.

[3] Andrews et al. (1990) suggest that the "death" of rehabilitation was the culmination of an historical process dating well before the watershed article by Robert Martinson (1974) declaring that "nothing works." The civil disturbances in American inner cities and college campuses in the 1960s, occurring in the midst of record homicide rates in the wake of an acute heroin epidemic, fueled conservative reactions that demanded retribution for lawbreakers who committed acts of violence. The antiscience underpinnings of conservative politicians were reinforced by critical theorists who denounced rehabilitation as a form of unregulated punishment. Literature reviews throughout this era reinforced the Martinson view (see, for example: Bailey, 1966; Wheeler and Robison, 1972; Wright and Dixon, 1977; Sechrest et al., 1979). Few scholars or politicians paid attention to Martinson's (1979) recant of his position on rehabilitation,

where he claimed that his conclusion of weak evidence for rehabilitation was misrepresented as a statement that rehabilitation does not work.

[4] Greenwood's optimism was not widely shared among his RAND colleagues who worked with the same data. For example, Chaiken and Chaiken (1982) claimed that at best, only 30 percent of the "high rate" offenders could be predicted from a combination of legal and extralegal variables such as employment and drug histories. When confined to legal variables, the prediction rate dropped well below 15 percent. Like Martinson before him, Greenwood also recanted (see: Greenwood and Zimring, 1985; Greenwood and Turner, 1987).

[5] For example, the role of delinquent peer groups as a risk factor in violent or nonviolent offending diminishes with age. Rates of co-offending decline with age (Reiss, 1986), and the character of violent crimes also tends to change from the expressive to the instrumental over the life course (Megargee, 1982).

[6] Whitehead and Lab (1989) required a phi coefficient of greater than .20 in 2 x 2 comparisons. This threshold often required large effect sizes (recidivism reductions). They explicitly rejected as effective programs those that achieved significant recidivism reductions but small effect sizes. Accordingly, they were making a statistical power argument on experiments (Weisburd, 1993) based on the false rejection of the null hypothesis.

[7] The other two studies involved mixed caseloads of violent and "serious" offenders, generally chronic property offenders. *see* Gruenwald, Laurence and West (1985), and Barton and Butts (1990).

[8] Diffusion of treatments was not an issue. The programs were geographically separated by 300 miles, and control youths returning to the community were supervised by state parole workers who had no contact with the county juvenile court staff who supervised the reintegration of the experimental group.

References

Agee, V. L. 1979. *Treatment of the Violent Incorrigible Adolescent.* Lexington, Massachusetts: Lexington Books.

Agee, V. L. and B. McWilliams. 1984. The Role of Group Therapy in the Therapeutic Community in Treating the Violent Juvenile Offender. In R. Mathias, P. DeMuro, and R. A. Allinson, eds. *Violent Juvenile Offenders: An Anthology*. San Francisco: National Council on Crime and Delinquency.

American Psychological Association. 1993. *Violence and Youth: Psychology's Response, Volume I*. Washington D.C.: American Psychological Association.

Anderson, E. 1994. The Code of the Streets. *The Atlantic Monthly*. May.

Andrews, D. A., I. Zinger, R. D. Hoge, J. Bonta, P. Gendreau, and F. T. Cullen. 1990. Does Correctional Treatment Work? A Clinically Relevant and Psychologically Informed Meta-analysis. *Criminology*. 28: 369-397.

Armstrong, T., ed. 1991. *Intensive Interventions with High-Risk Youths: Promising Approaches in Probation and Parole*. Monsey, New York: Criminal Justice Press.

Bakal, Y. and M. Polsky. 1979. *Reforming Corrections for Juvenile Offenders: Alternatives and Strategies*. Lexington, Massachusetts: Lexington Books.

Barton, W. H. and J. Butts. 1990. Viable Options: Intensive Supervision Programs for Juvenile Delinquents. *Crime and Delinquency*. 36: 238-56.

Bernard, T. J. 1990. Angry Aggression among the "Truly Disadvantaged." *Criminology*. 28: 73-96.

Beschner, G. M. and A. Friedman. 1986. *Teen Drug Use*. Lexington, Massachusetts: D. C. Heath and Company.

Blumstein, A., J. Cohen, and D. Nagin. 1979. *Deterrence and Incapacitation: Estimating the Effects of Criminal Sanctions on Crime Rates*. Washington, D.C.: National Academy Press.

Browne, A., and K. Williams. 1993. Gender, Intimacy, and Lethal Violence: Trends from 1976 through 1987. *Gender and Society*. 7: 78-98.

Bursik, R. J., Jr. and H. Grasmick. 1993. *Neighborhoods and Crime*. New York: Lexington Books.

Byrne, J., A. Lurigio, and C. Baird. 1989. The Effectiveness of the New Intensive Supervision Programs. *Research in Corrections*. 2 (2): 1-75.

Campbell, A. 1986. The Streets and Violence. In A. Campbell and J. Gibbs, eds. *Violent Transactions: The Limits of Personality*. New York: Basil Blackwell.

Centers for Disease Control and Prevention. 1991. *Healthy People 2000*. Atlanta, Georgia: U.S. Department of Health and Human Services.

———. 1992. *Proceedings of the Third National Injury Control Conference*. Atlanta, Georgia: U.S. Department of Health and Human Services.

Chaiken, J. and M. Chaiken. 1982. *Varieties of Criminal Behavior*. Report R-2814-NIJ. Santa Monica, California: The RAND Corporation.

Cohen, J. and J. A. Canela-Cacho. 1994. Incarceration and Violent Crime: 1965-88. In Albert J. Reiss, Jr. and Jeffrey A. Roth, eds. *Understanding and Preventing Violence, Volume 4: Consequences and Control*. Washington, D.C.: National Academy Press.

Cohen, S. 1988. *Statistical Power for the Behavioral Sciences*, 2nd Edition. Hillsdale, New Jersey: Lawrence Erlbaum Associates.

Cullen, F. T. and K. E. Gilbert. 1982. *Reaffirming Rehabilitation*. Cincinnati: Anderson.

Currie, E. 1989. *Confronting Crime*. New York: Pantheon.

Curtis, L. A. 1975. *Violence, Race, and Culture*. Lexington, Massachusetts: Lexington Books.

Davidson, W. S. III, R. Gottschalk, L. Gensheimer, and J. Mayer. 1984. *Interventions with Juvenile Delinquents: A Meta-Analysis of Treatment Efficacy*. Washington, D.C.: Office of Juvenile Justice and Delinquency Prevention.

Dembo, R., L. Williams, J. Fagan, and J. Schmeidler. 1993. The Relationships of Substance Involvement and Other Delinquency over Time in a Sample of Juvenile Detainees. *Criminal Behavior and Mental Health*. 3:158-197.

Elliott, D. S., S. S. Ageton, and R. Canter. 1979. An Integrated Theoretical Perspective on Delinquent Behavior. *Journal of Research in Crime and Delinquency*. 16: 3-27.

Elliott, D. S., D. Huizinga, and S. Menard. 1989. *Multiple Problem Youth*. New York: Springer-Verlag.

Fagan, J. A. 1989. The Social Organization of Drug Use and Drug Dealing among Urban Gangs. *Criminology*. 27:501-536.

———. 1990a. Treatment and Reintegration of Violent Delinquents: Experimental Results. *Justice Quarterly*. 7:233-263.

———. 1990b. Social and Legal Policy Dimensions of Violent Juvenile Crime. *Criminal Justice and Behavior*. 17:93-133.

———. 1990c. Intoxication and Aggression. In M. Tonry and J. Q. Wilson, eds. *Drugs and Crime—Crime and Justice: An Annual Review of Research, Volume 13*. Chicago: University of Chicago Press.

———. 1991. Community-based Treatment of Mentally disordered Juvenile Offenders. *Journal of Clinical Child Psychology*. 20: 42-50.

———. 1993a. Set and Setting Revisited: Influences of Alcohol and Other Drugs on the Social Context of Violence. In Susan E. Martin, ed. *Alcohol and Violence: Approaches to Interdisciplinary Research* (Research Monograph). Rockville, Maryland: National Institute on Alcohol Abuse and Alcoholism.

———. 1993b. Social Structure and Spouse Assault. In Brian Forst, ed. *The Socio-economics of Crime and Justice*. New York: M. A. Sharpe.

———. 1994. Legal and Illegal Work: Crime, Work and Unemployment. Paper presented at the Metropolitan Assembly on Urban Problems. Evanston, Illinois: Center for Urban Affairs and Policy Analysis, Northwestern University, October.

Fagan, J. A. and A. Browne. 1994. Violence Between Spouses and Intimates. In A. J. Reiss, Jr. and J. A. Roth. *Understanding and Preventing Violence, Volume 3*. Washington, D.C.: National Academy Press.

Fagan, J. A and K. Chin. 1990. Violence as Regulation and Social Control in the Distribution of Crack. In Mario de la Rosa, Bernard Gropper, and Elizabeth Lambert, eds. *Drugs and Violence* (NIDA Research Monograph No. 103). National Institute of Drug Abuse, Rockville Maryland: U.S. Public Health Administration.

Fagan, J. and M. Forst. (In press). Risks, Fixers and Zeal: Treatment Innovation and Implementation for Violent Juvenile Offenders. *Criminal Justice and Behavior.*

Fagan, J. A. and S. J. Jones. 1984. Toward a Theoretical Model for Treatment Interventions with Violent Juvenile Offenders. In R. Mathias, P. DeMuro, and R. A. Allinson, eds. *Violent Juvenile Offenders: An Anthology.* San Francisco: National Council on Crime and Delinquency.

Fagan, J. A., and C. Reinarman. 1991. The Social Context of Intensive Supervision: Ecological and Organizational Influences on Probation Services for Violent Adolescents. In Troy Armstrong, ed. *Intensive Interventions with High-Risk Youths: Promising Approaches in Probation and Parole*. Monsey, New York: Criminal Justice Press.

Fagan, J. A., and S. Wexler. 1988. Explanations of Adolescent Sex Offenses among Violent Juvenile Offenders. *Journal of Adolescent Research*. 3(3-4):363-385.

Feld, B. C. 1977. *Neutralizing Inmate Violence*. Cambridge, Massachusetts: Ballinger.

Felson, R. B. 1982. Impression Management and the Escalation of Aggression and Violence. *Social Psychology Quarterly*. 45:245-54.

———. 1993. Predatory and Dispute-related Violence: A Social Interactionist Approach. In R. V. Clarke and M. Felson, eds. *Routine Activity and Rational Choice*. New Brunswick, New Jersey: Transaction.

Frazier, C. B. 1978. The Use of Life History Interviews in Deviance Research. *Qualitative Sociology*. 1: 1-28.

Garrett, C. 1985. Effects of Residential Treatment on Adjudicated Delinquents: A Meta-analysis. *Journal of Research in Crime and Delinquency*. 22: 287-308.

Gelles, R. J. and M. A. Straus. 1979. Determinants of Violence in the Family: Toward a Theoretical Integration. In W. Burr, R. Hill, F. I. Nye, and I. L. Triss, eds. *Contemporary Theory about the Family*. New York: Free Press.

Gendreau, P. and R. R. Ross. 1979. Effectiveness of Correctional Treatment: Bibliotherapy for Cynics. *Crime and Delinquency*. 25: 463-489.

———. 1987. Revivification of Rehabilitation: Evidence from the 1980s. *Justice Quarterly*. 4: 349-408.

Gibbs, J. 1986. Alcohol Consumption, Cognition, and Context: Examining Tavern Violence. In A. Campbell and J. Gibbs, eds. *Violent Transactions: The Limits of Personality*. New York: Basil Blackwell.

Goldstein, P. J. 1985. The Drugs-violence Nexus: A Tri-partite Conceptual Framework. *Journal of Drug Issues*. 15:493-506.

Goldstein, P. J., H. H. Brownstein, P. Ryan, and P. A. Belluci. 1989. Crack and Homicide in New York City, 1989: A Conceptually Based Event Analysis. *Contemporary Drug Problems*. 16:651-687.

Gottfredson, D. 1986. Youth Employment, Crime and Schooling. *Developmental Psychology*. 21: 419-32.

Gottfredson, M., and T. Hirschi. 1990. *A General Theory of Crime*. Stanford, California: Stanford University Press.

Greenwood, P. and A. Abrahamse. 1982. *Selective Incapacitation*. Santa Monica, California: The RAND Corporation.

Greenwood, P. and S. Turner. 1987. Selective Incapacitation Revisited: Why the High Rate Offenders are Hard to Predict. Report R-3397-NIJ. Santa Monica, California: The RAND Corporation.

———. 1993. Evaulation of the Paint Creek Youth Center: A Residential Program for Serious Delinquents. *Criminology*. 31:263-279.

Greenwood, P. and F. Zimring. 1985. *One More Chance: The Pursuit of Intervention Strategies for Chronic Juvenile Offenders*. Santa Monica, California: The RAND Corporation.

Gruenewald, P., S. Laurence, and B. West. 1985. National Evaluation of the New Pride Replication Program: Executive Summary. Washington, D.C.: Office of Juvenile Justice and Delinquency Prevention.

Hartstone, E. C. and J. Cocozza. 1983. Violent Youth: The Impact of Mental Health Treatment. *International Journal of Law and Psychiatry.*

Hawkins, J. D. and J. G. Weis. 1980. *The Social Development Model for Delinquency Prevention*. Seattle, Washington: Center for Law and Justice, University of Washington.

Henglerr, S. W., G. B. Melton, L. A. Smith, S. L. Foster, J. H. Hanley, and C. M. Hutchison. 1993. Assessing Violent Offending in Serious Juvenile Offenders. *Journal of Abnormal Child Psychology*. 21:233-43.

Huessman, R. 1988. An Information-processing Model for the Development of Aggression. *Aggressive Behavior.* 14:13-24.

Katz, J. 1988. *Seductions of Crime*. New York: Basic Books.

Lab, S. P. and J. T. Whitehead. 1988. An Analysis of Juvenile Correctional Treatment. *Crime and Delinquency*. 34:60-83.

Land, K. C., P. L. McCall, and L. E. Cohen. 1990. Structural Covariates of Homicide Rates: Are There Any Invariances Across Time and Space. *American Journal of Sociology*. 95:922-963.

Levitt, John L., Thomas N. Young, and Donnell Pappenfort. 1979. *Achievement Place: The Teaching-Family Treatment Model in a Group Home Setting*. Washington, D.C.: U.S. Government Printing Office.

Lewis, D. O., S. S. Shanock, J. H. Pincus, and G. H. Glaser. 1979. Violent Juvenile Delinquents: Psychiatric, Neurological, Psychological, and Abuse Factors. *Journal of the American Academy of Child Psychiatry.* 2:591-602.

Lewis, D.O., S. S. Shanock, M. Grant, and E. Ritvo. 1984. Homicidally Aggressive Young Children: Neuropsychiatric and Experiential Correlates. In R. Mathias, P. DeMuro, and R. A. Allinson, eds. *Violent Juvenile Offenders: An Anthology.* San Francisco: National Council on Crime and Delinquency.

Lipsey, M. W. 1992. Juvenile Delinquency Treatment: A Meta-analytic Inquiry into the Variability of Effects. In Thomas Cook, ed. *Meta-Analysis for Explanation: A Casebook*. New York: Russell Sage Foundation Press.

Lipton, D., R. Martinson, and J. Wilks. 1975. *The Effectiveness of Correctional Treatment: A Survey of Treatment Evaluation Studies*. New York: Praeger Press.

Logan, C. H. 1972. Evaluation Research in Crime and Delinquency: A Reappraisal. *Journal of Criminal Law, Criminology, and Police Science*. 63:378-387.

Martinson, R. 1974. What Works? Questions and Answers about Prison Reform. *The Public Interest.* 35:22-54.

———. 1979. Symposium on Sentencing. *Hofstra Law Review.* 7:243-58.

McEwen, C. G. 1978. *Designing Correctional Organizations for Youths: Dilemmas of Subcultural Development.* Cambridge, Massachusetts: Ballinger.

Megargee, E. I. 1982. Psychological Deteminants and Correlates of Criminal Violence. In M. E. Wolfgang and N. A. Weiner, eds. *Criminal Violence.* Beverly Hills: Sage.

Mincy, Ronald B. 1994. Conclusions and Implications. In R. B. Mincy, ed. *Nurturing Young Black Males.* Washington, D.C.: Urban Institute Press.

Minuchin, R. 1974. *Families and Family Therapy.* Cambridge, Massachusetts: Harvard University Press.

Moffitt, T. 1990. The Neuropsychology of Juvenile Delinquency: A Critical Review. In M. Tonry and N. Morris, eds. *Crime and Justice: An Annual Review of Research, Volume 12.* Chicago: University of Chicago Press.

Oliver, W. 1994. *The Violent Social World of Black Men.* New York: Lexington Books.

Palmer, T. 1994. *A Profile of Correctional Effectiveness and New Directions for Research.* Albany, New York: SUNY Press.

Patterson, G. R., J. B. Reid, and T. Dishion. 1992. *Antisocial Boys: A Social Interactional Approach, Volume 4.* Eugene, Oregon: Castilia.

Prentky, R. A. 1990. Sexual Violence. Paper commissioned for the Panel on the Understanding and Control of Violent Behavior. Washington, D.C.: National Research Council, March 1.

Ramp, K., C. J. Braukmann, M. M. Wolf. 1979. The Teaching-Family Model of Group Home Treatment for Juvenile Offenders. In *Drug Abuse, Mental Health, and Delinquency: Summary of Proceedings of Practitioners' Conference on Juvenile Offenders with Serious Drug, Alcohol, and Mental Health Problems.* Washington, D.C.: Office of Juvenile Justice and Delinquency Prevention.

Reiss, A. J., Jr., 1986. Co-offender Influences on Criminal Careers. In A. Blumstein, J. Cohen, J. Roth, and C. Visher, eds. *Criminal Careers and "Career Criminals," Volume 1.* Washington, D.C.: National Academy Press.

Reiss, A. J. Jr., and J. A. Roth. 1993. *Understanding and Preventing Violence, Volume 1.* Washington, D.C.: National Academy Press.

Rezmovic, E. L. 1984. Assessing Treatment Implementation amid the Slings and Arrows of Reality. *Evaluation Review.* 8:187-204.

Rothman, K. J. 1986. *Modern Epidemiology*. Boston: Little Brown.

Royo, S. 1994. Legal and Illegal Social Control in the Treatment Retention of Drug Offenders. Doctoral dissertation, School of Criminal Justice, Rutgers University.

Sampson, R. J. 1987. Urban Black Violence: The Effect of Male Joblessness and Family Disruption. *American Journal of Sociology.* 93:348-382.

Sampson, R. J. and J. H. Laub. 1993. *Crime in the Making*. Cambridge, Massachusetts: Harvard University Press.

Sampson, R. J. and J. Lauritsen. 1994. Individual and Community Factors in Violent Offending. In A. J. Reiss, Jr. and J. A. Roth, eds. *Understanding and Preventing Violence, Volume* 3. Washington, D.C.: National Academy Press.

Scheirer, M. A. and E. L. Rezmovic. 1983. Measuring the Degree of Program Implementation: A Methodological Review. *Evaluation Review*. 7:599-633.

Sechrest, L., S. O. White, and E. D. Brown. 1979. *The Rehabilitation of Criminal Offenders: Problems and Prospects.* Washington, D.C.: National Academy Press.

Shannon, Lyle. 1991. *Changing Patterns of Delinquency and Crime.* Boulder, Colorado: Westview Press.

Sherman, L. W. 1992. The Influence of Criminology on Criminal Law: Evaluating Arrests for Misdemeanor Domestic Violence. *Journal of Criminal Law and Criminology.* 83:1-45.

Sommers, I. and D. Baskin. 1992. Sex, Race, Age, and Violent Offending. *Violence and Victims*. 7:191-201.

Sontheimer, H. and L. Goodstein. 1993. An Evaluation of Juvenile Intensive Aftercare Probation: Aftercare Versus System Response Effects. *Justice Quarterly.* 10:197-227.

Straus, M. A. and R. J. Gelles. 1990. How Violent Are American Families? Estimates from the National Family Violence Re-survey and Other Studies. In M. A. Straus and R. J. Gelles, eds. *Physical Violence in American Families: Risk Factors and Adaptations to Violence in 8,145 Families*. New Brunswick, New Jersey: Transaction.

Taylor, R. and J. Covington. 1988. Neighborhood Changes in Ecology and Violence. *Criminology*. 26:553-89.

Thornberry, T., M. D. Krohn, A. J. Lizotte, and D. Chard-Wierschem. 1993. The Role of Juvenile Gangs in Facilitating Delinquent Behavior. *Journal of Research in Crime and Delinquency*. 30:55-87.

Tolan, P. H., R. E. Cromwell, and M. Brasswell. 1986. Family Therapy with Delinquents: A Critical Review of the Literature. *Family Process*. 25:619-650.

Tolan, P. H. and N. G. Guerra. 1994. What Works in Reducing Adolescent Violence? An Empirical Review of the Field. Unpublished. Boulder, Colorado: Center for the Study and Prevention of Violence, University of Colorado.

Tolan, P. H. and M. E. Mitchell. 1989. Families and the Therapy of Antisocial and Delinquent Behavior. *Journal of Psychotherapy and the Family*. 6:29-48.

Toothaker, L. 1993. *Multiple Comparison Procedures*. Newbury Park, California: Sage.

Weis, J. G. and J. Sederstrom. 1981. *The Prevention of Serious Delinquency: What to Do?* Washington, D.C.: Office of Juvenile Justice and Delinquency Prevention.

Weisburd, D. 1993. Design Sensitivity in Criminal Justice Experiments: Reassesing the Relationship Between Sample Size and Statistical Power. In M. Tonry, ed. *Crime and Justice: An Annual Review of Research, Volume 17*. Chicago: University of Chicago Press.

Weisz, J. R., B. R. Walter, G. A. Fernandez, and V. A. Mikov. 1990. Arrests among Emotionally Disturbed Violent and Assaultive Individuals Following Minimal Versus Lengthy Intervention through North Carolina's Willie M Program. *Journal of Consulting and Clinical Psychology*. 58:720-728.

Whitehead, J. T. and S. P. Lab. 1989. A Meta-analysis of Juvenile Correctional Treatment. *Journal of Research in Crime and Delinquency*. 26:276-296.

Wolfgang, M. E., T. P. Thornberry, R. Figlio. 1987. *From Boy to Man, from Delinquency to Crime.* Chicago: University of Chicago Press.

TREATMENT FOR PRISONERS WITH MAJOR MENTAL DISORDERS[1]

7

Marnie E. Rice

Grant T. Harris

Mental Health Center
Penetanguishene, Ontario
Canada

Introduction

There are many seriously disturbed people in prisons. One might assume that the criminal justice system's laws about diminished capacity and insanity would ensure that offenders with mental disorder would be sent to hospitals instead of prisons. Experience and research show

---

[1]This chapter originally was prepared for the National Coalition for the Mentally Ill in the Criminal Justice System. It is similar to the presentation the authors made at the ICCA conference. Thanks are due to Vern Quinsey and members of the Coalition, especially Joel Dvoskin, for helpful comments on an earlier version and to Fred Tobin for bringing material regarding female offenders to our attention.

otherwise. Recent research shows that many persons with psychoses are convicted and sentenced (Rice and Harris, 1990; Teplin and Pruett, 1992). A surprisingly large proportion of prisoners, perhaps greater than 15 percent suffer from a psychotic or other major mental disorder (Hodgins and Coté, 1990; Motiuk and Porporino, 1991; Steadman, Fabisiak, Dvoskin, and Holohean, 1987; Teplin, 1990; Wormith and Borzecki, 1985).

There is accumulating evidence suggesting that persons currently experiencing psychotic symptoms are at increased risk of violent behavior (Hodgins, 1992; Klassen and O'Connor, 1988; Monahan, 1992; Taylor et al., 1994). There is also evidence that trends towards "deinstitutionalization" of mental hospitals have been accompanied by increased rates of incarceration for seriously mentally ill persons (Palermo, Smith, and Liska, 1991; Penrose, 1939; *see also* Steadman, Monahan, Duffee, Hartstone, and Robbins, 1984). The characteristics that predict criminal recidivism among mentally disordered offenders are essentially the same as those that predict recidivism among offenders in general (Bonta, Hanson, and Law, in press; Feder, 1992; Harris, Rice, and Quinsey, 1993; Rice and Harris, 1992; Rice, Harris, Lang, and Bell, 1990; Rice, Quinsey, and Houghton, 1990).

How does it happen that persons with psychoses or other major mental disorders end up in prison? This occurs partly as a deliberate result of social or institutional policy (in other words, persons who are psychotic but whose criminal act was minor or not seen as being a direct result of the psychosis are not usually considered for an insanity defense; Rice and Harris, 1990); partly because some persons are already in prison at the time their psychosis becomes apparent; and partly by accident (Teplin and Pruett, 1992; Toch, 1982; Toch and Adams, 1987). It is important to note, however, that the high incidence of psychosis in prison is not primarily directly caused by a cruel and unusual environment driving sane prisoners mad (Bonta and Gendreau, 1990; Wormith, 1984; Zamble and Porporino, 1988). The higher proportion of inmates with psychoses in segregation and special handling units is more likely due to the difficulties they present to staff and other inmates than to their mental disturbance being caused by segregation (Adams, 1986; Hodgins and Coté, 1991; Gendreau and Bonta, 1987).

Without question, the presence in prisons of inmates with major mental disorder presents serious problems for institutional staff and other inmates. In addition, most prisons are profoundly ill-equipped to manage and treat psychotic disorders, and traditional methods of isolation, chemical restraint, and transfer may exacerbate symptoms (Toch, 1982;

Toch and Adams, 1987; 1989). In this chapter, we discuss a psychosocial approach to the assessment and treatment of inmates with major mental disorder. The approach we advocate meets all the *desiderata* for mental health services in prison described in *Ruiz v. Estelle* (Jemelka, Trupin, and Chiles, 1989; *see also* Thyer, 1995). First, however, there are several key issues that should be addressed.

Key Issues

Diagnosis Versus Problems and Symptoms

Not all persons who qualify for a psychiatric diagnosis of major mental illness are disturbed or disruptive, in need of, or amenable to treatment. Conversely, not all disturbed or disruptive inmates qualify for a diagnosis of psychosis. In this chapter, we argue that all important clinical and administrative issues pertain to symptoms and other problems experienced by disturbed inmates and not to the diagnosis *per se*. There are several bases for this assertion:

First, though persons with schizophrenia, for example, may exhibit slightly more violence than citizens in general, characteristics that predict the occurrence of violence pertain to current symptomatology (Link and Stueve, 1994; Swanson, Holzer, Ganju, and Jono, 1990; Swanson, Borum, Sartz, and Monahan, 1996; Taylor et al., 1994), and to history of aggression (Harris and Varney, 1986; Rice and Harris, 1992; McNiel and Binder, 1994). Among mentally disordered offenders released to the community, severity of schizophrenic deficit and schizophrenic subtype are found to be unrelated to aggression (Bonta et al., in press; Rice and Harris, 1992).

Second, several studies of psychiatric patients (Harris, Hilton, and Rice, 1993), forensic patients (Rice and Harris, 1988; Rice, Harris, Quinsey, 1996), and prisoners with mental disorder (Sommers and Baskin, 1991) have shown that the type of psychiatric treatment delivered is, at best, weakly related to diagnosis and much more strongly related to presenting symptoms, other problems, and social factors.

Third, in several studies of psychiatric patients (Harris, Hilton, and Rice, 1993; Harris and Rice, 1990) and mentally disordered offenders (Quinsey, Cyr, and Lavallee, 1988; Rice and Harris, 1988; Rice, Harris, and Quinsey, 1996), we examined subjects' clinical presentation with cluster analyses. In every case, clinically useful (with respect to treatment and supervision needs) subgroups depended not upon psychiatric diagnosis but instead upon current interpersonal problems, skill deficits, criminal history, and current symptomatology. Thus, although a significant minority of prisoners qualify for psychiatric diagnoses, we conclude that treatment decisions cannot and should not be based solely or directly upon diagnosis.

Classification and Clinical Assessment

Classification of prisoners is a longstanding practice in corrections. Typically, inmates are sorted into institutions or areas within institutions based on security requirements. Levels range from maximum security for those judged to be the most likely to escape and the most dangerous to very open settings for inmates judged to be of low risk for escape and violence (Ekstedt and Griffiths, 1988). It also has been persuasively argued that, in addition to risk, classification also should reflect needs (Andrews, Bonta, and Hoge, 1990; Bonta and Gendreau, 1992). These authors assert that correctional classification should facilitate rehabilitation by targeting the criminogenic needs of relatively high risk offenders. In addition, we believe it is sensible to classify inmates based on their behavior within prison.

Our work on mentally disordered offenders (Rice and Harris, 1988; Rice, Harris, and Quinsey, 1996; *see also* Quinsey, Cyr, and Lavallee, 1988) suggests that several relevant subgroups emerge when the clinical presentations of offenders are examined in detail:

1. Relatively low-risk offenders who exhibit few problem behaviors in prison

2. High risk offenders who exhibit few problem behaviors in prison

3. High risk offenders who present significant management problems (violence, theft, threats, escape, noncompliance, insolence, lies, property destruction, and so forth)

4. Inmates of varying levels of risk who exhibit psychotic symptoms (delusions, hallucinations, confusion, and so forth) and social withdrawal (sometimes called negative symptoms of psychosis) while in prison

5. A small group of inmates with serious mental disturbances who exhibit active psychotic symptoms, social withdrawal, and severe management problems while in prison

This latter group, those with serious mental disturbances, is also likely to exhibit serious skill deficits (illiteracy, lack of vocational skills, and so forth) and to appear depressed and even suicidal (Bland, Newman, Dyck, and Orn, 1990; Florez and Holley, 1989). The characterization of the latter two subgroups matches the case material provided by Toch (1982) and Toch and Adams (1987) on disturbed-nondisruptive and disturbed-disruptive inmates, respectively. We propose that correctional systems identify persons in these latter two groups as the primary clientele of mental health services and provide specific treatment for them. In the remainder of this chapter, we describe the assessment and treatment of the significant minority of inmates who exhibit such severe problems.

Before beginning, however, there are three points to make. First, treatment and rehabilitation aimed at reducing criminal recidivism are indicated for many offenders in the first three groups (Andrews, Zinger, Hoge, Bonta, Gendreau, and Cullen, 1990; Rice and Harris, 1997; Rice, Harris, and Quinsey, 1996). Second, such rehabilitation is also indicated for the inmates in the latter two groups, but clinicians and prison administrators are likely to regard amelioration of the psychotic symptoms (and other problem behaviors) as a higher priority. As treatment improves such problems, one would expect an offender with mental disorder to be "reclassified" into his or her appropriate risk/needs category. Third, services for psychiatric patients are almost always directed towards the overarching goal of successful adjustment to the community.

By analogy it has been argued that the goal of services for inmates with mental disorder should be successful adjustment to the "normal" prison population (Dvoskin and Steadman, 1989) to permit participation in rehabilitation programs and other activities. It goes almost without saying that this idea rests on the assumption that correctional institutions are safely and humanely run. No ethical clinician would assist in preparing inmate clients for reintegration into a "community" where they were likely to be the victims of violence and exploitation (Roth, 1980).

Just as diagnosis cannot be equated with assessment of clinical problems, assessment of clinical problems cannot be equated with correctional classification. Classification officers charged with sorting incoming prisoners only can be expected to make educated guesses about which inmates present significant clinical problems. There are several reasons for this: First, not all clinical problems are easily detected. For example, our research on subgroups of mentally disordered offenders (Rice and Harris, 1988; Rice, Harris, and Quinsey, 1996), and over a decade of combined experience on an admission ward for the most disturbed mentally disordered offenders in Ontario, clearly show that many seriously disturbed inmates are not (or not always) disruptive. Rather, they are extremely withdrawn and seclusive. Second, much disturbed and disruptive behavior, no matter how pathological it seems, is profoundly controlled by the social environment (Rice, Harris, Varney, and Quinsey, 1989; Rice, Harris, and Quinsey, 1994). Third, as is discussed next, many inmates exhibit some signs of disturbance or pathology on admission to prison, but that disturbance constitutes a "situational reaction" that quickly resolves itself (Zamble and Porporino, 1988).

Clinical Services For Inmates With Mental Disorder

To address these difficulties, a progressive system for providing service to inmates with mental disorder has been proposed (Cohen and Dvoskin, 1992; Dvoskin and Steadman, 1989; Greene, 1988; James and Gregory, 1980). Under such a system, inmates pass through increasingly selective screens (and increasingly intensive clinical services) starting with very liberal screening of inmates in the general population. Those assessed to be in need of more than "crisis intervention" become candidates for "outpatient" assessment and treatment. Outpatients in need of greater services are moved to the institution's "clinic," and clinic patients in need of the most intensive services move to the highly specialized services available in the "hospital." Most of the services can be located either within prisons or in separate institutions operated by public mental health agencies.

To us, this approach makes good sense with the following provisos: 1) Especially at the early stages, extra care is needed to ensure that disturbed but nondisruptive inmates can receive services. At every stage, correctional staff (officers and clinicians) will be happy to see that the most disruptive inmates get transferred to the next step, but our research (Harris and Rice, 1992) and experience shows that withdrawn patients and inmates often are unnoticed or even preferred by institutional staff. 2) As much as possible, clinical services rather than patients should do the traveling. If the goal of service is successful adjustment to the prison environment, it is appropriate to evaluate the antecedents, problem behaviors, and consequences in that environment (Kazdin, 1993). As is discussed next, problems of generalization of treatment effects are minimized if that treatment occurs in the "home" environment. 3) Clinical services should be at least as much behavioral and psychosocial as pharmacological. There is abundant evidence that the resolution of the disturbed and disturbing behavior of mentally disordered offenders cannot come from exclusively from reliance on drugs (Harris, 1989; Harris and Rice, 1997a; 1997b; Rice and Harris, 1997a; Rice, Harris, and Quinsey, 1996; Rice, Harris, Quinsey, and Cyr, 1990).

Clinical Assessment

In this chapter, we take the strong view that traditional medical/psychiatric approaches to the treatment of offenders with mental disorder are inadequate. The problems inherent in basing policy and clinical decisions on psychiatric diagnosis already have been discussed. In assessing clinical needs and evaluating treatment, our position is the same: typical clinical observations are irrelevant (or nearly so). As we have discussed at length elsewhere (Rice and Harris, 1997a; Rice, Harris, Quinsey, and Cyr, 1990; Rice et al., 1996), typical clinical observations as recorded in institutional files or noted in discussions among staff lack sufficient reliability and validity. Unfortunately, however, there is abundant evidence that clinically important behaviors are grossly underreported, that even highly qualified clinical staff do not agree about the meaning of clinical terms (such as delusional, depressed, disturbed, agitated) and that observations are not recorded in a sufficiently systematic (in time or context) fashion to permit useful comparability (Rice et al., 1990). Accurate decisions about who needs treatment, how much, and for what problems cannot be made using diagnoses or traditional clinical observations.

One response to these difficulties in traditional clinical practice was the rise of behavior therapy and behavioral assessment. We advocate the use of behavioral observation methods in the assessment of the clinical problems for mentally disturbed prisoners. Time sampling behavioral observation systems (for example, Paul and Lentz, 1977) provide the highest quality data and also can be used to evaluate any intervention that is indicated in the treatment of inmates with mental disorder.

In addition to behavioral observation techniques, assessment of clinical problems can be informed by a number of paper and pencil questionnaires, checklists, and rating scales completed by staff or patients. Some valuable general measures completed by clinical staff are the Psychotic Reaction Profile (Lorr, O'Connor, and Stafford, 1960), and the MACC Behavior Adjustment Scale (Ellsworth, 1971). Valuable self-report measures include the Correctional Institutions Environment Scale

(Moos, 1975), and the Social Performance Survey Schedule (SPSS: Lowe and Cautela, 1978; Monti, 1983). Useful tools for the assessment of assaultiveness, anger, and aggression include the Overt Aggression Scale (completed by clinical staff) (Yudofsky, Silver, Jackson, Endicott, and Williams, 1986), and the self-report measures, the Special Hospitals Assessment of Personality and Socialization (SHAPS; Blackburn, 1987), and several other self-report assessments of anger and temper control problems (Buss and Durkee, 1957; Novaco, 1975; Siegel, 1985; 1986; Spielberger, Johnson, Russell, Crane, Jacobs, and Warden, 1985).

An expanded version of the Brief Psychiatric Rating Scale (BPRS; Lukoff, Liberman, and Nuechterlein, 1986; Overall and Gorham, 1962) may be a useful supplement to behavioral observations in the assessment of positive psychotic symptoms. Finally, as discussed, many persons suffering from schizophrenia or other serious disorders will exhibit only extreme social withdrawal as presenting problems. The SPSS (Miller and Funabiki, 1984), MACC (Ellsworth, 1971; Helzel and Rice, 1985; Rice, 1983), and NOSIE (Dvoskin and Steadman, 1989; Honigfeld, Gillis, and Klett, 1966) have been shown to be useful with offenders with mental disorder. In addition, the Socialization Level Scale (Aumack, 1962; Rice, 1983) and measures of assertion (Harris and Rice, 1984; McCormick, 1984) also may be valuable.

Pharmacological Treatment

Many inmates with mental disturbances will be candidates for drug treatment. Of course, there is abundant and unequivocal evidence that neuroleptics reduce the positive symptoms of schizophrenia (agitation, hallucinations, and delusions) and that lithium is the treatment of choice for bipolar disorder. The most revolutionary change in the history of the treatment of mental disorder was the advent of phenothiazine drugs. These drugs have profoundly altered the nature and duration of psychiatric hospitalization, and greatly have improved the quality of life for many persons diagnosed with schizophrenia (Rice, Harris, Quinsey, and Cyr, 1990). Furthermore, newer antipsychotic drugs offer hope that more patients will be helped by drugs and that the effects of treatment will be more complete (Chouinard et al., 1993; Heinrich, et al., 1994; Peuskens, 1995; Pickar, Owen, Litman, Konicki, Gutierrez, and Rappoport, 1992; Reid, 1995; Reid, Mason, and Toprac, 1994; Tollefson et al., 1997) In addition, there is suggestive evidence that other psychotropic drugs reduce the aggression and agitation of other institutionalized individuals (Eichelman, 1988; Rice, Harris, Varney, and Quinsey, 1989).

Psychological treatments require institutional administration to engage in extensive planning and to have considerable control over the behavior of staff at all levels, while the delivery of drugs alone rarely requires such a high degree of effective administrative control. Because drugs might seem cheaper and easier to deliver than therapy programs, why do we so strongly advocate behavioral methods described next?

Neuroleptic drugs are completely effective neither for all psychotic symptoms nor for all patients. Harris (1989) showed that patients in a maximum-security institution for mentally disordered offenders exhibited different responses to being admitted and receiving neuroleptic drugs. Many responded quickly and within a month or two were sufficiently stable to be considered for transfer. Many others, however, did not respond positively to drug administration and remained in the institution for many months or years. Neither increasing nor decreasing neuroleptic dose, nor changing to different drugs were associated with improvements in behavior or eventual transfer. Although new antipsychotic drugs promise to help more patients than traditional neuroleptics, it is still inevitable that any ward, unit, or institution for disturbed and disruptive inmates will be populated by those who are partial or complete drug nonresponders.

Even when neuroleptic drugs have demonstrably positive effects, some patients resist taking them and initiate expensive legal battles in their efforts to resist. In fact, there is evidence that the best predictor of future drug refusal is the severity of some side effects (dysphoria and akasthesia) upon initial drug administration (Van Putten, May, and Marder, 1984). Drug refusal appears to be an especially common precursor to being identified as a mentally disordered inmate (Smith, 1989). Inmates also might be even less likely to take medication if they perceive that the drugs are offered to keep them quiet and compliant rather than to help them with their own serious personal difficulties. There are behavioral and cognitive-behavioral methods that improve medication compliance (Meichenbaum and Turk, 1987; Wittlin, 1988), but in the end, though an essential part of the clinical armamentarium, it must be concluded that drugs will not suffice as the only clinical tool for prisoners with mental disorder (Harris, 1989; Rice et al., 1989; Rice, Harris, Quinsey, and Cyr, 1990).

Behavioral Treatment

What other form(s) of therapy should be provided for inmates with mental disorder? Should it be psychotherapy, milieu therapy, cognitive therapy, cognitive-behavior therapy, or what? Whatever the value of other approaches in general, the empirical literature is unequivocal in supporting the use of behavioral treatment for inmates with mental disorder (Andrews et al., 1990; Harris and Rice, 1992; Rice et al., 1989; 1996; Rice, Harris, Quinsey, and Cyr, 1990). It is commonplace to hear that treatment should be prescriptive. However, for the most part, the only form of prescriptiveness supported by empirical literature for the present population is attention to the antecedents, specific behaviors, and consequences that characterize behavior therapy. We propose a two-pronged behavioral approach. The first prong is the use of token economies, and the second is the provision of skills training for specific behavioral deficits. Although therapeutic community or milieu programs are common in clinical settings, clinicians are unlikely to regard the most disturbed and disruptive inmates as candidates for such a program. Furthermore, Paul and Lentz (1977) reported data showing that a token economy was more effective than an equally intensive therapeutic community program.

The existing literature strongly favors token economy programs as comprehensive systems to promote independent, prosocial, cooperative behavior; to extinguish (and sometimes penalize) dependent, crazy, antisocial behavior; to promote therapeutic client-staff interactions; to guide discharge and transfer decisions, and to encourage clients to participate in other skills teaching programs (Harris and Rice, 1992; Milan, 1987; Rice and Harris, in press; Rice et al., in press; Rice, Harris, Quinsey, and Cyr, 1990). Token economies can be individualized to target specific problem behaviors—shaping and reinforcing desired prosocial conduct (being in a good mood, helping others, talking about realistic topics, leaving one's cell, and so forth) and extinguishing or punishing undesirable conduct (assault, property destruction, threatening, yelling, and so forth).

Behavioral techniques designed to rapidly suppress self-injurious and assaultive behavior in institutions include differential reinforcement of incompatible behaviors, extinction, time-out, overcorrection-restitution, and contingent punishment. There is also evidence that suppression of these problem behaviors can be achieved through the use of contingent required relaxation and time-out plus response cost. Specific behavioral consequences can be accomplished without the use of a token economy, of course (Wong, Slama, and Liberman, 1987; Wong, Woolsey, Innocent, and Liberman, 1988), but a token economy is an invaluable tool when many or most inmates exhibit similar problem behaviors and deficits.

Token economy programs have been shown to improve and maintain many of the adaptive and prosocial behaviors of patients exhibiting a variety of problems in a variety of institutional settings (Rice et al., 1990). For example, the self-care, life skills and social adjustment of institutionalized adolescents and delinquents, as well as the academic performance, work, life skills, and interpersonal behavior of adult and adolescent correctional inmates all have been reported to have been improved by token economy programs. Token economies also produce improvements in self-help behaviors, attendance at other programs, work, compliance, shortened length of hospital stay, and less recidivism in chronic psychiatric patients (Rice, Harris, Quinsey, and Cyr, 1990).

The overwhelming evidence of their effectiveness demands that clinicians planning therapeutic efforts in secure treatment institutions seriously consider the use of token economy programs (Rice, Harris, Quinsey, and Cyr, 1990). However, significant difficulties will face a clinician who proposes to implement a token economy program in an institution where staff are accustomed to a traditional custodial environment (Harris and Rice, 1992; Rice, Harris, Quinsey, and Cyr, 1990; *see also* Backer, Liberman, and Kuehnel, 1986). Appropriately trained and oriented staff are essential to the effective operation of a token economy. The effectiveness of a behavioral program can be undermined even when only a minority of staff fail to carry out program duties because customary staff practice is incompatible with effective behavioral treatment: deviant and dependent patient behaviors are reinforced and independent behaviors are extinguished. Laws (1974) asserted that custodially oriented ward staff should not operate a token economy and instead behaviorally trained staff should be specifically hired. As much as possible, one would seek an organization with staff specifically selected and trained for the program (Paul and Lentz, 1977).

Although it has been reported that token economy treatment can generalize to post-institutional environments (Paul and Lentz, 1977), such generalization is difficult to ensure (Rice, Quinsey, and Houghton, 1990). Certain steps improve generalization (Kazdin, 1993), but whether behaviors acquired or strengthened in institutional reinforcement systems generalize or not, program managers require systems to monitor behavior, enforce reasonable rules, make security decisions and encourage patients in the specific skill building programs (for which there is evidence of generalization) that form the other part of our recommended behavioral approach. As discussed in the Inmates Rights section below, token economics have no serious rivals as management systems for offenders with mental disorder (Rice, Harris, Quinsey, and Cyr, 1990).

The second prong of our recommended behavioral approach is applicable to all inmates in need of mental health services and consists of specific skill training. This behavioral technology usually is provided for small groups of inmates at a time. The training methods comprise shaping, coaching, modeling, practicing role-play, and providing feedback. The technology has been applied to general social skills associated with making and keeping friends (Rice, 1983; Rice and Josefowitz, 1983); heterosocial skills (Quinsey, Chaplin, Maguire, and Upfold, 1987), anger management or aggression replacement (Goldstein and Glick, 1987), assertion (Harris and Rice, 1992; Rice and Chaplin, 1979), interpersonal problem solving (Ross and Fabiano, 1985; Ross, Fabiano, and Ewles, 1988), conversation skills (Liberman, Mueser, and Wallace, 1986), and the management of positive psychotic symptoms (Liberman, 1988; MacKain and Streveler, 1990). Because patients with psychoses exhibit such obvious and gross deficits in interpersonal behavior, considerable effort has gone into teaching them social skills.

There is substantial evidence that social skill training produces lasting treatment effects and can increase community adjustment and reduce hospitalization (Beck, Menditto, Baldwin, Angelone, and Maddox, 1991; Benton and Schroeder, 1990; Corrigan, 1991; Etscheidt, 1991; Liberman, Van Putten, Barringer, Mintz, Bowen, Kuehnel, Aravagiri, and Marder, 1994; Tarrier, Beckett, Harwood, Baker, Yusupoff, and Ugarteburu, 1993). Although not specifically directed towards remediation of positive psychotic symptomatology (bizarre talk and actions, and so forth), a common result of standard social skills training is that patients are reported, and report themselves, to have significant reductions in such psychotic symptoms (Rice, Harris, Quinsey, and Cyr, 1990). Liberman, Neuchterlein, and Wallace 1982; Liberman, Kopelowicz, and Young, 1994 make cogent arguments for a concerted training effort aimed at teaching: basic cognitive/conversational skills such as staying on topic, focusing attention, ignoring distractions, handling stimulus overload, delaying responses, employing appropriate voice volume, and developing greater fluency; basic interpersonal social identification skills such as the accurate identification of others' emotions, predicting the impact of social behaviors, and the identification of others' social status; and coping strategies such as compromising, repeating requests, refusing to comply, and escaping (*see also* Wallace, 1982). Good examples of comprehensive social learning, token economy, and pharmacological treatments for severely disordered psychiatric patients may be found in Liberman et al. (1994); Marder et al. (1996), and Menditto et al. (1996).

Other Treatment Issues

Seclusion and mechanical restraint are frequently used to reduce disruptive behavior (c.f. Harris, Rice, and Preston, 1989). However, their use often depends as much upon such factors such as staffing levels and the absence of structured activity as upon the nature of the problematic behavior itself. In addition, there is evidence that the use of behavioral treatments drastically can reduce the necessity for seclusion and restraint with no corresponding reductions in staff morale or safety (Davidson, Hemingway, and Wysocki, 1984).

It is important to note that disturbed disruptive inmates or patients can cause much friction within the ranks of institutional staff. Front line staff invariably seek to punish disruptive behaviors but frequently fail to reinforce appropriate responses. Even in token economy programs, there appears to be a continual tendency for front line staff to lobby for more and larger penalties for misbehaviors but to give fewer and fewer rewards (Bassett and Blanchard, 1977; Harris and Rice, 1992).

There is every reason to suppose that, in a general (nontoken economy) ward environment, patients who exhibit management problems would live in a de facto program that was almost entirely aversive. That is, prosocial behaviors would largely be extinguished and there would be aversive consequences (in the form of restraints, seclusion, loss of privileges, scolding, and so forth) for aggressive or disruptive behavior. Also, working with such patients can be stressful and frustrating for staff because of the effort required to effect patient improvement and because of the uncooperativeness and litigiousness of the patients. Staff are also at high risk for both real and specious charges of abuse and misconduct. In work with intrafamilial aggression, Patterson (1982; 1985) described an analogous phenomenon called *coercive family process* in which all family members attempt to control each others' behavior through an implicit means of using exclusively negative reinforcement and punishment. Those who have worked on wards for the management of problem patients can recognize a nearly identical process in operation (Quinsey, 1981; Rice, 1985).

A final approach to the reduction of violent behavior in institutions is founded on quite a different understanding of the problem. It is based on the assumption that institutional violence is not solely the product of individual pathology but stems primarily, instead, from problems in the way patients and staff typically interact. That is, while staff regard their own behavior as reasonable, expected, and "part of the job," patients often regard the same staff behaviors as provocative, insensitive and arbitrary. Thus, Rice and her colleagues (Rice et al., 1989; Rice, Helzel, Varney, and Quinsey, 1985) developed and evaluated a five-day staff training course that emphasized early recognition of patients' disturbance, early verbal intervention to calm or defuse upset behavior and, as a last resort, safe and effective techniques for manual restraint and self-defense. The course was positively received, reduced assaults, lowered workdays lost due to patient-caused injuries, improved ward morale, and resulted in increased staff ratings of their own effectiveness and patients' ratings of self-esteem.

Isn't Prison Depressing?

So far, we have not addressed the assessment and treatment of the symptoms and other problems associated with depression. These problems include inactivity (psychomotor retardation); agitation; expressions of sadness, worthlessness, and hopelessness; threatened and attempted suicide; sleeplessness; anxiety; and sometimes anger. In a comprehensive and enlightening study, Zamble and Porporino (1988) showed that a very large number of prisoners report problems associated with depression and anger, especially early in their sentences. The authors point out that this is, to some extent, deliberate: prisoners are supposed to be unhappy about being in prison.

In addition, depression can be the iatrogenic result of inconsistent and punitive staff behavior. Of course, some offenders have real and serious problems in other domains that cause them to be unhappy (marital discord, financial losses, addiction, and so forth). Zamble and Porporino also showed that many of the most serious problems of depression resolve themselves relatively quickly with little or no intervention. Then, most prisoners "do their time" in what Zamble and Porporino term an intellectual and personal "deep freeze" in which they deal with problems much in the ways they do on the street: using avoidance, escaping, and, occasionally, employing impulsive antisocial conduct.

There, however, will be a significant minority of inmates whose problems of depression do not quickly resolve themselves. What clinical services should be provided for such persons? The treatment of major depression has received considerable scientific attention in recent years. There have also been efforts to distil those scientific data available in the public domain into useful advice for clinicians who treat unipolar depression (such as the American Psychiatric Association, 1993). That advice seems sensible and fits traditional clinical lore: Supportive counseling is indicated for mild situational depression, psychotherapy is indicated for moderate depression, and somatic therapy (drugs or electroconvulsive therapy) combined with psychotherapy is required for moderate to severe depression.

In our view, a fair reading of the available literature, however, calls some of this advice into question. A comprehensive set of meta-analyses, narrative reviews, and multisite treatment evaluations (Antonuccio, Danton, and DeNelsky, 1995; Blatt, Zuroff, Quinlan and Pilkonis, 1996; Elkin et al., 1989; 1995; Evans et al., 1992; Greenberg, Bornstein, Greenberg, and Fisher, 1992; Hollon, Shelton, and Loosen, 1991; Hollon, et al., 1992; Kupfer et al., 1992; Lipsey and Wilson, 1993; Robinson, Berman, and Neimeyer, 1990; Shea et al., 1989; 1992; Shelton, Hollon, Purdon, and Loosen, 1991; Sotsky et al., 1991; Sweet and Loizeaux, 1991) leads to somewhat different conclusions:

(1) Both cognitive-behavioral therapy and drugs (imipramine is the best-studied to date, but newer antidepressants are likely to be at least as effective as imipramine; Rickels, Schweizer, Fox, and Weise, 1994) are effective in the treatment of acute depression. However, treatment effects are smaller when patients' (versus clinicians') ratings are used for the evaluation, and when greater efforts are made to control the effects of expectancies and the theoretical allegiance of the investigators.

(2) Psychotherapies (usually in the form of cognitive, behavioral or cognitive-behavioral treatments) are equivalent to each other in effectiveness and to pharmacotherapy in the treatment of acute depression regardless of initial symptom severity or type of unipolar depression.

(3) Cognitive-behavioral treatment during the acute phase of depression and continuing drug treatment are effective (and

equally so) in reducing the likelihood of relapse regardless of initial severity.

(4) The combination of cognitive-behavioral therapy and drugs provided during acute treatment is not much more effective than either alone, except that cognitive-behavioral therapy (with or without drugs) appears to lower the risk of relapse.

(5) The attrition rates for all forms of treatment are high (25 to 50 percent) and the personal characteristics that predict attrition and response to treatment are unknown. Also unknown are the mechanisms responsible for the positive effects of drugs and electroconvulsive therapy and the specific features of interpersonal, cognitive, behavioral and cognitive-behavioral psychotherapy responsible for clinical improvement.

Consequently, our advice for treating problems of depression is little different than for treating other serious mental difficulties. Assessment should involve evaluation of the specific antecedents, behaviors, and consequences of depression. Some self-report measures also may be helpful (Beck and Beck, 1972; Hamilton, Stephens, and Allen, 1967; Rehm, 1981; Zung, 1969). Based on the meta-analyses and multisite studies cited, inmates with persistent and acute depression should be offered a choice between cognitive-behavioral therapy (group or individual) or ongoing pharmacotherapy. Those who fail to respond to their first choice should be encouraged to try the alternate mode of treatment. Electroconvulsive therapy may be indicated for severely depressed inmates who fail to respond to both other forms of treatment.

Some Illustrative Treatment Programs

By far, the most powerful demonstration of the effects of behavioral treatment for psychiatric patients is that of Gordon Paul and his colleagues (Paul and Lentz, 1977). Working with very chronic and disturbed mental patients, Paul and his colleagues demonstrated that the specific behavioral techniques in a token economy were responsible for profound improvements in the severity of psychiatric symptoms, and the development of interpersonal skills and adaptive functioning. The token economy program was much more effective and less expensive than standard hospital care. The results of this study also showed that the behavioral improvements were maintained when the patients and programs were transferred to the community and resulted in very low rates of rehospitalization.

Paul also developed a comprehensive technology to monitor patient and staff behaviors and demonstrated that the positive effects of the program occurred because the staff interacted with the patients in a manner very different from that found in a traditional hospital setting. Patients who participated in the program were maintained on far less medication (85 percent were drug-free). Although one might think such a program would be very costly, Paul and Lentz reported that it (including the detailed behavioral observation methods described) was effectively delivered with a staff that was no larger nor more highly qualified (though with much different training, of course) than that on traditional psychiatric wards. Paul's demonstration shows what is possible when an institution or service is organized specifically to deliver effective psychosocial treatment.

Milan and his colleagues (Milan, 1987) have convincingly demonstrated that behavioral programs can be effectively delivered in prisons. Using a cell block token economy for imprisoned felons, they demonstrated that contingent token reinforcement was responsible for increases in a variety of behaviors ranging from maintenance activities and personal hygiene to participation in educational programs. These improvements were achieved without deprivation of recreational opportunities or the imposition of other aversive consequences. Milan and his colleagues also demonstrated that response chaining could be used to develop behaviors that otherwise were never performed by the inmate participants.

In a separate series of demonstrations, Ayllon and Milan (Milan, 1987) showed that behavioral programs in prison could produce large changes in academic and vocational skills compared to typical institutional routines. Furthermore, these investigators provided evidence that behavioral programs were acceptable to prisoners and that some skills generalized to the postrelease community. Milan (1987) also examined legal judgments concerning the use of behavioral programs and concluded that the courts have never prohibited the use of effective and clinically sound behavioral programs. Rather, the courts have forbidden the use of some arbitrary, coercive, and clinically unsound practices that skilled behaviorists would eschew anyway. Milan also noted the lack of behavioral work published since 1980, especially in institutions for mentally disordered offenders, and attributed this dearth to a host of professional, political, and administrative barriers to effective programming. The reappearance of strong behavioral programs for forensic patients in the 1990s is an encouraging sign (cf. Beck et al., 1991).

Finally, other investigators have shown that behavioral programs can be effectively delivered to prison inmates with mental disorder. Based on the work of Liberman (1988), MacKain and Streveler (1990) described a comprehensive psychosocial rehabilitation program for mentally ill offenders. The program was provided for both acutely disturbed "inpatients" and "day treatment" inmates who resided on regular prison ranges. Skills training (comprising modeling, shaping, practicing role-play and using videotaped feedback) was provided on such diverse topics as life skills, medication, self-management, communication skills, anger management, recreation, avoiding substance abuse, and stress management.

Special Populations

In this section, we consider whether special treatment procedures are required for three specific groups of offenders with a mental disorder: HIV positive inmates, sex offenders, and females.

Mentally Disordered HIV Positive Inmates

Both incarcerated individuals and persons with severe mental disorder are at higher risk for human immunodeficiency virus (HIV) infection and acquired immune deficiency syndrome (AIDS) than the general population (Cournos et al., 1991; Lurigio, 1989). Because of impaired judgment regarding drug injection and sexual behavior, as well as vulnerability to victimization, inmates suffering from major mental disorder may be at particularly high risk of infection by HIV both before and after incarceration.

In addition, psychiatric symptoms are common in HIV positive persons in all phases of HIV-related illness (Evans and Perkins, 1990). Dementia beginning with social withdrawal and impaired concentration, and then worsening gradually until there is severe poverty of speech, global cognitive impairment, and loss of muscle control occurs in a proportion of HIV positive individuals. Sometimes the dementia may be the only sign of AIDS. In other cases, there may be dementia secondary to acute infections. Suicide, suicidal ideation, depression, and anxiety are common. There is some evidence that an HIV-related organic mood disorder may exist, and both major depression and manic syndromes have been reported (Evans and Perkins, 1990; Lyketsos et al., 1993).

There is some evidence that HIV-related mental disorders, especially major depression, respond to antiviral treatments. In addition, traditional psychotropic medication including antidepressants, antianxiety agents, neuroleptics, and psychostimulants can be used for symptomatic treatment. However, patients with HIV infection seem to be especially sensitive to many psychotropic drugs, so very low dosages are recommended (Evans and Perkins, 1990). Of course, all of the psychosocial treatments are applicable for HIV-positive inmates just as they are for other inmates with mental disorder.

One of the most common concerns of staff who work with HIV-positive inmates is the possibility of infection via blood spills or bites during a violent altercation (Lurigio, 1989). Although there is no evidence that any correctional officer or person in any of a number of other occupations where contact through blood spills or bites is thought to be likely (such as police officers, paramedics or firefighters) has contacted HIV infection through the performance of their duties (Lurigio, 1989), it cannot be concluded that it is impossible (Belbot and del Carmen, 1991).

Because of the increasing numbers of cases of AIDS in prisons and the rapid pace of knowledge and laws about this topic, ongoing AIDS-related education should be an important topic for both inmates and staff who work with inmates. Although correctional officers mostly favor mandatory testing and the segregation of HIV-positive inmates (Lurigio, 1989), the courts to this point have neither required nor forbidden either. Neither segregation nor mandatory testing is standard practice for both practical and humanitarian reasons (Belbot and del Carmen, 1991).

At this point, then, universal precautions should be used with all inmates. Staff training in verbal methods to prevent and intervene in violent incidents (for example, Rice et al., 1989) is especially important for staff who work with mentally disordered and other inmates at high risk for HIV infection. When physical intervention must be used with aggressive inmates known to be HIV-positive, great caution is indicated and special equipment such as restraining blankets and retractable needles should be used (Cournos, Empfield, Horwath, and Schrage, 1990). Finally, AIDS education and protective devices (condoms and dental dams) and should be made available even though there may be explicit rules prohibiting sex (Cournos et al., 1990). Skills in negotiation and assertiveness in sexual situations have been shown to be related to HIV-risk behavior among the chronically mentally ill, and should thus be targetted for treatment in high-risk settings (Kelly et al., 1995).

Mentally Disordered Sex Offenders

The idea that sex offenders, or many of them, at least, suffer from a mental disorder and therefore are in need of treatment has been debated at length. Until the late 1970s, the majority of U.S. states had statutes that allowed the indeterminate confinement of mentally disordered sex offenders (Monahan and Davis, 1983). Throughout the 1980s, the trend was towards repeal of these laws. Most recently, however, there has been a trend towards reenactment of special laws to indefinitely detain and treat the most serious sex offenders (usually child molesters, rapists and sexual murderers) who qualify for the label *sexual predator.* Contrary to the earlier laws, which were viewed as a less severe sanction than prison (Monahan and Davis, 1983), the most recent U.S. laws are designed to detain the most serious offenders beyond the end of whatever sentence they received.

Only a minority of sex offenders, even within psychiatric settings, qualify for a diagnosis of major mental disorder as discussed in earlier parts of this chapter (Sturgeon and Taylor, 1980), and most sex offender treatment programs specifically exclude acutely psychotic offenders (Marques, Nelson, West, and Day, 1994; Pithers, Martin, and Cumming, 1989). The diagnosis most commonly responsible for a designation as a "mentally disordered" sex offender is a paraphilia (almost always pedophilia or sexual sadism) in the *Diagnostic and Statistical Manual of Mental Disorders* (DSM-III-R, American Psychiatric Association, 1987). Although a diagnosis of antisocial personality disorder is very common among sex offenders, it usually was not sufficient to qualify for a classification as a "mentally disordered" sex offender (Monahan and Davis, 1983) under the previous generation of special laws. However, antisocial personality disorder is explicitly recognized as qualifying under the new generation of "sexual predator" statutes (Rice and Harris, in press).

In the rest of this chapter, we have approached treatment from the point of view of alleviating the suffering of the afflicted inmate so that he or she can live in the regular prison community. Although in some cases treatment might have the effect of reducing the likelihood of recidivism, that has not been the explicit purpose of treatment. On the other hand, the purpose of treatment programs for sex offenders, whether labelled mentally disordered or not, is to reduce the likelihood of sexual recidivism.

There is little question that the most popular current treatments for sex offenders are cognitive-behavioral and pharmacological (Becker, 1992; Bloom, Bradford, and Kofoed, 1988; Laws, 1989; Maletzky, 1991). There seems to be general agreement that other forms of group or individual therapy for sexual aggressors have not been shown to be effective (Furby, Weinrott, and Blackshaw, 1989; Marshall, Jones, Ward, Johnston, and Barbaree, 1991; Quinsey, 1984; Quinsey, Harris, Rice, and Lalumière, 1993). Moreover, at least some outcome studies of treatment, including at least one behavioral treatment, done with the very serious offenders seen in most institutional programs for mentally disordered sex offenders have been failures (Frisbee and Dondis, 1965; Hanson, Steffy, and Gauthier, 1993; Rice, Quinsey, and Harris, 1991).

A very ambitious program for incarcerated sex offenders was undertaken at Atascadero State Hospital (Marques, Day, Nelson, Miner, and West, 1992). The program was based upon relapse prevention, a cognitive-behavioral treatment strategy in which participants learn to recognize and interrupt the chain of events leading to relapse. The focus of both assessment and treatment was the identification and alteration of the links in the chain, from broad lifestyle factors (such as substance abuse) and cognitive distortions to lack of specific skills (such as heterosocial skills, or anger management) and deviant sexual arousal patterns. The program was very intensive and lasted for two years during incarceration, followed by a one-year aftercare program designed to maintain treatment gains and reintegrate offenders into the community. The program included an evaluation of both in-treatment changes and long-term treatment effects using a design which included volunteer subjects who were randomly assigned to treatment or control groups, as well as a matched nonvolunteer control group. The followup is not yet completed, but preliminary data are available on 108 men who completed at least one year of treatment, 9 men who began treatment but who dropped out before one year, 108 volunteer controls, and 110 nonvoluntary controls (Marques et al., 1994). The average time at risk is about three years. Unfortunately, the data so far are not encouraging inasmuch as reoffense rates among the groups are not significantly different.

There have been more encouraging results from less well-controlled (Marshall and Barbaree, 1988) and uncontrolled (Maletzky, 1991; Pithers and Cumming, 1989) studies of behavioral and cognitive-behavioral treatments for sex offenders, especially child molesters, treated in the community. However, the effectiveness of cognitive-behavioral programs, especially for serious offenders, remains to be demonstrated (Harris, Rice and Quinsey, in press; Quinsey, et al., 1993; Rice, Harris, and Quinsey, in press).

Pharmacologic treatments including antiandrogens (cyproterone acetate and medroxyproxgesterone acetate) and, more recently, fluoxetine, have been recommended as additions to cognitive-behavioral treatments for offenders who ruminate or masturbate excessively, or who have high plasma testosterone levels (Becker, 1992; Bloom, Bradford, and Kofoed, 1988). Although positive results have been reported for an uncontrolled evaluation of a combined behavioral, cognitive-behavioral, and pharmacological treatment program for offenders in the community (Maletzky, 1991), controlled studies that involve antiandrogen treatment suggest that dropout rates are so high that it is impossible to tell whether the treatment is effective (Fedoroff, Wisner-Carlson, Dean, and Berlin, 1992; Hucker, Langevin, and Bain, 1988).

Aside from the discouraging results so far about the effectiveness of any treatments for incarcerated sex offenders, much progress has been made in the prediction of which offenders are most likely to reoffend (Quinsey, Harris, Rice, and Cormier, in press; Rice and Harris, 1997b). Aside from factors known to predict recidivism (such as age, number of previous offenses) among offenders in general, some factors specific to sex offenders have been identified. Deviant sexual arousal, and level of psychopathy have been shown to predict recidivism among sex offenders (Quinsey, Rice, Harris, and Lalumière, 1995; Rice and Harris, 1997b; Rice, Harris, and Quinsey, 1990). Rapists have higher levels of violent recidivism than child molesters (Quinsey, Rice, Harris, and Lalumière, 1995). Among child molesters, those who have male victims have higher recidivism rates (Quinsey, Rice, Harris, and Lalumière, 1995; Rice, Quinsey, and Harris, 1991). Furthermore, it appears as though offenders who drop out of treatment have worse outcomes than both treated and unselected untreated offenders (Marques et al., 1994).

Female Offenders with Mental Disorder

Although women form but a small fraction of persons held in prison, some data suggest that they exhibit a higher rate of psychological disturbance than incarcerated men. Moreover, compared to men, they are more likely to be sent to secure hospitals than to prisons. There also is some evidence that although women respond better to prison and psychiatric hospitalization (in terms of recidivism) than men, they are harder to manage in the institution (Prins, 1980). Contrary to findings in society in general, there is little evidence among institutionalized persons with mental disorder that males are more violent (Rice et al., 1989).

Although high proportions of mental disorder have been found among female offenders, their disorders fall mostly into the personality disorder category rather than into the category of psychosis or major mental disorder (Guze, 1976; Prins, 1980). Similar to the findings for male offenders, psychological distress seems to be highest upon admission to prison (Hurley and Dunne, 1991). When the presence of a major mental disorder is compared for male and female offenders (rarely done in the same study), the rates do not seem to be very different (Daniel, Robins, Reid, and Wilfley, 1988; Guze, 1976; Menzies, Chunn, and Webster, 1992) although there may be more affective disorder among women (Herjanic, Henn, and Vanderpearl, 1977). Similarly, studies of recidivism among female offenders have shown the best predictors to be similar to those for men—age, previous criminal history, marital status, education, and diagnosis of antisocial personality disorder, and drug dependence (Cloniger and Guze, 1973; Martin, Cloninger, and Guze, 1978). Instruments designed to predict criminal recidivism among male offenders also have been found to work well for female offenders (Bonta, Pang, and Wallace-Capretta, 1995; Coulson, 1993).

Among psychiatric patients, there is considerable evidence that females are more likely than males to have been victims of abuse, especially sexual abuse (Carmen, Rieker, and Mills, 1984; Jacobson and Richardson, 1987). Diagnoses most commonly said to be associated with sexual abuse histories include post-traumatic stress disorder, borderline personality disorder, multiple personality disorder, substance abuse, and psychosis (Firsten, 1990), although in one study that compared diagnoses of abused and nonabused patients, no differences were found (Carmen et al., 1984). Sexual abuse histories are also common among female offenders, especially sex offenders (Travin, Cullen, and Potter, 1990), self-mutilators (Wilkins and Coid, 1991), and recidivist offenders (Long, Sultan, Kiefer, and Schrum, 1984). Although long-term psychotherapy, hypnotherapy, and pharmacotherapy are frequently recommended (Choy and Bossett, 1992; Kluft, 1987; Sonnenberg, 1988), there are few data to inform these recommendations. By contrast, there are promising data for short-term cognitive-behavioral treatments for victims of sexual or physical abuse (Foa, Rothbaum, Riggs, and Murdock, 1991; Foa, Rothbaum, and Steketee, 1993; Sultan and Long, 1988).

At the present time, there is virtually no literature on the treatment of female offenders suffering from major mental disorder. However, based on the available literature concerning both female offenders and female psychiatric patients, there is little reason to believe that the recommended treatments would be any different from those recommended for males.

Administrative Considerations In Providing Treatment In Prisons

Staffing Issues

Although there are many strong opinions, and many sets of standards that address staffing issues in correctional institutions (for example, the American Public Health Association's Standards for Health Services in Correctional Institutions, 1976; the American Association of Correctional Psychologists' Standards for Psychological Services in Adult Jails and Prisons, 1980), there are virtually no data on the selection of a staffing model for the provision of mental health services to incarcerated inmates. In studies that have attempted to identify the characteristics of effective psychiatric programs more generally (Collins, Ellsworth, Casey, Hickey, and Hyer, 1984; Ellsworth et al., 1979) none of the following had any relationship to program effectiveness: the staff/patient ratio, the qualifications or experience of the nursing staff, or the presence of a qualified psychiatrist. By contrast, stability of frontline ward staff-shift assignments was related to program effectiveness. Obviously, there must be limits to the statement that numbers and qualifications of staff do not matter, and the authors urge caution in the interpretation of their results, but the findings lead us to question standards- and credentials-oriented approaches to measuring the quality of mental health services. Instead, we advocate a focus on measures of program integrity and program effectiveness as ways to evaluate the quality of services (*see*, for example, McGrew, Bond, Dietzen, and Salyers, 1994; Rice, Harris, Quinsey, and Cyr, 1990).

Social scientists who have studied the prison environment have argued strongly that greater interaction between correctional officers and inmates can make the prison environment less stressful (Levinson, 1982). Similarly, in programs in which prison officers are encouraged to interact and develop relationships with prisoners, there is evidence of psychological and psychiatric improvement at least while inmates remain in that environment (Gunn and Robertson, 1982).

In another study (Harris, Rice, and Cormier, 1994; Rice, Harris, and Cormier, 1992), it was found that men with psychoses involved in a highly intensive therapeutic community program in a maximum-security hospital that relied heavily on patient interaction with very low numbers of professional staff of any discipline had lower rates of criminal and violent recidivism upon release than did a similar group of men sentenced to prison (although the opposite was true for psychopaths). Similar to findings reported by Gunn and Robertson (1982) and Moos (1975), there was widespread agreement that the program eliminated the normal prison subculture and improved the attitudes and morale of both staff and patients (Barker, 1980), at least while they were in the program.

Because there is no evidence that high numbers of professional staff increase program effectiveness, because one goal of mental health treatment for inmates is to return them to a regular prison environment, because there is evidence that positive effects can occur when frontline staff have combined treatment and security duties, and because it is likely to be less expensive, we advocate a staffing model in which staff assigned to a unit housing mentally disordered inmates have dual treatment and security functions. In such a unit, as in other units for mentally disordered offenders, tensions between treatment goals and security goals will be inevitable (Rice and Harris, 1993), but we believe that the advantages of such a model outweigh the disadvantages (Johnson and Price, 1981).

Similarly, we believe that rather than relying primarily on one discipline (usually nursing) to provide the frontline staff of residential treatment units for mentally disordered offenders, consideration should be given to selecting frontline staff from disciplines that have the training most suited to the particular programs being offered. For example, in token economy programs, high proportions of persons with backgrounds in behavioral psychology might be most appropriate whereas in the skills training programs, high proportions of staff with backgrounds in occupational therapy might be appropriate. Of course, some staff with nursing backgrounds would be required in most programs, but the proportion could be much lower than is currently customary.

There has been considerable debate about whether inpatient treatment units for inmates with mental disorder should be located in institutions under the administration of health authorities or correctional authorities. We know of few data to inform this debate. Jurisdictions where mental health services are administered by correctional departments may be at greater risk for litigation about the quality of care (Metzner, Fryer, and Usery, 1990). On the other hand, others have noted (Gearing, Heckel, and Matthey, 1980) that the transfer from prison to hospital, or indeed, even from one institution to another (Dell, 1980), often serves as an opportunity to screen out undesirable but deserving patients. It also leads to interinstitutional rivalries where the best interests of prospective patients gets lost; for example "blacklisting" institutions that refuse to take their clients back when treatment is deemed to have been successful.

Perhaps more important than whether the treatment unit is under the jurisdiction of health or correctional authorities is the question of the knowledge base of program managers and their supervisors. Unless they have some knowledge about mental health issues and psychosocial treatment approaches in the programs for which they are responsible, they are unlikely to recognize or reward desirable behaviors in their subordinates. Gendreau (1988) refers to the "MBA syndrome" in which managers are construed as a generic entity who need only know about how to manage. By contrast, managers who are familiar with something of the theory and practice of treatment will be much more likely to base promotional practices on treatment-relevant performance. Moreover, they will be able to model pro-treatment attitudes and values that frequently are not valued sufficiently in psychiatric settings for mentally disordered offenders.

Aside from the numbers and professional disciplines of the staff, how should staff be selected to work with mentally disordered inmates? Studies suggest that staff who are most likely to succeed with correctional or mentally disordered offender populations are those who use authority to enforce rules but in a nonconfrontational (firm but fair) manner, who model prosocial (and anticriminal) attitudes and behaviors, and who are at the same time empathic and interpersonally skilled (Andrews and Kiessling, 1980; Andrews et al., 1990). Unfortunately, typical institutional practice often selects staff for exactly the wrong characteristics (Johnson and Price, 1981).

Because of the power differences between inmates and staff in correctional and psychiatric settings, it has been argued that there is a tendency for staff to become more authoritarian and to treat the inmates or patients less humanely over time. This phenomenon was dramatically illustrated in the Stanford Prison Experiment (Zimbardo, 1973). In addition, as discussed, there is good evidence that much of the violence that occurs in institutions is iatrogenic and that staff training can reduce the number of assaultive incidents. In fact, there is evidence that a staff training course that includes sections on interviewing and employing mediation skills, as well as safe physical techniques to be used when the situation requires them, can lead to increased staff and patient morale as well as reduce the level of institutional violence (Rice et al., 1989; Rice et al., 1985).

Inmate-Patient Rights Issues

The basic philosophy underlying various professional standards for the provision of mental health care in institutions is that it should be equivalent to that available in the community (Steadman, McCarty, and Morrissey, 1989). Furthermore, there is general agreement that inmates have a right to health care including mental health care while in prison (Ferguson, 1988; Fifth United Nations Congress on the Prevention of Crime and the Treatment of Offenders, 1975; Joliffe, 1984; Wishart and Dubler, 1983). At least part of the rationale for this right comes from the acknowledgment that mentally disordered offenders are particularly vulnerable in prisons, and there is substantial evidence that this is the case (Morrison, 1991).

Rights regarding treatment include both the right to treatment and the right to refuse treatment. Regarding first the right to treatment, in countries where there is no national health care program (and thus no specific entitlement to health care), it might seem that inmates are actually much better off than other citizens (Wishart and Dubler, 1983). Yet, despite their legal right to adequate care, it is widely acknowledged that there are significant numbers of inmates suffering from major mental disorders who do not receive treatment while in prison (Hodgins and Coté, 1990; James, Gregory, Jones and Rundell, 1980). Part of the reason for this, as discussed earlier, is that many of the inmates with severe mental disorders do not stand out to untrained observers; they are quiet and withdrawn and do not call attention to themselves, or ask for treatment. For this reason, mental health professionals have an obligation to do more than passively accept referrals. A system such as that described by Condelli, Dvoskin, and Holanchock (1992) is a good example of an efficient system of identifying inmates in need of treatment.

Once identified as in need of treatment, there is little guidance in the literature as to what a patient's rights are regarding the nature of treatment. There have been occasional legal rulings that have made some specific recommendations regarding treatment of psychiatric patients (such as *Wyatt v. Stickney*, 1972 described in Slovenko, 1973). There has also been a Canadian attempt to develop principles regarding quality of treatment for psychiatric patients that are sufficiently specific to guide practice, and were designed to include mentally disordered offenders held in secure treatment units (Rice, Harris, Sutherland, and Leveque, 1990).

Much has been written about the right of psychiatric patients to refuse treatment (for example, Appelbaum, 1988) with heated debate on both sides of the issue. More recently, the issue has been reframed as "competence to consent to treatment" (Appelbaum and Grisso, 1995). In most psychiatric settings, the issues regarding forced treatment have pertained to pharmacological treatment only. However, in prisons, the right to refuse treatment also has encompassed nonpharmacological treatments, especially behavior modification (Friedman, 1975; Schwitzgebel, 1974; Martin, 1975; Law Reform Commission of Canada, 1985). One of the most difficult tasks facing mental health practitioners in corrections concerns what to do about those inmates who are obviously severely ill but who adamantly refuse all forms of treatment. James et al. (1980) have presented data suggesting that up to 20 percent of prisoners with severe mental disorder would require involuntary treatment.

Involuntary treatment issues in prison commonly have involved the question of transfer from a prison to a mental hospital, and it has been argued that providing treatment on-site in a prison would get around the requirement of a hearing before transfer. It also has been suggested that the standard for the prison equivalent of civil commitment should be somewhat higher than in nonprison society as the standard should refer to dangerousness within the prison rather than dangerousness within society at large (*Vitek v. Jones* discussed in Churgin, 1983).

In our view, many of the problems about forced treatment, especially behavioral treatments, arise because of a mistaken belief that there is a meaningful distinction between treatment and nontreatment environments. In fact, every institution has some form of management system in place in which consequences are applied to influence the behavior of the residents. The only choice program leaders have is how specific to be about which behaviors will be promoted and which will be discouraged. In most institutions, although the leaders make a set of rules and regulations, they do not make a coherent plan to influence the behaviors and attitudes of the inmates or patients. There is good reason to believe that in the absence of a coherent plan, individual staff members and other patients each apply their own consequences for behavior, and much of this is inconsistent, disorganized, and clinically destructive (Positano, Sanford, Elzinga, and James, 1990; Quinsey, Harris, and Rice, 1987). There is evidence that under these conditions, the institution will be more coercive, punitive, and less therapeutic (Buehler, Patterson, and Furniss, 1966; Gelfand, Gelfand, and Dobson, 1967; Harris and Rice, 1992).

For wardwide or institutionwide environments, there can be unplanned and/or unknown consequences of behavior, but that is not "no treatment" in the same sense that there can be a nontreatment alternative to drugs, electroconvulsive therapy, or individual counseling. This view seems to lead to a logical and ethical dilemma:

(1) Unless a prison's administration employs a coherent, systematic, and noncoercive approach, the institutional environment will be dangerous and will make some inmates with mental disorder worse.

(2) The more coherent, systematic, and noncoercive such an approach is, the more closely it must embody the principles of psychosocial treatment or behavior therapy.

(3) Behavior therapy is a recognized and effective form of clinical treatment.

(4) An inmate with mental disorder has (as does everyone else) the right to decline unwanted treatment.

This dilemma pits ethical values against each other (Canadian Psychological Association, 1988); "respect for the dignity of individual persons" versus "responsible caring" and the Hippocratic injunction to "do no harm." There is no established way to resolve such a dilemma. However, elsewhere we have described a compromise in which the latter obligation (to do no harm) takes slight precedence. Thus, despite patients' rights to be free of unwanted therapy, we argued that an institution has an overriding obligation to have in place a system to discourage dangerous and destructive behavior and to promote cooperative safe, prosocial conduct. We argued further that such an obligation holds even though such a system also might alleviate psychological suffering and/or increase adaptation to regular prison or society in general (Quinsey et al., 1987; Rice, Harris, Sutherland, and Leveque, 1990).

What can be done, then, for patients who refuse all forms of treatment? We argue that there is little to be gained by entering into an extended legal battle to win the authority to treat a patient against his or her will. Rather, we advocate the use of humane management techniques in such a case and turning the noncompliance issue into one of collaboration between the patient and the treatment providers wherein both take responsibility for producing a treatment program to which the patient can adhere (Appelbaum and Hoge, 1986; Corrigan, Liberman, and Engel, 1990). Although this may not be easy, it is the duty of treatment staff to continue to offer treatment even when it is unappreciated.

Conclusions

Although there is little evidence that prison causes much serious mental disorder, there is considerable evidence that serious mental disorder is much more prevalent in prisons than in society in general. In this chapter, we assert that the provision of mental health services to prisoners should be driven by inmates' interpersonal difficulties, skill deficits, criminal history, and current symptoms. We identified two classes of consumers of such services: disturbed-disruptive inmates who exhibit active psychotic symptoms, anger, unhappiness, withdrawal, aggression and other institutional management problems; and disturbed-nondisruptive inmates who exhibit active psychotic symptoms, unhappiness, and withdrawal, but only rarely exhibit problems of institutional management. We advocate that services for inmates suffering from mental disturbance be provided via a series of successively more selective screens that ensure that disturbed-nondisruptive inmates are identified and treated, that services are delivered in an environment that most closely resembles the "normal" prison environment, and that services include behavioral and psychosocial treatments as well as pharmacological ones.

In this chapter, we take the view that behavioral assessment and treatment in the form of time-sampling behavioral checklists, behavioral analysis, token economies, and behavioral skills training are the treatments of choice for most mentally disordered inmates. A good example of the use of many aspects of this behavioral approach is the work of MacKain and Streveler (1990). Pharmacotherapy is a very useful adjunct in many cases.

For units devoted to the treatment of inmates with mental disorder, we advocate multidisciplinary teams that include behavioral technicians and correctional officers. Program standards should reflect measures of program integrity rather than professional credentials. Selection and training of staff should eschew confrontational, authoritarian personality styles and methods in favor of persons and methods that emphasize empathy, democratic techniques, and interpersonal skill. Inmates with mental disorder have moral and, in some jurisdictions, legal rights to treatment. They also have a right to decline unwanted treatment, but this cannot remove the obligation of administrators to provide an environment that promotes prosocial, independent, responsible, nonsymptomatic behavior. In considering several subgroups of inmates with mental disorder (those with HIV infection, sex offenders and female prisoners), we find no evidence to motivate a change in our overall advice:

Triage and referral decisions should be based on interpersonal problems, skill deficits, and current symptoms; assessment and treatment should be primarily behavioral.

Future Research

Though we cite empirical work in support of most of the recommendations made in this chapter, there are many unanswered questions about the treatment of offenders with mental disorder. With few exceptions, there have been no studies of the effectiveness of treatments specifically for felon prisoners with a mental disorder. There is virtually no empirical literature on the treatment of female offenders with a mental disorder. It is unlikely that one program or therapy will prove effective in reducing all forms of criminal and psychiatric recidivism. Rather, the appropriate question is, "What services, provided to offenders with which characteristics, in what settings yield reductions in which classes of recidivism?" (Andrews et al., 1990; West, 1980). Important issues concern the role of clinical follow-up and community supervision, whether services that improve community adjustment and quality of life also reduce recidivism, and the cost-effectiveness of services for offenders with a mental disorder.

References

Adams, K. 1986. The Disciplinary Experiences of Mentally Disordered Inmates. *Criminal Justice and Behavior.* 13:297-316.

American Association of Correctional Psychologists (AACP). 1980. Standards for Psy- chology Services in Adult Jails and Prisons. *Criminal Justice and Behavior.* 7:81-127.

American Psychiatric Association. 1987. *Diagnostic and Statistical Manual of Mental Disorders, Third Edition, Revised.* Washington, D.C.: American Psychiatric Association.

———. 1993. Practice Guideline for Major Depressive Disorder in Adults. *American Journal of Psychiatry.* 150:1-26.

American Public Health Association (APHA). 1976. *Standards for Health Services in Correctional Institutions.* Washington, D.C.: American Public Health Association.

Andrews, D. A., J. Bonta, and R. D. Hoge. 1990. Classification for Effective Rehabilitation. *Criminal Justice and Behavior.* 17:20-52.

Andrews, D. A. and J. J. Kiessling. 1980. Program Structure and Effective Correctional Practices: A Summary of the Cavic Research. In R R. Ross and P. Gendreau, eds. *Effective Correctional Treatment*. Toronto: Butterworths.

Andrews, D. A., I. Zinger, R. D. Hoge, J. Bonta, P. Gendreau, and F. T. Cullen. 1990. Does Correctional Treatment Work: A Clinically Relevant and Psychologically Informed Meta-analysis. *Criminology*. 28:369-404.

Antonuccio, D. O., W. G. Danton, and G. Y. DeNelsky. 1995. Psychotherapy Versus Medication for Depression: Challenging the Conventional Wisdom with Data. *Professional Psychology: Research and Practice*. 26:574-585.

Appelbaum, P. S. 1988. The Right to Refuse Treatment with Antipsychotic Medications: Retrospect and Prospect. *American Journal of Psychiatry*. 145:413-419.

Appelbaum, P. S. and T. Grisso. 1995. The MacArthur Treatment Competence Study. *Law and Human Behavior*. 19:105-126.

Appelbaum, P. S. and K. Hoge. 1986. The Right to Refuse Treatment: What the Research Reveals. *Behavioral Sciences and the Law*. 4:279-292.

Aumack, L. 1962. A Social Adjustment Behavior Rating Scale. *Journal of Clinical Psychology*. 18:436-441.

Barker, T. E., R. P. Liberman, and T. G. Kuehnel. 1986. Dissemination and Adoption of Innovative Psychosocial Interventions. *Journal of Consulting and Clinical Psychology*. 54:111- 118.

Barker, E. T. 1980. The Penetanguishene Program: A Personal Review. In H. Toch, ed. *Therapeutic Communities in Corrections*. New York: Praeger.

Bassett, J. E. and E. B. Blanchard. 1977. The Effect of the Absence of Close Supervision on the Use of Response Cost in a Prison Token Economy. *Journal of Applied Behavior Analysis*. 10:375-379.

Beck, A. T. and R. W. Beck. 1972. Screening Depressed Patients in Family Practice: A Rapid Technique. *Post-graduate Medicine*. 52:81-85.

Beck, N. C., A. A. Menditto, L. Baldwin, E. Angelone, and M. Maddox. 1991. Reduced Frequency of Aggressive Behavior in Forensic Patients in a Social Learning Program. *Hospital and Community Psychiatry*. 42:750-752.

Becker, J. V. 1992. Sexual Deviance. *Current Opinion in Psychiatry*. 5:788-791.

Belbot, B. A. and R. V. del Carmen. 1991. AIDS in Prison: Legal Issues. *Crime and Delinquency*. 37: 135-153.

Benton, M. K., and H. E. Schroeder. 1990. Social Skills Training with Schizophrenics: A Meta-analytic Evaluation. *Journal of Consulting and Clinical Psychology*. 58:741-747.

Blackburn, R. 1987. Special Hospitals Assessment of Personality and Socialization. *Personality and Individual Differences*. 8:81-93.

Bland, R. C., S. C. Newman, R. J. Dyck, and H. Orn. 1990. Prevalence of Psychiatric Disorders and Suicide Attempts in a Prison Population. *Canadian Journal of Psychiatry*. 35:407-413.

Blatt, S. J., D. M. Quinlan, D. C. Zuroff, and P. A. Pilkonis. 1996. Interpersonal Factors in Brief Treatment of Depression: Further Analyses of the National Institute of Mental Health Treatment of Depression Collaborative Research Program. *Journal of Consulting and Clinical Psychology*. 64:162-171.

Bloom, J. D., J. Bradford, and L. Kofoed. 1988. An Overview of Psychiatric Treatment Approaches to Three Offender Groups. *Hospital and Community Psychiatry*. 39:151-158.

Bonta, J. and P. Gendreau. 1990. Reexamining the Cruel and Unusual Punishment of Prison Life. *Law and Human Behavior*. 14:347-372.

———. 1992. Coping with Prison. In P. Suedfueld and P. E. Tetlock, eds. *Psychology and Social Policy*. New York: Hemisphere Publishing.

Bonta, J., R. Hanson, and M. Law. (in press). The Prediction of Criminal and Violent Recidivism among Mentally Disordered Offenders: A Meta-analysis. *Psychological Bulletin*.

Bonta, J., B. Pang, and S. Wallace-Capretta. 1995. Predictors of Recidivism among Incarcerated Female Offenders. *The Prison Journal*. 75:277-294.

Buehler, R. E., G. R. Patterson, and J. M. Furniss. 1966. The Reinforcement of Behavior in Institutional Settings. *Behaviour Research and Therapy*. 4:157-167.

Buss, A. H. and A. Durkee. 1957. An Inventory for Assessing Different Kinds of Hostility. *Journal of Consulting Psychology*. 21:343-349.

Canadian Psychological Association. 1988. *Canadian Code of Ethics for Psychologists*. Old Chelsea, Quebec: Canadian Psychological Association.

Carmen, E., P. P. Rieker, and T. Mills. 1984. Victims of Violence and Psychiatric Illness. *American Journal of Psychiatry*. 141:378-383.

Chouinard, G., B. Jones, G. Remington, D. Bloom, D. Addington, G. W. MacEwan, A. Labelle, L. Beauclair, and W. Arnott. 1993. A Canadian Multicenter Placebo-controlled Study of Fixed Doses of Risperidone and Haloperidol in the Treatment of Chronic Schizophrenic Patients. *Journal of Clinical Psychopharmacology*. 13:25-40.

Choy, T. and F. Bossett. 1992. Post-traumatic Stress Disorder: An Overview. *Canadian Journal of Psychiatry*. 37:578-583.

Churgin, M. J. 1983. The Transfer of Inmates to Mental Health Facilities. In J. Monahan and H. J. Steadman, eds. *Mentally Disordered Offenders: Perspectives from Law and Social Science*. New York: Plenum.

Cloninger, C. R. and S. B. Guze. 1973. Psychiatric Disorders and Criminal Recidivism. *Archives of General Psychiatry*. 29:266-269.

Collins, J. F., R. B. Ellsworth, N. A. Casey, R. B. Hickey, and L. Hyer. 1984. Treatment Characteristics of Effective Psychiatric Programs. *Hospital and Community Psychiatry*. 35:601- 605.

Cohen, F. and J. Dvoskin. 1992. Inmates with Mental Disorders: A Guide to Law and Practice. *Mental and Physical Disability Law Reporter*. 16:462-470.

Condelli, W. S., J. Dvoskin, and H. Holanchock. 1992. *Intermediate Care Programs for Inmates with Psychiatric Disorders*. Manuscript submitted for publication.

Corrigan, P. W. 1991. Social Skills Training in Adult Psychiatric Populations: A Meta-analysis. *Journal of Behavior Therapy and Experimental Psychiatry*. 22:203-210.

Corrigan, P. W., R. P. Liberman, and J. D. Engel. 1990. From Noncompliance to Collaboration in the Treatment of Schizophrenia. *Hospital and Community Psychiatry*. 41:1203-1211.

Coulson, G. 1993. Using the Level of Supervision Inventory in Placing Female Offenders in Rehabilitation Programs or Halfway Houses. *The International Association of Residential and Community Alternatives (IARCA) Journal on Community Corrections*. 12-13.

Cournos, F., M. Empfield, E. Horwath, and H. Schrage. 1990. HIV Infection in State Hospitals: Case Reports and Long-term Management Strategies. *Hospital and Community Psychiatry*. 41:163-166.

Cournos, F., M. Empfield, E. Horwath, K. McKinnon, I. Meyer, H. Schrage, C. Currie, and B. Agosin. 1991. HIV Seroprevalence among Patients Admitted to Two Psychiatric Hospitals. *American Journal of Psychiatry*. 148:1225-1230.

Daniel, A. E., A. J. Robins, J. C. Reid, and D. E. Wilfley. 1988. Lifetime and Six-month Prevalence of Psychiatric Disorders among Sentenced Female Offenders. *Bulletin of the American Academy of Psychiatry and Law*. 16:333-342.

Davidson, N. A., M. J. Hemingway, and T. Wysocki. 1984. Reducing the Use of Restrictive Procedures in a Residential Facility. *Hospital and Community Psychiatry*. 35:164-167.

Dell, S. 1980. Transfer of Special Hospital Patients to the NHS. *British Journal of Psychiatry*. 136:222-234.

Dvoskin, J. A. and H. J. Steadman. 1989. Chronically Mentally Ill Inmates: The Wrong Concept for the Right Services. *International Journal of Law and Psychiatry*. 12:203-210.

Eichelman, B. 1988. Toward a Rational Pharmacotherapy for Aggressive and Violent Behavior. *Hospital and Community Psychiatry*. 39:31-39.

Ekstedt, J. W. and C. T. Griffiths. 1988. *Corrections in Canada: Policy and Practice*. Toronto: Butterworths.

Elkin, I., R. D. Gibbons, M. T. Shea, S. M. Sotsky, J. T. Watkins, and P. A. Pilkonis. 1995. Initial Severity and Differential Treatment Outcome in the National Institute of Mental Health Treatment of Depression Collaborative Research Program. *Journal of Consulting and Clinical Psychology*. 63:841-847.

Elkin, I., T. Shea, J. T. Watkins, S. D. Imber, S. M. Sotsky, J. F. Collins, D. R. Glass, P. A. Pilkonis, W R. Leber, J. P. Docherty, S. J. Fiester, and M. B. Parloff. 1989. National Institute of Mental Health Treatment of Depression Collaborative Research Program. *Archives of General Psychiatry*. 46:971-982.

Ellsworth, R. B. 1971. *The MACC Behavioral Adjustment Scale*. Los Angeles, California: Western Psychological Services.

Ellsworth, R. B., J. F. Collins, N. A. Casey, J. Schoonover, J. Hickey, T. Hyer, T. Twemlow, and R. Nesselroade. 1979. Some Characteristics of Effective Psychiatric Treatment Programs. *Journal of Consulting and Clinical Psychology*. 47:799-817.

Etscheidt, S. 1991. Reducing Aggressive Behavior and Improving Self-control: A Cognitive-behavioral Training Program for Behaviorally Disordered Adolescents. *Behavior Disorders*. 16:107-115.

Evans, M. D., S. D. Hollon, R. J. DeRubeis, J. M. Piasecki, W. M. Grove, M. J. Garbey, and V. B. Tuason. 1992. Differential Relapse Following Cognitive Therapy and Pharmacotherapy for Depression. *Archives of General Psychiatry*. 49:802-808.

Evans, D. L. and D. O. Perkins. 1990. The Clinical Psychiatry of AIDS. *Current Opinion in Psychiatry*. 3:96-102.

Feder, L. 1992. A Profile of Mentally Ill Offenders and Their Adjustment in the Community. *The Journal of Psychiatry and Law*. 79-96.

Fedoroff, J. P., R. Wisner-Carlson, S. Dean, and F. S. Berlin. 1992. Medroxy-progesterone Acetate in the Treatment of Paraphillic Sexual Disorders. *Journal of Offender Rehabilitation*. 18:109-123.

Ferguson, G. 1988. Le Droit Aux Soins de Santé Mentale en Milieu Carcéral. *Criminologie*. 21:13-26.

Fifth United Nations Congress on the Prevention of Crime and the Treatment of Offenders. 1975. *Health Aspects of Avoidable Maltreatment of Prisoners and Detainees*. New York: United Nations.

Firsten, T. 1990. An Exploration of the Role of Physical and Sexual Abuse for Psychiatrically Institutionalized Women. (Unpublished report). Toronto.

Florez, J. A. and H. Holley. 1989. Predicting Suicide Behaviours in Incarcerated Settings. *Canadian Journal of Psychiatry*. 34:668-413.

Foa, E. B., B. O. Rothbaum, D. S. Riggs, and T. B. Murdock. 1991. Treatment of Posttraumatic Stress Disorder in Rape Victims: A Comparison Between Cognitive-behavioral Procedures and Counseling. *Journal of Consulting and Clinical Psychology*. 59:715-723.

Foa, E. B., B. O. Rothbaum, and G. S. Steketee. 1993. Treatment of Rape Victims. *Journal of Interpersonal Violence*. 8:256-276.

Friedman, P. R. 1975. Legal Regulation of Applied Behavior Analysis in Mental Institutions and Prisons. *Arizona Law Review*. 17:40-104.

Frisbie, L. V. and E. H. Dondis. 1965. *Recidivism among Treated Sex Offenders* (Mental Health Research Monograph, No. 5). Sacramento: California Department of Mental Hygiene.

Furby, L., M. R. Weinrott, and L. Blackshaw. 1989. Sex Offender Recidivism: A Review. *Psychological Bulletin*. 105:3-30.

Gearing, M., R. V. Heckel, and W. Matthey. 1980. The Screening and Referral of Mentally Disordered Inmates in a State Correctional System. *Professional Psychology*. 11:849-854.

Gelfand, D. M., S. Gelfand, and S. Dobson. 1967. Unprogrammed Reinforcement of Patients' Behavior in a Mental Hospital. *Behaviour Research and Therapy*. 5:201-207.

Gendreau, P. 1988, August. *Principles of Effective Treatments for Offenders*. Paper presented at a conference on the Antisocial Personality: Research, Assessment and Treatment Programs, Midland, Ontario.

Gendreau. P. and J. Bonta. 1987. Solitary Confinement Is Not Cruel and Unusual Punishment: People Sometimes Are. *Canadian Journal of Criminology*. 26:467-478.

Goldstein, A. P. and B. Glick. 1987. *Aggression Replacement Training: A Comprehensive Intervention for Aggressive Youth*. Champaign, Illinois: Research Press.

Greenberg, R. P., R. F. Bornstein, M. D. Greenberg, and S. Fisher. 1992. A Meta-analysis of Antidepressant Outcome Under "Blinder" Conditions. *Journal of Consulting and Clinical Psychology*. 60:664-669.

Greene, R. T. 1988. A Comprehensive Mental Health Care System for Prison Inmates: Retrospective Look At New York's Ten Year Experience. *International Journal of Law and Psychiatry*. 11:381-389.

Gunn, J. and G. Robertson. 1982. An Evaluation of Grendon Prison. In J. Gunn and D. P. Farrington, eds. *Abnormal Offenders, Delinquency, and the Criminal Justice System*. New York: Wiley.

Guze, S. B. 1976. *Criminality and Psychiatric Disorders*. New York: Oxford University Press.

Hamilton, J., L. Stephens, and P. Allen. 1967. Controlling Aggressive and Destructive Behavior in Severely Retarded Institutionalized Residents. *American Journal of Mental Deficiency*. 71:852-856.

Hanson, R. K., R. A. Steffy, and R. Gauthier. 1993. Long-term Recidivism of Child Molesters. *Journal of Consulting and Clinical Psychology*. 61:646-652.

Harris, G. T. 1989. The Relationship Between Neuroleptic Drug Dose and the Performance of Psychiatric Patients in a Maximum Security Token Economy Program. *Journal of Behavior Therapy and Experimental Psychiatry*. 20:57-67.

Harris, G. T., N. Z. Hilton, and M. E. Rice. 1993. Patients Admitted to Psychiatric Hospital: Presenting Problems and Resolution at Discharge. *Canadian Journal of Behavioural Science*. 25:267-285.

Harris, G. T., and M. E. Rice. 1984. Mentally Disordered Firesetters: Psychodynamic Versus Empirical Approaches. *International Journal of Law and Psychiatry*. 7:19-34.

———. 1990. An Empirical Approach to Classification and Treatment Planning for Psychiatric Inpatients. *Journal of Clinical Psychology*. 46:3-14.

———. 1992. Reducing Violence in Institutions: Maintaining Behaviour Change. In R. D. Peters, R. J. McMahon, and V. L. Quinsey, eds. *Aggression and Violence Throughout the Lifespan*. Newbury Park, California: Sage.

———. 1997a. Mentally Disordered Offenders: What Research Says About Effective Service. In C. D. Webster and M. A. Jackson, eds. *Impulsivity: Theory, Assessment and Treatment.* New York: Guilford Press.

———. 1997b. Risk Appraisal and Management of Violent Behavior. *Psychiatric Services.* 48:1168-1176.

Harris, G. T., M. E. Rice, and C. A. Cormier. 1994. Psychopaths: Is a Therapeutic Community Therapeutic? *Therapeutic Communities.* 15:283-300.

Harris, G. T., M. E. Rice, and D. L. Preston. 1989. Staff and Patient Perceptions of the Least Restrictive Alternatives for the Short Term Control of Disturbed Behavior. *Journal of Psychiatry and Law.* 17:239-263.

Harris, G. T., M. E. Rice, and V. L. Quinsey. 1993. Violent Recidivism of Mentally Disordered Offenders: The Development of a Statistical Prediction Instrument. *Criminal Justice and Behavior.* 20:315-335.

———. (in press). Appraisal and Management of Risk in Sexual Aggressors: Implications for Criminal Justice Policy. *Psychology, Public Policy and Law.*

Harris, G. T. and G. W. Varney. 1986. A Ten Year Study of Assaults and Assaulters on a Maximum Security Psychiatric Unit. *Journal of Interpersonal Violence.* 1:173-191.

Heinrich, K., E. Kliesser, E. Lehmann, E. Kinzler, et al.1994. Risperidone Versus Clozapine in the Treatment of Schizophrenic Patients with Acute Symptoms: A Double Blind, Randomized Trial. *Progress in Neuro-Psychopharmacology and Biological Psychiatry.* 18:129-137.

Helzel, M. F. and M. E. Rice. 1985. On the Validity of Social Skills Assessments: An Analysis of Role-play and Ward Staff Ratings of Social Behaviour in a Maximum Security Setting. *Canadian Journal of Behavioural Science.* 17:400-411.

Herjanic, M., F. A. Henn, and R. H. Vanderpearl. 1977. Forensic Psychiatry: Female Offenders. *American Journal of Psychiatry.* 134:556-558.

Hodgins, S. 1992. Mental Disorder, Intellectual Deficiency, and Crime. *Archives of General Psychiatry.* 49: 476-483.

Hodgins, S. and G. Coté.1990. Prevalence of Mental Disorders among Penitentiary Inmates in Quebec. *Canada's Mental Health.* March. 1-4.

———. 1991. The Mental Health of Penitentiary Inmates in Isolation. *Canadian Journal of Criminology.* 175-182.

Hollon, S. D., R. J. DeRubeis, M. D. Evans, M. J. Wiemer, M. J. Garvey, W. M. Grove, and V. B. Tuason. 1992. Cognitive Therapy and Pharmacotherapy for Depression: Singly and in Combination. *Archives of General Psychiatry.* 49:774-781.

Hollon, S. D., R. C. Shelton, and P. T. Loosen. 1991. Cognitive Therapy and Pharmacotherapy For Depression. *Journal of Consulting and Clinical Psychology*. 59: 88-99.

Honigfeld, G., R. D. Gillis, and C. J. Klett. 1966. NOSIE-30: A Treatment Sensitive Behavior Scale. *Psychological Reports*. 19:180-182.

Hucker, S., R. Langevin, and J. Bain. 1988. A Double Blind Trial of Sex Drive Reducing Medication in Pedophiles. *Annals of Sex Research*. 1:227-242.

Hurley, W. and M. P. Dunne. 1991. Psychological Distress and Psychiatric Morbidity in Women Prisoners. *Australian and New Zealand Journal of Psychiatry*. 25:461-470.

Jacobson, A. and B. Richardson. 1987. Assault Experiences of 100 Psychiatric Inpatients: Evidence of the Need for Routine Inquiry. *American Journal of Psychiatry*. 144:908-913.

James, J. F. and D. Gregory. 1980. Improving Psychiatric Care for Prisoners. *Hospital and Community Psychiatry*. 31:671-673.

James, J. F., D. Gregory, R. K. Jones, and O. H. Rundell. 1980. Psychiatric Morbidity in Prisons. *Hospital and Community Psychiatry*. 31: 674-677.

Jemelka, R., E. Trupin, and J. A. Chiles. 1989. The Mentally Ill in Prisons: A Review. *Hospital and Community Psychiatry*. 40:481-491.

Johnson, R. and S. Price. 1981. The Complete Correctional Officer: Human Service and the Human Environment of Prison. *Criminal Justice and Behavior*. 8:343-373.

Joliffe, K. 1984. *Penitentiary Medical Services*. Programs Branch User Report. Ministry of the Solicitor General of Canada.

Kazdin, A. E. 1993. Evaluation in Clinical Practice: Clinically Sensitive and Systematic Methods of Treatment Delivery. *Behavior Therapy*. 24:11-45.

Kelly, J. A., D. A. Murphy, K. J. Sikkema, A. M. Somiai, G. W. Mulry, M. I. Fernandez, J. G. Miller, and L. Y. Stevenson. 1995. Predictors of High and Low Levels of HIV-Risk Behavior among Adults with Chronic Mental Illness. *Psychiatric Services*. 46:813-818.

Klassen, D. and W. A. O'Connor. 1988. Crime, Inpatient Admissions, and Violence among Male Mental Patients. *International Journal of Law and Psychiatry*. 11:305-312.

Kluft, R. P. 1987. An Update on Multiple Personality Disorder. *Hospital and Community Psychiatry*. 38:363-373.

Kupfer, D. J., E. Frank, J. M. Perel, C. Cornes, A. G. Mallinger, M. E. Thase, A. B. McEachran, and V. J. Grochocinski. 1992. Five-year Outcome for Maintenance Therapies in Recurrent Depression. *Archives of General Psychiatry*. 49:769-773.

Law Reform Commission of Canada. 1985. *Behaviour Alteration and the Criminal Law*. Working paper 43. Ottawa: Ministry of Supply and Services Canada.

Laws, D. R. 1974. The Failure of a Token Economy. *Federal Probation*. 1:33-38.

———, ed. 1989. *Relapse Prevention with Sex Offenders*. New York: Guilford Press.

Levinson, R. B. 1982. Try Softer. In R. Johnson and H. Toch, eds. *The Pains of Imprisonment*. Beverly Hills: Sage.

Liberman, R. P.. Ed. 1988. *Psychiatric Rehabilitation of Chronic Mental Patients*. Washington, D.C.: American Psychiatric Press Inc.

Liberman, R. P., A. Kopelowicz, and A. S. Young. 1994. Biobehavioral Treatment and Rehabilitation of Schizophrenia. *Behavior Therapy*. 25:89-107.

Liberman, R. P., K. T. Mueser, and C. J. Wallace. 1986. Social Skills Training for Schizophrenic Individuals at Risk for Relapse. American *Journal of Psychiatry*. 143:523-526.

Liberman, R. P., K. H. Nuechterlein, and C. J. Wallace. 1982. Social Skills Training and the Nature of Schizophrenia. In J. P. Curran and P. M. Monti, eds. *Social Skills Training*. New York: Guilford.

Liberman, R. P., T. Van Putten, D. Barringer, J. Mintz, L. Lowen, T. G. Kuehnel, M. Aravagiri, and S. R. Marder. 1994. Optimal Drug and Behavior Therapy for Treatment-refractory Schizophrenic Patients. *American Journal of Psychiatry*. 151:756-759.

Link, B. G. and A. Stueve. 1994. Psychotic Symptoms and the Violent/illegal Behavior of Mental Patients Compared to Community Controls. In J. Monahan and H. J. Steadman, eds. *Violence and Mental Disorder: Developments in Risk Assessment*. Chicago: University of Chicago Press.

Lipsey, M. W. and D. B. Wilson. 1993. The Efficacy of Psychosocial, Educational, and Behavioral Treatment. *American Psychologist*. 48:1181-1209.

Long, G. T., F. E. Sultan, S. A. Kiefer, and D. M. Schrum. 1984. The Psychological Profile of the Female First Offender and the Recidivist: A Comparison. *Journal of Offender Counseling Services and Rehabilitation*. 9:119-123.

Lorr, M., J. P. O'Connor, and J. W. Stafford. 1960. The Psychotic Reaction Profile. *Journal of Clinical Psychology*. 16:241-246.

Lowe, M. R. and J. R. Cautela. 1978. A Self-report Measure of Social Skill. *Behavior Therapy*. 9:535-544.

Lukoff, D., R. P. Liberman, and K. H. Nuechterlein. 1986. Symptom Monitoring in the Rehabilitation of Schizophrenic Patients. *Schizophrenia Bulletin*. 12:578-602.

Lurigio, A. J. 1989. Practitioners' Views on AIDS in Probation and Detention. *Federal Probation*. 53:16-24.

Lyketsos, C. G., A. L. Hanson, M. Fishman, A. Rosenblatt, P. R. McHugh, and G. J. Treisman, 1993. Manic Syndrome Early and Late in the Course of HIV. *American Journal of Psychiatry*. 150: 326-327.

MacKain, S. J. and A. Streveler. 1990. Social and Independent Living Skills for Psychiatric Patients in a Prison Setting. *Behavior Modification*. 14:490-518.

Maletzky, B. M. 1991. *Treating the Sexual Offender*. Newbury Park, California: Sage.

Marder, S. R., W. C. Wirshing, J. Mintz, J. McKenzie, K. Johnston, T. A. Eckman, M. Lebell, K. Zimmerman, and P. R. Liberman. 1996. Two-year Outcome of Social Skills Training and Group Psychotherapy for Outpatients with Schizophrenia. *American Journal of Psychiatry*. 153:1585-1592.

Marques, J. K., D. M. Day, C. Nelson, M. H. Miner, and M. A. West. 1992. *The Sex Offender Treatment and Evaluation Project: Fourth Report to the Legislature in Response to PC 1365*. Sacramento: California State Department of Mental Health.

Marques, J. K., C. Nelson, M. A. West, and D. M. Day. 1994. The Relationship Between Treatment Goals and Recidivism among Child Molesters. *Behaviour Research and Therapy*. 32:577-588.

Marshall, W. L. and H. E. Barbaree. 1988. The Long-term Evaluation of a Behavioral Treatment Program for Child Molesters. *Behavior Research and Therapy*. 26:499-511.

Marshall, W. L., R. Jones, T. Ward, P. Johnston, and H. E. Barbaree. 1991. Treatment Outcome with Sex Offenders. *Clinical Psychology Review*. 11:465-485.

Martin, R. 1975. *Legal Challenges to Behavior Modification*. Champaign, Illinois: Research Press.

Martin, R. L., R. Cloninger, and S. B. Guze. 1978. Female Criminality and the Prediction of Recidivism. *Archives of General Psychiatry*. 35:207-213.

McCormick, I. A. 1984. A Simple Version of the Rathus Assertiveness Schedule. *Behavioral Assessment*. 7:95-99.

McGrew, J. H., G. R. Bond, L. Dietzen, and M. Salyers. 1994. Measuring the Fidelity of Implementation of a Mental Health Program Model. *Journal of Consulting and Clinical Psychology*. 62:670-678.

McNiel, D. E. and R. L. Binder. 1994. Screening for Risk of Inpatient Violence. *Law and Human Behavior*. 18:579-586.

Meichenbaum, D. and D. C. Turk. 1987. *Facilitating Treatment Adherence: A Practitioner's Guidebook.* New York: Plenum Press.

Menditto, A. A., N. C. Beck, P. Stuve, J. A. Fisher, M. Stacy, M. B. Logue, and L. J. Baldwin. 1996. Effectiveness of Clozapine and a Social Learning Program for Severely Disabled Psychiatric Inpatients. *Psychiatric Services.* 47:46-51.

Menzies, R. J., D. E. Chunn, and C. D. Webster. 1992. Female Follies: The Forensic Psychiatric Assessment of Women Defendants. *International Journal of Law and Psychiatry.* 15:179-193.

Metzner, J. L., G. E. Fryer, and D. Usery. 1990. Prison Mental Health Services: Results of a National Survey of Standards, Resources, Administrative Structure, and Litigation. *Journal of Forensic Sciences.* 35:433-438.

Milan, M. A. 1987. Token Economy Programs in Closed Institutions. In E. K. Morris and C. J. Braukmann, eds. *Behavioral Approaches to Crime and Delinquency: A Handbook of Application, Research, and Concepts.* New York: Plenum.

Miller, L. S., and D. Funabiki. 1984. Predictive Validity of the Social Performance Survey Schedule for Component Interpersonal Behaviors. *Behavioral Assessment.* 6:33-44.

Monahan, J. 1992. Mental Disorder and Violent Behavior. *American Psychologist.* 47:511-521.

Monahan, J. and S. K. Davis. 1983. Mentally Disordered Sex Offenders. In J. Monahan and H. J. Steadman, eds. *Mentally Disordered Offenders: Perspectives from Law and Social Science.* New York: Plenum.

Monti, P. M. 1983. The Social Skills Intake Interview: Reliability and Convergent Validity Assessment. *Journal of Behavior Therapy and Experimental Psychiatry.* 14:305-310.

Moos, R. H. 1975. *Evaluating Correctional and Community Settings.* New York: Wiley.

Morrison, E. F. 1991. Victimization in Prison: Implications for the Mentally Ill Inmate and for Health Professionals. *Archives of Psychiatric Nursing.* 5:17-24.

Motiuk, L. L. and F. J. Porporino. 1991. *The Prevalence, Nature and Severity of Mental Health Problems among Federal Male Inmates in Canadian Penitentiaries.* Ottawa: Correctional Service Canada.

Novaco, R. W. 1975. *Anger Control.* Toronto: D.C. Heath.

Overall, J. E. and D. R. Gorham. 1962. The Brief Psychiatric Rating Scale. *Psychological Reports.* 19:799-812.

Palermo, G. B., M. B. Smith, and F. J. Liska. 1991. Jails Versus Mental Hospitals: A Social Dilemma. *International Journal of Offender Therapy and Comparative Criminology*. 35:97-106.

Patterson, G. R. 1982. *Coercive Family Process: A Social Learning Approach.* Eugene, Oregon: Castalia.

Patterson, G. R. 1985. A Microsocial Analysis of Anger and Irritable Behavior. In M. A. Chesney and R. H. Rosenman, eds. *Anger and Hostility in Cardiovascular and Behavioral Disorders*. New York: Hemisphere.

Paul, G. L. and R. J. Lentz. 1977. *Psychosocial Treatment of Chronic Mental Patients: Milieu Versus Social Learning Programs*. Cambridge, Massachusetts: Harvard University Press.

Penrose, L. S. 1939. Mental Disease and Crime: Outline of a Comparative Study of European Statistics. *British Journal of Medical Psychology*. 18:1-15.

Peuskens, J. 1995. Risperidone in the Treatment of Patients with Chronic Schizophrenia: A Multi-national, Multi-centre, Double-blind, Parallel-group Study Versus Haloperidol. *British Journal of Psychiatry.* 166:712-726.

Pickar, D., R. R. Owen, R. E. Litman, E. Konicki, R. Gutierrez, and M. H. Rapaport. 1992. Clinical and Biologic Response to Clozapine in Patients with Schizophrenia. *Archives of General Psychiatry*. 49:345-353.

Pithers, W. D. and G. F. Cumming. 1989. Can Relapses Be Prevented? Initial Outcome Data from the Vermont Treatment Program for Sexual Aggressors. In D. R. Laws, ed. *Relapse Prevention with Sex Offenders*. New York: Guilford.

Pithers, W. D., G. R. Martin, and G. F. Cumming. 1989. Vermont Treatment Program for Sexual Aggressors. In D. R. Laws, ed. *Relapse Prevention with Sex Offenders.* New York: Guilford Press.

Positano, S., D. A. Sandford, R. H. Elzinga, and J. E. James. 1990. Virtue Rewarded: Reinforcement and Punishment in an Acute Psychiatric Admission Ward. *Journal of Behavior Therapy and Experimental Psychiatry*. 21:257-262.

Prins, H. 1980. *Offenders, Deviants, or Patients?* New York: Tavistock.

Quinsey, V. L. 1981. The Long Term Management of the Mentally Disordered Offender. In S. J. Hucker, C. D. Webster, and M. Ben-Aron, eds. *Mental Disorder and Criminal Responsibility.* Toronto: Butterworths.

———. 1984. Sexual Aggression: Studies of Offenders against Women. In D. Weisstub, ed. *Law and Mental Health: International Perspectives, Vol. 1*. New York: Pergamon.

Quinsey, V. L., T. C. Chaplin, A. Maguire, and D. Upfold. 1987. The Behavioral Treatment of Rapists and Child Molesters: An Example of an Institutional Program. In E. K. Morris and C. J. Braukmann, eds. *Behavioral Approaches to Crime and Delinquency: Application, Research, and Theory*. New York: Plenum.

Quinsey, V. L., M. Cyr, and Y. Lavallee. 1988. Treatment Opportunities in a Maximum Security Psychiatric Hospital. *International Journal of Law and Psychiatry*. 11:179-194.

Quinsey, V. L., G. T. Harris, and M. E. Rice. 1987. Review of "Behaviour Alteration and the Criminal Law," Law Reform Commission of Canada. *Canadian Psychology*. 28:85-87.

Quinsey, V. L., G. T. Harris, M. E. Rice, and C. A. Cormier. (in press). *Violent Offenders: Appraising and Managing Risk*. Washington, D.C.: American Psychological Association Press.

Quinsey, V. L., G. T. Harris, M. E. Rice, and M. L. Lalumière. 1993. Assessing Treatment Efficacy in Outcome Studies of Sex Offenders. *Journal of Interpersonal Violence*. 8:512-523.

———. 1995. The Actuarial Prediction of Sexual Recidivism. *Journal of Interpersonal Violence*. 10:85-105.

Reid, W. H. 1995. The Treatment of Psychosis: Resetting the Drug Cost Thermostat. *Journal of Clinical Psychiatry*. 55:166-168.

Reid, W. H., M. Mason, and M. Toprac. 1994. Saving in Hospital Bed-days Related to Treatment with Clozapine. *Hospital and Community Psychiatry*. 45:261-264.

Rhem, L. P. 1981. Assessment of Depression. In M. Hersen and A. S. Bellack, eds. *Behavioral Assessment: A Practical Handbook, 2nd ed.* New York: Pergamon Press.

Rice, M. E. 1983. Improving the Social Skills of Males in a Maximum Security Psychiatric Setting. *Canadian Journal of Behavioural Science*. 15:43-51.

———. 1985. Violence in the Maximum Security Hospital: In M. H. Ben-Aron, S. J. Hucker, and C. D. Webster, eds. *Clinical Criminology: The Assessment and Treatment of Criminal Behaviour.* Toronto: M and M Graphics.

Rice, M. E. and T. C. Chaplin. 1979. Social Skills Training for Hospitalized Male Arsonists. *Journal of Behavior Therapy and Experimental Psychiatry*. 10:105-108.

Rice, M. E. and G. T. Harris. 1988. An Empirical Approach to the Classification and Treatment of Maximum Security Psychiatric Patients. *Behavioral Sciences and the Law*. 6:497-514.

———. 1990. The Predictors of Insanity Acquittal. *International Journal of Law and Psychiatry*. 13:217-224.

———. 1992. A Comparison of Criminal Recidivism among Schizophrenic and Nonschizophrenic Offenders. *International Journal of Law and Psychiatry*. 15:397-408.

———. 1993. Ontario's Maximum Security Hospital at Penetanguishene: Past, Present and Future. *International Journal of Law and Psychiatry*. 16:195-215.

———. 1997a. Cross-validation and Extension of the Violence Risk Appraisal Guide for Child Molesters and Rapists. *Law and Human Behavior.* 21:231-241.

———. 1997b. Treatment of Adult Offenders. In D. Stoff, J. Breiling, and J. D. Maser, eds. *Handbook of Antisocial Behavior.* New York: Wiley.

———. (in press). Sexual Aggressors. In D. Faigman, ed. *Modern Scientific Evidence, Vol. 3*. St. Paul, Minnesota: West Publishing Co.

Rice, M. E., G. T. Harris, and C. Cormier. 1992. Evaluation of a Maximum Security Therapeutic Community for Psychopaths and Other Mentally Disordered Offenders. *Law and Human Behavior*. 16:399-412.

Rice, M. E., G. T. Harris, C. Lang, and V. Bell. 1990. Recidivism among Male Insanity Acquittees. *Journal of Psychiatry and Law*. 18:379-403.

Rice, M. E., G. T. Harris, and V. L. Quinsey. 1990. A followup of Rapists Assessed in a Maximum Security Psychiatric Facility. *Journal of Interpersonal Violence*. 5:435-448.

———. 1994. Control in the Psychiatric Setting: Adults. In M. Hersen, R. Ammerman and L. Sisson, eds. *Handbook of Aggressive and Destructive Behavior in Psychiatric Patients*. New York: Plenum.

———. 1996. Treatment of Forensic Patients. In B. Sales and S. Shaw, eds. *Mental Health Policy and the Law: Research, Policy and Practice*. New York: Carolina Academic Press.

———. (in press). Treating Adult Sex Offenders. In J. B. Ashford, B. D. Sales, and W. Reid, eds. *Treating Adults and Juvenile Offenders with Special Needs*. Washington, D.C.: American Psychological Association.

Rice, M. E., G. T. Harris, V. L. Quinsey, and M. Cyr. 1990. Planning Treatment Programs in Secure Psychiatric Facilities. In D. Weisstub, ed. *Law and Mental Health: International Perspectives*. New York: Pergamon.

Rice, M. E., G. T. Harris, D. Sutherland, and J. Leveque. 1990. Principles Regarding Treatment of Patients in Psychiatric Institutions. *Canada's Mental Health*. 18-24.

Rice, M. E., G. T. Harris, G. W. Varney, and V. L. Quinsey. 1989. *Violence in Institutions: Understanding, Prevention, and Control.* Toronto: Hans Huber.

Rice, M. E., M. F. Helzel, G. W. Varney, and V. L. Quinsey. 1985. Crisis Prevention and Intervention Training for Psychiatric Hospital Staff. *American Journal of Community Psychology.* 13:289-304.

Rice, M. E. and N. Josefowitz. 1983. Assertion, Popularity, and Social Behavior in Maximum Security Psychiatric Patients. *Corrective and Social Psychiatry and Journal of Behavior Technology Methods and Therapy.* 29:97-104.

Rice, M. E., V. L. Quinsey, and G. T. Harris. 1991. Sexual Recidivism among Child Molesters Released from a Maximum Security Psychiatric Institution. *Journal of Consulting and Clinical Psychology.* 59:381-386.

Rice, M. E., V. L. Quinsey, and R. Houghton. 1990. Predicting Treatment Outcome and Recidivism among Patients in a Maximum Security Token Economy. *Behavioral Sciences and the Law.* 8:313-326.

Rickel, K., E. Schweizer, I. Fox, and C. Weise. 1994. Nefazodone and Imipramine in Major Depression: A Placebo-controlled Trial. *British Journal of Psychiatry.* 164:802-805.

Robinson, L. A., J. S. Berman, and R. A. Neimeyer. 1990. Psychotherapy for the Treatment of Depression: A Comprehensive Review of Controlled Outcome Research. *Psychological Bulletin.* 108:30-49.

Ross, R. R. and E. A. Fabiano. 1985. *Time To Think: A Cognitive Model of Delinquency Prevention and Offender Rehabilitation.* Johnson City, Tennessee: Institute of Social Science and Arts Inc.

Ross, R. R., E. A. Fabiano, and C. D. Ewles. 1988. Reasoning and Rehabilitation. *International Journal of Offender Therapy and Comparative Criminology.* 32:29-335.

Roth, L. H. 1980. Correctional Psychiatry. In W. J. Curran, A. L. McGarry, and C. S. Petty, eds. *Modern Legal Medicine, Psychiatry, and Forensic Science.* Philadelphia: F. A. Davis.

Schwitzgebel, R. K. 1974. *Development and Legal Regulation of Coercive Behavior Modification Techniques with Offenders.* Rockville, Maryland: National Institute of Mental Health.

Shea, M. T., I. Elkin, S. D. Imber, S. M. Sotsky, J. T. Watkins, J. F Collins, P. A. Pikonis, E. Beckham, D. R. Glass, R. T. Dolan, and M. B. Parloff. 1992. Course of Depressive Symptoms over Follow-up: Findings from the National Institute of Mental Health Treatment of Depression Collaborative Research Program. *Archives of General Psychiatry.* 49:782-787.

Shea, I. E., J. T. Watkins, S. D. Imber, S. M. Sotsky, J. F. Collins, D. R. Glass, P. A. Pilkonis, W. R. Leber, J. P. Docherty, S. J. Fiester, and M. B. Parloff. 1989. National Institute of Mental Health Treatment of Depression Collaborative Research Program: General Effectiveness of Treatments. *Archives of General Psychiatry*. 46:971-982.

Shelton, R. C., S. D. Hollon, S. E. Purdon, and P. T. Loosen. 1991. Biological and Psychological Aspects of Depression. *Behavior Therapy*. 22:201-228.

Siegel, J. M. 1985. The Measurement of Anger as a Multidimensional Construct. In M. A. Chesney and R. H. Rosenman, eds. *Anger and Hostility in Cardiovascular and Behavioral Disorders*. New York: Hemisphere.

———. 1986. The Multidimensional Anger Inventory. *Journal of Personality and Social Psychology*. 51:191-200.

Slovenko, R. 1973. *Psychiatry and Law*. Boston: Little Brown.

Smith, L. D. 1989. Medication Refusal and the Rehospitalized Mentally Ill Inmate. *Hospital and Community Psychiatry*. 40:491-496.

Sommers, I. and D. R. Baskin. 1991. Assessing the Appropriateness of the Prescription of Psychiatric Medications in Prison. *The Journal of Nervous and Mental Disease*. 179:267-273.

Sonnenberg, S. M. 1988. Victims of Violence and Post-traumatic Stress Disorder. *Psychiatric Clinics of North America*. 11:581-590.

Sotsky, S. M., D. R. Glass, M. T. Shea, P. A. Pilkonis, J. E. Collins, I. Elkin, J. Watkins, S. D. Imber, W. R. Leber, J. Moyer, and M. E. Oliveri. 1991. Patient Predictors of Response to Psychotherapy and Pharmacotherapy: Findings in the National Institute of Mental Health Treatment of Depression Collaborative Research Program. *American Journal of Psychiatry*. 148:997-1008.

Spielberger, C. D., E. H. Johnson, S. F. Russell, R. J. Crane, G. A. Jacobs, and T. J. Warden. 1985. The Experience and Expression of Anger: Construction and Validation of an Anger Expression Scale. In M. A. Chesney and R. H. Rosenman. Eds. *Anger and Hostility in Cardiovascular and Behavioral Disorders*. New York: Hemisphere.

Steadman, H. J., S. Fabisiak, J. Dvoskin, and E. J. Holohean. 1987. A Survey of Mental Disability among State Prison Inmates. *Hospital and Community Psychiatry*. 38:1086-1090.

Steadman, H. J., D. W. McCarty, and J. P. Morrissey. 1989. *The Mentally Ill in Jail: Planning for Essential Services*. New York: The Guilford Press.

Steadman, H. F., J. Monahan, B. Duffee, E. Hartstone, and P. C. Robbins. 1984. The Impact of State Mental Hospital Deinstitutionalization on United States Prison Populations, 1968-1978. *The Journal of Criminal Law and Criminology*. 75:474-490.

Sturgeon, V. H. and J. Taylor. 1980. Report of a Five-year Follow-up Study of Mentally Disordered Sex Offenders Released from Atascadero State Hospital in 1973. *Criminal Justice Journal*. 4:31-63.

Sultan, F. E. and G. T. Long. 1988. Treatment of the Sexually/physically Abused Female Inmate: Evaluation of an Intensive Short-term Intervention Program. *Journal of Offender Counseling, Services and Rehabilitation*. 131-143.

Swanson, J. W., R. Borum, M. S. Swartz, and J. Monahan. 1996. Psychotic Symptoms and Disorders and the Risk of Violent Behaviour in the Community. *Criminal Behaviour and Mental Health*. 6:317-338.

Swanson, J. W., C. E. Holzer, V. K. Ganju, and R. T. Jono. 1990. Violence and Psychiatric Disorder in the Community: Evidence from the Epidemiologic Catchment Area Surveys. *Hospital and Community Psychiatry*. 41:761-770.

Sweet, A. A., and A. Loizeaux. 1991. Behavioral and Cognitive Treatment Methods: A Critical Comparative Review. *Journal of Behavior Therapy and Experimental Psychiatry*. 22:159-185.

Tarrier, N., R. Beckett, S. Harwood, A. Baker, L. Yusupoff, and I. Ugarteburu. 1993. A Trial of Two Cognitive-behavioural Methods of Treating Drug-resistant Residual Psychotic Symptoms in Schizophrenic Patients: I. Outcome. *British Journal of Psychiatry*. 162:524-532.

Taylor, P. J., P. Garety, A. Buchanan, A. Reed, S. Wessely, K. Ray, G. Dunn, and D. Grubin. 1994. Delusions and Violence. In J. Monahan and H. Steadman, eds. *Violence and Mental Disorder*. Chicago: The University of Chicago Press.

Teplin, L. A. 1990. The Prevalence of Severe Mental Disorder among Male Urban Jail Detainees: Comparison with the Epidemiologic Catchment Area Program. *American Journal of Public Health*. 80:663-669.

Teplin, L. A. and N. S. Pruett. 1992. Police as Streetcorner Psychiatrists: Managing the Mentally Ill. *International Journal of Law and Psychiatry*. 15:139-156.

Thyer, B. A. 1995. Promoting an Empiricist Agenda within the Human Services: An Ethical and Humanistic Imperative. *Journal of Behavior Therapy and Experimental Psychiatry*. 26:93-99.

Toch, H. 1982. The Disturbed Disruptive Inmate: Where Does the Bus Stop? *The Journal of Psychiatry and Law*. 327-349.

Toch, H. and K. Adams. 1987. The Prison as Dumping Ground: Mainlining Disturbed Offenders. *The Journal of Psychiatry and Law*. 539-553.

———. 1989. Coping: *Maladaption in Prisons*. New Brunswick: Transaction Books.

Tollefson, G. D., C. M. Beasley, P. V. Tran, J. S. Street, J. A. Krueger, R. N. Tamura, K. A. Graffeo, and M. E. Thieme. 1997. Olanzapine Versus Haloperidol in the Treatment of Schizophrenia and Schizoaffective and Schizophreniform Disorders: Results of an International Collaborative Trial. *American Journal of Psychiatry*. 154:457-465.

Travin, S., K. Cullen, and B. Protter. 1990. Female Sex Offenders: Severe Victims and Victimizers. *Journal of Forensic Sciences*. 35:140-150.

Van Putten, T., P. R. A. May, and S. R. Marder. 1984. Response to Antipsychotic Medication: The Doctor's and the Consumer's View. *American Journal of Psychiatry*. 161:16-19.

Wallace, C. J. 1982. The Social Skills Training Project of the Mental Health Clinical Research Center for the Study of Schizophrenia. In J. P. Curran and P. M. Monti, eds. *Social Skills Training*. New York: Guilford Press.

West, D. J. 1980. The Clinical Approach to Criminology. *Psychological Medicine*. 10:619-631.

Wilkins, J. and J. Coid. 1991. Self-mutilation in Female Remanded Prisoners: I. An Indicator of Severe Psychopathology. *Criminal Behavior and Mental Health*. 1:247-267.

Wishart, M. D. and N. N. Dubler, eds. 1983. *Health Care in Prisons, Jails and Detention Centers: Some Legal and Ethical Dilemmas*. New York: Department of Social Medicine, Montefiore Medical Center.

Wittlin, B. J. 1988. Practical Psycho-pharmacology. In R. P. Liberman, ed. *Psychiatric Rehabilitation of Chronic Mental Patients*. Washington, D.C.: American Psychiatric Press, Inc.

Wong, S. E., K. M. Slama, R. P. Liberman. 1987. Behavioral Analysis and Therapy for Aggressive Psychiatric and Developmentally Disabled Patients. In L. H. Roth, ed. *Clinical Treatment of the Violent Person*. New York: Guilford Press.

Wong, S. E., J. E. Woolsey, A. J. Innocent, and R. P. Liberman. 1988. Behavioral Treatment of Violent Psychiatric Patients. *Psychiatric Clinics of North American*. 11:569-579.

Wormith, J. S. 1984. Attitude and Behavior Change of a Correctional Clientele: A 3-year Follow-up. *Criminology*. 22:595-618.

Wormith, J. S. and M. Borzecki. 1985. *Mental Disorder in the Criminal Justice System*. Ottawa: Ministry of the Solicitor General.

Yudofsky, S. C., J. M. Silver, W. Jackson, J. Endicott, and D. Williams. 1986. The Overt Aggression Scale for the Objective Rating of Verbal and Physical Aggression. *American Journal of Psychiatry*. 143:35-39.

Zamble, E. and F. Porporino. 1988. *Coping, Behavior, and Adaptation in Prison Inmates*. New York: Springer-Verlag.

Zimbardo, P. G. 1973. The Psychological Power and Pathology of Imprisonment. In O. Milton and R. G. Wahler, eds. *Behavior Disorders: Perspectives and Trends*. Philadelphia: Lippincott.

Zung, W. K. 1969. A Cross-cultural Survey of Symptoms in Depression. *American Journal of Psychiatry*. 126:116-121.

ASSESSMENT, MANAGEMENT, AND TREATMENT OF SEX OFFENDERS

8

Vernon L. Quinsey, Ph.D.
Queen's University,
Kingston, Ontario,
Canada

Introduction

The history of the management and treatment of sex offenders has been driven by spectacular incidents of sexual recidivism within particular jurisdictions. Such incidents create strong political pressures on everyone assessing, treating, and making release decisions concerning sex offenders to either become more conservative or to make foolproof decisions. When faced with great uncertainty and strong pressure not to make errors, people are prone to look for certainty in technology or to defer to experts with special knowledge.

Sex offenders are, however, much like other offenders, and the issues of risk pertaining to them are identical. Although there is a technology of assessment and treatment that is specific to sex offenders, and a substantial proportion of them are undoubtedly paraphiliacs or sexual deviants, the technology of assessment and treatment that exists specifically for sex offenders is fallible and will not bear the weight of unrealistic expectations. There is no mark of Cain nor magic bullet of treatment to eliminate uncertainty.

Community harm in the form of sexual recidivism, however, can be reduced through careful release decisions guided by standardized predictive instruments and phallometric assessments, provision of treatment where appropriate, and programs of community risk management. Nevertheless, even with the best system of assessment, treatment, and management, some sex offenders inevitably will recidivate while under supervision. Thus, recidivism can occur either as the inevitable result of basing decisions on imperfect knowledge or as the result of carelessness or human error. It is important to make a sharp distinction between these two sources of recidivism. The adoption of formal policies for the assessment, treatment, and management of sex offenders should protect decision makers and service providers from being accused of human error when the fault lies in imperfect knowledge.

The goal of the approach recommended in this article is the improvement of the balance between the civil liberties of offenders and public safety by more accurately appraising risk. This risk then can be linked to dispositional decisions, including the provision of interventions designed to reduce it. Of course, dispositional decisions can be made using a variety of criteria, such as just deserts, general and special deterrence, offense seriousness, number of previous offenses, degree of recovery from mental illness, and so on. A variety of moral, legal, and historical rationales can be given for the use of particular criteria in making dispositional decisions. Regardless of the rationale for particular dispositional policies, however, community safety and the civil liberties of offenders are inevitably an issue. The only rational manner in which this issue can be addressed is through accurately appraising the dangerousness of individual sex offenders.

Prediction of Sexual Recidivism

Let us consider the art and science of predicting recidivism among sex offenders. First, it must be decided exactly what negative outcomes of release or relaxation of supervision are at issue. Policy could be concerned about psychiatric relapse, recidivism of any kind, violent recidivism, and/or sexual recidivism. The distinction among these is important because their likelihood for any given offender is very different. For example, in a sample of rapists and child molesters assessed at the Oak Ridge maximum-security psychiatric facility (Quinsey, Rice, and Harris, in press), 28 percent were convicted of a new sex offense, 40 percent were arrested or returned for a violent or sexual offense, and 57 percent were arrested or returned to Oak Ridge for any offense. If we were to be concerned with minor offenses or rehospitalization, therefore, we would be much more conservative in our decision making than if we concerned ourselves only with more serious (and rarer) phenomena.

Base Rate Issues

The literature on decision making suggests that the initial step in appraising the dangerousness of an individual is to establish the base rate or the expected likelihood that the person will commit a new violent or sex offense within a specified period of time (for example, Quinsey and Walker, 1992). The initial estimate of the probability with which a sex offender will commit a new sexual or violent offense only can be made by examining the results of follow-up studies of similar offenders. First, the relevant characteristics of the offender in question must be established, and then the frequency of violent and sexual recidivists among offenders with similar characteristics can be used to generate the probability. For clarity, it must be remembered that the focus of such predictive efforts is on the prospective identification of persons who will commit crimes, not on the prediction of the crimes themselves.

Assessors, therefore, must have a reasonable estimate of the base rate before they proceed. The base rate is a function of the rate at which violent crimes are committed and the duration of time that offenders are followed. Clearly, if the interval of time for which the question of dangerousness is relevant is short, then, it is likely that the base rate will be too low (for example, Villeneuve and Quinsey, in press).

The initial estimate of the likelihood of recidivism is determined primarily by static or historical variables. Although variables such as offense history cannot change with time, they are vital in anchoring clinical judgment in actuarial reality. One of the reasons this anchoring is so important is that unaided human judgment is remarkably insensitive to dramatic differences in base rate in a prediction context (Cannon and Quinsey, in press). The final appraisal of dangerousness is made by adjusting the initial estimate upward or downward according to dynamic variables such as progress in treatment and type and quality of supervision.

The importance of the initial estimate can be seen by considering a hypothetical treatment method that reduces recidivism by half: An offender whose expected likelihood of recidivism is 80 percent will have a likelihood of 40 percent after treatment, whereas one with an initial 10 percent probability will have a post-treatment probability of only 5 percent. (For an extensive discussion of these issues, *see* Webster, Harris, Rice, Cormier, and Quinsey, 1994.)

The base rate is most important when it is extreme. For example, if the expected probability of recidivism is very low, say 5 percent, then an appraisal of dangerousness must be 95 percent accurate to equal the accuracy of making a decision to release based solely on the base rate (for example, Quinsey, 1980). Predictions of sexual recidivism are worthwhile, therefore, only where the base rate is not extremely low or high. An individual prediction should not be made when the base rate for the population from which the assessed individual comes is too extreme.

Actuarial Assessment

Among sex offenders, a variety of historical factors, such as the number of previous sex offenses, predict the likelihood of sexual and violent recidivism. Among child molesters, the sex of the victim and the relationship of the victim to the offender are also important predictors. Intrafamilial (father-daughter incest) offenders have quite low recidivism rates. Among extrafamilial offenders, those with boy victims have double the recidivism rate of heterosexual offenders (for a review, *see* Quinsey, 1986).

In a recent study (Quinsey, Rice, and Harris, in press), 178 sex offenders who had been assessed at a maximum-security psychiatric facility were followed for an average of fifty-nine months to determine their opportunity to reoffend. Twenty-eight percent were convicted of a new sex offense and 40 percent were arrested, convicted, or returned to the psychiatric facility for a violent (including sex) offense. Rapists were more likely to recidivate than child molesters. Psychopathy, measures of previous criminal history, and phallometric indices of deviant sexual interests were found to be useful predictors of sexual recidivism.

A predictor scale was formed by weighting each of the fourteen predictors that was significant in the regression analyses by a number reflecting its univariate correlation with the criterion. The variables, in descending order of the size of their relationship with the criterion, were as follows: the Psychopathy Checklist—Revised (Hare, 1991), elementary school maladjustment, not having lived with both parents until age sixteen, property offense charges, prior criminal charges against persons, number of previous sexual offenses, history of sexual offenses against only female children (negative), never married or having lived common-law, age at index offense (negative), failure on prior conditional release or supervision, initial phallometric assessment indicating deviant sexual age or activity preferences, DSM-III criteria for any personality disorder, DSM-III criteria for schizophrenia (negative), and alcohol abuse history.

Linear relationships (r's = .45 and .46, respectively) were found between scores on the predictor scale and reconviction for a sexual offense and violent (including sexual) recidivism. When the selection ratio was set approximately equal to the base rate, there were 77 percent correct decisions and a relative improvement over chance of 44 percent for sexual reconvictions and 72 percent correct decisions and an RIOC of 42 percent for violent failure.

It is of interest that another actuarial instrument, the Statistical Risk Appraisal Guide (Harris, Rice, and Quinsey, 1993), developed using the same method on a larger sample of offenders (about 10 percent of whom were sex offenders), predicts sexual and violent recidivism on cross validation a bit better than the Psychopathy Checklist, which was derived exclusively from a sex offender sample. This observation is particularly useful because the general Statistical Risk Appraisal Guide does not require phallometric assessment. The predictors in this instrument are, in descending order of their relationship with violent or sexual recidivism: the Psychopathy Checklist-Revised, elementary school maladjustment, not having lived with both parents to age sixteen, adult property offenses, never having been married or lived common-law, age at index offense (negative), failure on prior conditional release or supervision, victim injury in index offense (negative), DSM-III criteria for any personality disorder, DSM-III criteria for schizophrenia (negative), female victim in index offense (negative), and history of alcohol abuse.

Using theoretically relevant and empirically tested predictors, therefore, predictive accuracy realistically can be expected to be in the 80 percent range. This is far from perfect, but it is much better than chance or relying on clinical intuition. The actuarial instruments developed by colleagues and this author provide probabilities of violent or sexual recidivism for particular levels of risk score, but these probabilities are only accurate for the population from which they were derived. However, because the predictors of violent recidivism in the actuarial instrument are similar to those that have been successfully used in a variety of contexts and because the derivation offender sample was quite heterogeneous, the instruments can be used to assign persons from different but similar populations to relative risk categories with some confidence. In other words, the actuarial instrument can rank the dangerousness of offenders in different populations relative to each other.

Incapacitation

The actuarial models described are designed to predict violent or sexual recidivism but do not otherwise directly address the seriousness of such recidivism. The anticipated seriousness of a violent offense (should one occur) is important in considering incapacitation, the long-term refusal of community access. Incapacitation should be considered where the actuarially determined risk of violent recidivism is high and when the offender being assessed has committed at least one very serious prior violent offense.

Dynamic Predictors

An actuarial estimate of risk may be adjusted in a conservative manner based upon the idiosyncratic aspects of the particular case (for an extensive discussion of this issue *see* Webster et al., 1994). Such adjustment might be indicated by therapeutic outcome, changed opportunities of offending, adequacy of supervision, current compliance with medication or supervision, and so on. It is usually the case with dynamic variables that intuition must be relied upon because of the absence of empirical information. Because of the well documented unreliability of clinical judgment in general, and clinical prediction of violent behavior in particular (Quinsey and Ambtman, 1979; Quinsey and Maguire, 1986), the reliability of clinical appraisals of dangerousness can be markedly increased by averaging the independently made judgments of different clinicians.

In the best circumstance, the clinicians considering an individual case have a theory that identifies the antecedents of violent or sexual offending for that offender. Such individualized theories often are cast in terms of relapse prevention (Laws, 1989). These antecedents are the clinical issues to be considered in adjusting actuarially determined risk.

Both the actuarial model and clinical appraisals rest upon a detailed and corroborated history. Assessments of dangerousness should not be based solely on offender self-report. This, however, does not imply that more information is necessarily better. Only some potential predictors in fact are related to violent recidivism. It is these that must be evaluated carefully. The consideration of irrelevant information simply confuses the issue.

Phallometric Assessment

As discussed previously, phallometric data from an initial assessment can be employed as a static predictor in an actuarial model. It can, however, also be employed to identify treatment targets and to monitor changes in sexual interest and, by inference, in the likelihood of committing a new sexual offense.

The probative value of phallometric assessments is often unknown because the discriminant and predictive validity of the procedures used in many sexual behavior laboratories have not yet been established. In these cases, it is not known whether, let alone how well, these assessments can differentiate sex offenders of various kinds from each other or from offenders who have not committed sex crimes; whether these assessments relate to important aspects of a sex offender's history; whether they predict sexual recidivism; or whether changes in phallometric assessment data occasioned by treatment are related to subsequent sexual recidivism. It has not been established that phallometric data collected using different procedures and stimuli have these various forms of validity (Quinsey and Laws, 1990); the stimuli and procedures that are used in a particular case have to be evaluated themselves.

Because phallometric assessments are not immune from faking (for example, Quinsey and Chaplin, 1988) and the motivation of most inmates is to "pass" them by appearing to have normative sexual interests, test results are more confidently interpreted if evidence of deviant sexual interests is found than if no deviant interests are found. Phallometric assessment reports, therefore, tend to be conservative with respect to risk.

Further, the question of validity of specialized procedures is best thought of as an incremental one. Specifically, what increase in predictive efficiency is achieved by a phallometric assessment? This is an important question because a number of instruments have been developed that are less expensive, easier to use, and well known to be related to general recidivism (Nuffield, 1982; Hare, 1985; Hare et al., 1990; Hart, Kropp, and Hare, 1988; the Level of Supervision Inventory, Andrews, 1989; Andrews, Kiessling, and Kominos, 1983; Andrews, 1989; Andrews et al., 1986) and violent and sexual recidivism (the Psychopathy Checklist, Hare and McPherson, 1984; the Statistical Risk Appraisal Guide, Harris, Rice and

Quinsey, 1993). A variety of methods of quantifying a person's history of sex offenses also are useful predictors of sexual recidivism.

The issue of the amount of incremental validity that is gained by specialized sex-offender assessment is connected to standardized measures of risk in another manner as well. An offender's history of sex offending is related in a direct way to the probability with which he will show deviant sexual interest in a phallometric assessment. Those with many sex offenses, who have chosen very young victims and who have selected male children as victims, are more likely to show deviant sexual interests in phallometric assessments.

Treatment of Sex Offenders: A Brief Overview

Policies concerning the treatment of sex offenders are necessarily complex because they relate simultaneously to sentencing, probation and parole policies, the civil liberties of offenders, community safety, and issues of treatment efficacy. Programs of treatment for sex offenders, therefore, must be developed in the context of a variety of policies dealing with offender disposition. In addition, sex offenders often are involved with mental health and social service agencies before, after, or instead of their involvement with the criminal justice system. Clearly, policies pertaining to treatment must be coordinated across a variety of agency and governmental jurisdictions. In view of these considerations, psychological or psychiatric treatments must be viewed as one of a variety of preventive interventions directed at reducing the probability of a sex offender committing a further offense. In the total context of social policies designed to prevent future sexual victimizations, therefore, sex-offender treatment programs are most sensibly evaluated in the same manner as incapacitation, special deterrence, community service, parole supervision, and other criminal justice interventions in terms of cost, efficacy, humaneness, and so forth. These various interventions, of course, are not usually incompatible with each other.

Actuarial Assessment and Treatment

The dimensional nature of risk scores can serve to direct the apportionment of treatment and supervisory resources. With respect to reducing the likelihood of recidivism, resources should be concentrated on higher-risk offenders. However, current actuarial models are historical in nature, the predictors included in them cannot change or are unlikely to change quickly. In particular, they cannot be made to change through active intervention. Although this is an unhappy situation for offenders who are assessed to be of high risk, most offenders are of moderate to low risk. It is likely that the most important consequence of using actuarial models is the identification of offenders who are low risk and require little, if any, intervention to reduce their risk.

Treatment can be focused on mental health needs, the likelihood of recidivism, or both. Although treatments designed to reduce general recidivism by addressing criminogenic needs among high-risk offenders have been shown to be modestly successful (Andrews, Zinger, Hoge, Bonta, Gendreau, and Cullen, 1990; Lipsey, 1992), the efficacy of treatments addressing mental health needs and any form of treatment for reducing the likelihood of violent or sexual crimes among serious adult offenders has not yet been demonstrated convincingly because of variability in outcome studies, methodological shortcomings, and few data (Quinsey, Rice, Harris, and Lalumiere, 1993).

Before discussing what characteristics sex-offender treatment programs should have and how these programs should be coordinated with other societal interventions, it may be helpful first to consider in more detail what we do and do not know about the efficacy of treatment programs for sex offenders. Broadly speaking, sex offender treatment programs employ three approaches: (a) pharmacological, in which the goal is to reduce sexual arousability and the frequency of deviant sexual fantasies through the use of anti-androgens (for example, Bradford, 1990; Berlin and Meinecke, 1981); (b) psychotherapeutic or evocative in which the goals include increasing offender empathy for the victims of sexual assault together with their sense of responsibility for their sexual crimes (for example, Frisbie and Dondis, 1965), and (c) cognitive-behavioral, where the object is to remedy skill deficits, alter cognitions that are believed to be related to sexual offending, and alter deviant patterns of sexual arousal or preference (for example, Abel et al., 1984; Griffiths, Quinsey, and Hingsburger, 1989; Marshall, Earls, Segal, and Drake, 1983; Quinsey, Chaplin, Maguire, and Upfold, 1987). These approaches are not mutually exclusive, and the trend has been in recent years for treatment programs to employ all three approaches to varying degrees.

In addition, many programs also employ a cognitive-behavioral relapse-prevention orientation borrowed from the substance abuse area in which the focus is on eliminating idiosyncratically defined precursors of relapse and teaching the offender more effective ways of coping with these precursors in an extensive period of follow-up supervision (Laws, 1989; Pithers, 1990; Pithers et al., 1988).

There is a substantial literature on all of these forms of sex offender treatment. Surveys of North American treatment programs can be found in Borzeck and Wormith (1987) and Knopp (1984). A *National Inventory of Treatment Programs for Child Sexual Abuse Offenders* has been prepared by the Canadian Child Welfare Association (1989). Reviews of the literature on the efficacy of treatment can be found in Bradford (1990), Dixen and Jenkins (1981), Kelly (1982), Langevin (1983), Marshall and Barbaree (1990), Quinsey (1973; 1977), Quinsey and Earls (1990), and Quinsey and Marshall (1983).

Relative to the number of sex offenders who are treated each year and the number of articles and books written about sex offender treatment, the evaluative outcome literature is astonishingly small. One is tempted to conclude that there are more authors with published opinions on the effectiveness of sex offender treatment than sex offenders in treatment outcome studies. With respect to evaluating the ultimate effect of treatment efforts directed toward reducing the recidivism rates of sexual offenders such as rapists and child molesters, there have been no experimental comparisons of different treatment approaches, almost no comparisons of treated and untreated sex offenders involving random assignment, and very few quasi-experimental studies that compare treated and untreated sex offenders, even without random assignment.

Variations in recidivism rates associated with different treatment programs are extremely hazardous to interpret. Differences among recidivism rates across studies are confounded with legal jurisdiction, cohort effects, duration of followup, offender characteristics, differential client attrition rates, differences in program integrity and amount of treatment, amount and quality of post-treatment supervision, and a host of other variables. In addition, recidivism measures tend to be noisy and result in comparisons of low statistical power. Even without attempting to attribute variations in recidivism to treatment program characteristics, the variation in recidivism rates in the published literature is truly remarkable (for reviews *see* Furby, Weinrott, and Blackshaw, 1989; Quinsey, 1984; 1986).

Although there have been no comparisons of different treatment approaches within the same study using random assignment of offenders to treatment conditions, there have been some recent treatment versus no treatment comparisons using matched designs or convenience samples and one comparison of a treatment with a no treatment control using random assignment. Unfortunately, the evidence from these studies is mixed.

Marshall and Barbaree (1988) obtained large differences in recidivism rates, as estimated by official police records and unofficial records of police and child protective agencies, between child molesters given cognitive-behavioral treatment in a community clinic and similar, but not randomly assigned clients given no treatment. Recidivism rates over approximately four years were 43 and 18 percent for untreated and treated extrafamilial heterosexual child molesters, respectively; 43 and 13 percent for extrafamilial homosexual child molesters, and 22 and 8 percent for untreated and treated heterosexual incestuous child molesters.

Quite different results were obtained by Rice, Quinsey, and Harris (1991), who determined the recidivism rates over an average 6.3 year followup period of 136 extrafamilial child molesters who had received phallometric assessment in a maximum security psychiatric institution from 1972 to 1983. Fifty of these offenders had participated in a behavioral program designed to alter inappropriate sexual age preferences, and some had received social skill and sex education programs as well (Quinsey, Chaplin, Maguire, and Upfold, 1987). Thirty-one percent of the subjects were convicted of a new sexual offense, 43 percent of the total were known to have committed a violent or sexual offense, and 58 percent were arrested for any offense or returned to the maximum-security institution. Behavioral laboratory treatment did not affect recidivism. Similar negative results were reported by Hanson, Steffy, and Gauthier (1993) in a retrospective evaluation of a treatment program for incarcerated child molesters involving milieu therapy, counseling, and modification of sexual preferences.

The difference in outcomes among the quasi-experimental treatment evaluations just reported illustrates the difficulties in arriving at definitive conclusions concerning treatment efficacy. Among the more important of the myriad of differences between these studies are the locus of the program (maximum-security psychiatric facility versus the community), severity of the offense history of the clients/patients treated in the program, differences in amount of client self-selection (including differential attrition), and differences in the amount of treatment received. Any or all of these or other confounded variables could be responsible for the markedly different results. Perhaps the strongest conclusion that one can draw from this literature is that the aspects of treatment, client population, supervision, and setting characteristics related to successful outcome are at present unknown.

Marques, Day, Nelson, and West (1994) have reported preliminary data from the most ambitious evaluation of sex-offender treatment yet undertaken. This prospective follow-up study involves the random assignment of offenders to a cognitive-behavioral treatment program or a nontreatment condition. Specifically, there are three groups in the study matched on age, criminal history, and offense type: ninety-eight treated offenders, ninety-seven men who volunteered but were not (randomly) selected for treatment, ninety-six men who refused treatment, and eight men who voluntarily withdrew or whose participation were terminated early in treatment.

Subjects were at risk for an average of thirty-four months. During this period 8.2 percent of the treated offenders, 13.4 percent of the untreated volunteers, 12.5 percent of the treatment refusers, and 37.5 percent of the early terminators committed a new sexual offense. These preliminary data indicate that a small treatment effect may be found with more subjects, and that noncompliance or withdrawal from treatment is a poor prognostic sign.

The status of the treatment outcome literature explains why treatment variables, such as exposure to a particular treatment or the outcome of a particular treatment, are not yet included in any actuarial model. Clearly, additional treatment program evaluation is the most pressing need in this area. The major implication of this observation is that progress in treatment must be interpreted very cautiously when assessing risk.

Supervision

Dangerousness appears to be inversely related to the quality and intensity of supervision. Some predictors also are relevant to supervision. Criminal versatility, one of the items on the Revised Psychopathy Checklist, refers to the variety of different kinds of criminal acts that an individual has committed. Criminally versatile offenders are more difficult to supervise than others because there are more potential types of crimes about which a supervisor should worry. The quintessential example of a nonversatile offender is an incestuous child molester who has molested his daughter and committed no other crimes. Supervision for this person ordinarily would be relatively simple because it involves only his access to his daughter.

Dynamic predictors can also be monitored postrelease to good advantage (Motiuk and Porporino, 1989; Quinsey and Walker, 1992). Unstable living conditions, noncompliance with medication or supervision, increased drinking, negative affect, and procriminal attitudes are all variables that are related to recidivism or relapse. These postrelease predictors can be used to titrate the amount of supervision an offender receives.

Developing Programs for Sex Offenders

Programs for sex offenders have to be developed in the context of imperfect but increasing knowledge. Currently, more is known about the characteristics of sex offenders than about the efficacy of treatment interventions or the etiology of sex offending. This conclusion has far reaching implications for the strategy of program development that should be adopted.

The first implication is that there is no identifiable "gold standard" treatment that could be adopted for use without further evaluation. There are interventions that have been shown to produce changes in theoretically relevant measures (such as social skills). However, there is no evidence that improvements in these measures are related to reduced recidivism. In the case of phallometric measurements of sexual preference, for example, it appears that treatment changes the relationship between phallometric measurement and recidivism; pre-treatment but post-treatment phallometric measures of sexual preference do not predict recidivism (for example, Rice, Quinsey, and Harris, 1991).

To say that treatments have not been evaluated convincingly, however, is neither to say that they do not work nor to assert that different approaches to treatment are of equivalent efficacy. In this author's view, the best option in these circumstances of relative ignorance is to adopt treatments that: (a) fit with what is known about the treatment of offenders in general; (b) have a convincing theoretical rationale in that they are motivated by what we know about the characteristics of sex offenders; (c) have been demonstrated to produce proximal changes in theoretically relevant measures; (d) are feasible in terms of acceptability to offenders and clinicians, cost, and ethical standards; (e) are described in sufficient detail that program integrity can be measured; and (f) can be integrated into existing supervisory procedures.

The second implication of this conclusion is that the treatment of sex offenders has to be viewed not simply as a matter of providing service to offenders and protecting the public but as a matter of program development. The key to successful program development is to design interventions in such a way that their evaluation tests the theory upon which they are based. Such a strategy is called "Program Development Evaluation" (Gottfredson, 1984).

Treatment of Offenders

Because sex offenders are by definition criminal offenders, it is reasonable to expect that principles of treatment that apply to offenders in general also apply to sex offenders. The support for a cognitive-behavioral approach to offender treatment in general is based on a much stronger and more extensive literature than for cognitive-behavioral approaches to sex-offender treatment. This more general literature, however, indirectly supports the cognitive-behavioral treatment of sex offenders.

The principles of offender treatment have perhaps been best conceptualized by Andrews (1980; 1982; Andrews et al., 1986; Gendreau and Andrews, in press) in terms of risk, need, and responsivity. Basically, Andrews and his colleagues argue that offender treatment is most effective when targeted at the criminogenic needs of high-risk cases; a similar argument, in the context of managing violent offenders, has been advanced by Quinsey and Walker (1992).

It is equally clear from the general literature on offender treatment that evocative, insight-oriented, nondirective, or milieu approaches either have been ineffective or have raised recidivism rates (Andrews, 1982; Gendreau and Andrews, 1990). In particular, an evaluation of the Social Therapy Unit milieu therapy program at Oak Ridge found very high post-release rates of violent recidivism among patients (including a substantial proportion of sex offenders) treated in this confrontational patient-led program. The rate of violent recidivism among psychopathic patients (defined by Hare's Psychopathy Checklist) was higher than that of similarly psychopathic offenders sent to prison (Harris, Rice, and Cormier, 1991; Rice, Harris, and Cormier, 1992). This program is important because it involved serious offenders and was implemented with great intensity and integrity. These findings raise very serious concerns about programs for psychopathic sex offenders that rely on these techniques.

Programs that foster anticriminal attitudes among inmates through exposure to anticriminal models do appear to be helpful. In speaking of the effectiveness of correctional and parole officers, Andrews (1982) puts it this way: ". . . attributes of the officer which are relevant to the supervision of offenders include a positive socio-emotional orientation (the relationship principle) in combination with the ability to establish anticriminal contingencies (the contingency principle)." Problem-solving and self-management skill acquisition appear to be helpful to inmates in learning to cope with problems without resorting to (or drifting toward) crime (Zamble and Porporino, 1988).

The implications of these conclusions from the literature on offender treatment can be applied to sex offender treatment programs that have not received evaluative attention. In fact, they must be applied because there is no other relevant information available to judge the appropriateness of an unevaluated program's rationale and practices.

Based upon the correctional treatment literature, characteristics of programs that have some hope of success in reducing recidivism include: a skill-based training approach; the modeling of prosocial behaviors and attitudes; a directive but nonpunitive orientation; a focus on modifying antecedents to criminal behavior; and a supervised community component to assess and teach the offender relevant skills.

Characteristics of programs that are likely to be ineffective or associated with increased recidivism include: confrontation without skill building; a nondirective approach; a punitive orientation; a focus on irrelevant (noncriminogenic) factors (for example, building an offender's self-esteem without modifying his procriminal attitudes); and the use of highly sophisticated verbal therapies, such as insight-oriented psychotherapy.

These observations on the characteristics of effective and ineffective programs for offenders, in general, are relevant to the characteristics of unevaluated programs for sex offenders, such as self-help groups. Of course, one cannot say whether these programs will be successful in reducing recidivism because they have not received evaluative attention in the form of comparative follow-up studies.

From the earlier discussion, however, we can make some educated guesses about whether self-help programs are likely to be successful. First, the issue is not limited to who provides the intervention (clinicians or offenders) but includes all of the other program characteristics. The characteristics of successful programs directed by clinicians are likely to be similar to the characteristics of successful programs operated by offenders. There are three exceptions, however. First, offender-led programs cannot effectively use authority. Authority is, of course, sometimes clinically indicated and sometimes indicated for reasons of public safety. Second, self-help groups do not contain the technical expertise for certain forms of assessment and treatment. Third, self-help or offender-led groups are much more likely than clinicians to be able to change the climate of institutional opinion in a pro-therapeutic direction and to provide ongoing support for offenders attempting to change.

The success of self-help groups depends upon the rationale and organization of the actual program. Self-help groups should not be seen as a substitute for more conventional treatment; indeed, one of the reasons for their development has been the limited availability of other sex-offender programs. Self-help groups would benefit from input from clinical staff and should be coordinated with other programs (the worst scenario would be that self-help and staff-led sex offender programs worked at cross purposes). It is obvious, on the other side of this issue, that sex offender programs of whatever kind cannot be successful unless they have meaningful input from offender clients.

Theoretical Rationale

The probability and type of recidivism is strongly affected by victim age, sex, and relationship to the offender, the seriousness and nature of the sex offense, and the number of previous sex offenses. Because sex offenders are heterogeneous even within categories defined by offense history, a focus of current research is to develop more differentiated taxonomies of sex offenders (Knight and Prentky, 1990). Because of this heterogeneity, sex-offender treatment programs should be organized to take account of these differences.

Perhaps the most important of these differences and the most relevant for the design of individual treatment programs, is the nature of the offender's sexual preferences. Some offenders have marked paraphilic (sexually deviant) interests in children, sadistic sexual assault, and so forth. These sexual preferences can be measured with varying degrees of adequacy by offender self-report, offense history, or phallometric assessment. The measurement of these interests is important because it provides clues to the motivation underlying the offense, an idea as to the nature of possible future acts of sexual aggression, and a focus for a treatment intervention. Although phallometric measurement is usually the most accurate method of measuring sexual preferences, it is more useful in a treatment as opposed to a release-decision context. Phallometric assessment data can be faked and is more likely to yield misleading results when offenders are highly motivated to appear to have normal sexual preferences. With respect to phallometric data gathered before and after treatment, therefore, continued evidence of inappropriate sexual preferences is a bad prognostic sign but a reduction in such interest is not necessarily a good sign.

Other offender characteristics are related to the probability of treatment success and the design of individual programs. Alcohol abuse is a common problem among sex offenders, as it is among offenders more generally. Such problems can, if not effectively addressed, undermine treatment effectiveness by reducing offender compliance and self control.

The limitations of current treatment technology also interact with individual differences among offenders. Variations in the seriousness of offense history are among the most important of these. In view of the limitations of current treatment technology, it cannot be expected that very serious sexual offenders, such as serial murderers, will or should be viewed as less of a risk as a result of progress in a treatment program.

This brief description of offender characteristics, although incomplete, suggests an individualized treatment planning process that uses the results of a variety of standardized assessments to formulate a theory of offender motivation from which the practitioner can choose a combination of specific interventions designed to prevent recidivism. Thus, for an individual offender, any or all of a variety of interventions, such as treatments designed to reduce sexual arousability, modify inappropriate sexual preferences, control drinking, improve assertive or heterosocial skills, secure employment, prevent depression, and so forth might be appropriate. Quinsey and Earls (1990) have explicated this approach in more detail.

This approach is consistent with what is usually described as a behavioral, cognitive-behavioral, or, more broadly, a social-learning based treatment model. At present, this model is, with the exception of antiandrogenic medication or castration, the only approach that enjoys any evidence of effectiveness in reducing sexual recidivism.

Acceptability to Clinicians

The cognitive-behavioral model is currently the most widely accepted by clinicians working with nonincestuous sex offenders in North America. This wide acceptance of a cognitive behavioral approach among clinicians has important implications. First, it means that it is easier for additional clinicians to be trained in its use than in other therapies because of the variety of sites where such programs are in operation. Second, these programs have been in existence long enough for several of them to have developed treatment program manuals (for example, Abel et al., 1984).

Although sex-offender treatment programs are common, and most clinicians believe that at least some sex offender treatment must occur in the community, there is a reluctance on the part of community residential facilities to accept sex offenders. This reluctance must be dealt with on several levels: by the development of supervisory policies that address safety issues, by educating the public and the people responsible for these facilities, and by arranging financial contingencies.

Acceptability to Offenders

Although sex offenders generally prefer individual treatment or counseling (Langevin, Wright, and Handy, 1988), individual treatment is characteristic of a setting rather than a specific intervention. Cognitive-behavioral interventions typically employ both group and individual treatments and are acceptable to a substantial proportion of sex offenders. Antiandrogen medication is rejected as a treatment modality by a larger proportion of sex offenders (Hucker, Langevin, and Bain, 1988; Langevin, Wright, and Handy, 1988; Langevin, et al., 1979), although there are certainly enough who comply with this form of treatment to make its use feasible.

Developmentally handicapped sex offenders have been shown to respond well to a cognitive-behavioral approach if it is tailored to their particular needs (Griffiths, Quinsey, and Hingsburger, 1989). Programs for these offenders require greater attention to informed consent issues but these can be overcome, particularly with the help of advocacy organizations.

Of course, sex offenders, as a group, are not distinguished by their enthusiasm for treatment, regardless of the form it takes. Motivating sex offenders to enter and persist in treatment is an important aspect of any treatment program and, as noted, treatment dropouts appear to have high recidivism rates (Marques et al., 1994). Pretreatment identification of treatable problems in a group context has proven useful in encouraging sex offenders to enter treatment (for example, Quinsey et al., 1987).

Supervision

The literature suggests, and most practitioners have come to believe, that sex offender treatment programs must involve community follow-up because that is where offenders must learn to control their behavior. The institutional adjustment of sex offenders, unfortunately, is unrelated to the probability of their committing a sex offense in the community. Obviously, such community treatment involves ongoing supervision. Supervision might be facilitated profitably, in high-risk cases, through the use of antiandrogenic drugs and electronic surveillance. In any event, community treatment, as a follow-up to institutional programs or as a program in itself, involves teaching sex offenders to avoid high-risk situations and acquire skills for coping with such situations when they occur. A high priority for the continuing development of such community programs is the detailed study of the circumstances surrounding supervisory failure.

Both supervision and treatment must be concentrated on sex offenders who present the greatest danger to the public in terms of the probability of their committing a new offense and its likely seriousness. Such high-risk cases are those best suited for intensive supervision and supervised community living situations. It is vital that these offenders not be released from medium- or maximum-security institutions directly to the community.

Conclusions

Because of the relatively greater empirical support for the efficacy of the cognitive-behavioral approach to the treatment of sex offenders (particularly in proximal-outcome evaluations); the preponderance of treatment programs employing this approach; the existence of detailed treatment manuals; the relatively short-term nature of these interventions; their compatibility with intensive supervision, antiandrogenic medication, and a relapse-prevention strategy; and the support for cognitive-behavioral treatments of offenders, more generally, cognitive-behavioral treatment strategies for sex offenders have no serious rivals.

There are, however, serious limitations and reservations concerning the cognitive-behavioral treatment of sex offenders. The follow-up literature is extremely weak; reductions in recidivism among more serious offenders have not yet been convincingly demonstrated. Cognitive-behavioral programs vary in the intensity, duration, and many of the details of their treatments. It is simply not known which, if any, of these differences are associated with greater efficacy, although there is a growing consensus that sex offender programs should be focused on the community adjustment of sex offenders.

References

Abel, G. G., et al. 1984. *The Treatment of Child Molesters.* (Available from SBC-TM, 722 W. 168th St., Box 17, New York, New York 10032).

Andrews, D. A. 1980. Some Experimental Investigations of the Prin-ciples of Differential Association Through Deliberate Manipulation of the Structure of Service Systems. *American Sociological Review.* 45:448-462.

———. 1982. *The Supervision of Offenders: Identifying and Gaining Control over the Factors Which Make a Difference.* Report to the Solicitor General of Canada.

———. 1989. Recidivism Is Predictable and Can Be Influenced: Using Risk Assessments to Reduce Recidivism. *Forum on Corrections Research.* 1:11-18.

Andrews, D. A. et al. 1986. The Construct Validity of Interview-based Risk Assessment in Corrections. *Canadian Journal of Behavioural Science.* 18:460-470.

Andrews, D. A., J. J. Kiessling, and S. Kominos. 1983. *The Level of Supervision Inventory (LSI-6): Interview and Scoring Guide.* Toronto: Ontario Ministry of Correctional Services.

Andrews, D. A., J. J. Kiessling, S. Mickus, and D. Robinson. 1986. The Construct Validity of Interview-based Risk Assessment in Corrections. *Canadian Journal of Behavioural Science.* 18:460-470.

Andrews, D. A., J. J. Kiessling, D. Robinson, and S. Mickus. 1986. The Risk Principle of Case Classification: An Outcome Evaluation with Young Adult Probationers. *Canadian Journal of Criminology.* 28:377-384.

Andrews, D. A., I. Zinger, R. D. Hoge, J. Bonta, P. Gendreau, and F. T. Cullen. 1990. Does Correctional Treatment Work? A Clinically Relevant and Psychologically Informed Meta-analysis. *Criminology.* 28:369-404.

Barbaree, H. E. and W. L. Marshall. 1988. Deviant Sexual Arousal, Offense History, and Demographic Variables as Predictors of Reoffense among Child Molesters. *Behavioral Sciences and the Law.* 6:267-280.

Berlin, F. S. and C. F. Meinecke. 1981. Treatment of Sex Offenders with Antiandrogenic Medication: Conceptualization, Review of Treatment Modalities, and Preliminary Findings. *American Journal of Psychiatry.* 138:601-607.

Borzeck, M. and J. S. Wormith. 1987. A Survey of Treatment Programmes for Sex Offenders in North America. *Canadian Psychology.* 28:30-44.

Bradford, J. M. W. 1990. The Antiandrogen and Hormonal Treatment of Sex Offenders. In W. L. Marshall, D. R. Laws, and H. E. Barbaree, eds. *Handbook of Sexual Assault: Issues, Theories, and Treatment of the Offender.* New York: Plenum.

Canadian Child Welfare Association. 1989. *National Inventory of Treatment Programs for Child Sexual Abuse Offenders.* Ottawa: National Clearinghouse on Family Violence, Health and Welfare.

Cannon, C. K. and V. L. Quinsey. (in press). The Likelihood of Violent Behavior: Predictions, Postdictions, and Hindsight Bias. *Canadian Journal of Behavioural Science.*

Dixen, J. and J. O. Jenkins. 1981. Incestuous Child Abuse: a Review of Treatment Strategies. *Clinical Psychology Review.* 1:211-222.

Frisbie, L. V. and E. H. Dondis. 1965. *Recidivism among Treated Sex Offenders.* California Mental Health Research Monographs, No. 5. State of California Department of Mental Hygiene.

Furby, L., M. R. Weinrott, and L. Blackshaw. 1989. Sex Offender Recidivism: A Review. *Psychological Bulletin.* 105:3-30.

Gendreau, P. and D. A. Andrews. 1990. Tertiary Prevention: What the Meta-analysis of the Offender Treatment Literature Tells Us about "What Works." *Canadian Journal of Criminology.* 32:173-184.

Gottfredson, G. D. 1984. A Theory-ridden Approach to Program Evaluation: a Method for Stimulating Research-implementer Collaboration. *American Psychologist.* 39:1101-1112.

Griffiths, D. M., V. L. Quinsey, and D. Hingsburger. 1989. *Changing Inappropriate Sexual Behavior: A Community-based Approach for Persons with Developmental Disabilities.* Toronto: Brookes.

Hanson, R. K., R. A. Steffy, and R. Gauthier. 1993. Long-term Recidivism of Child Molesters. *Journal of Consulting and Clinical Psychology.* 61:646-652.

Hare, R. D. 1991. *Manual for the Revised Psychopathy Checklist.* Toronto: Multi-Health Systems.

Hare, R. D. et al. 1990. The Revised Psychopathy Checklist: Reliability and Factor Structure. *Psychological Assessment: A Journal of Consulting and Clinical Psychology.* 2:1-4.

Hare, R. D. and L. M. McPherson. 1984. Violent and Aggressive Behavior by Criminal Psychopaths. *International Journal of Law and Psychiatry.* 7:35-50.

Harris, G. T., M. E. Rice, and C. A. Cormier. 1991. Psychopathy and Violent Recidivism. *Law and Human Behavior.* 15:625-632.

Harris, G. T., M. E. Rice, and V. L. Quinsey. 1993. Violent Recidivism of Mentally Disordered Offenders: The Development of a Statistical Prediction Instrument. *Criminal Justice and Behavior.* 20:315-335.

Hart, S. D., P. R. Kropp, and R. D. Hare. 1988. Performance of Male Psychopaths Following Conditional Release from Prison. *Journal of Consulting and Clinical Psychology.* 56:227-232.

Hucker, S., R. Langevin, and J. Bain. 1988. A Double Blind Trial of Sex Drive Reducing Medication in Pedophiles. *Annals of Sex Research.* 1:227-242.

Kelly, R. J. 1982. Behavioral Reorientation of Pedophiliacs: Can it Be Done? *Clinical Psychology Review.* 2:387-408.

Knight, R. A. and R. A. Prentky. 1990. Classifying Sexual Offenders: The Development and Corroboration of Taxonomic Models. In W. L. Marshall, D. R. Laws, and H. E. Barbaree, eds. *The Handbook of Sexual Assault: Issues, Theories, and Treatment of the Offender.* New York: Plenum.

Knopp, F. H. 1984. *Retraining Adult Sex Offenders: Methods and Models.* Syracuse, New York: Safer Society Press.

Langevin, R. 1983. *Sexual Strands: Understanding and Treating Sexual Anomalies in Men.* Hillsdale, New Jersey: Erlbaum.

Langevin, R., et al. 1979. The Effectiveness of Assertiveness Training, Provera and Sex of Therapist in the Treatment of Genital Exhibitionism. *Journal of Behavior Therapy and Experimental Psychiatry.* 10:275-282.

Langevin, R., P. Wright, and L. Handy. 1988. What Treatment Do Sex Offenders Want? *Annals of Sex Research.* 1:363-385.

Laws, D. R., ed. 1989. *Relapse Prevention with Sex Offenders.* New York: Guilford Press.

Lipsey, M. W. 1992. Juvenile Delinquency Treatment: A Meta-analytic Inquiry into the Variability of Effects. In T. D. Cook et al., eds. *Meta-analysis for Explanation: A Casebook.* New York: Russell Sage Foundation.

Marques, J. K., D. M. Day, C. Nelson, and M. A. West. 1994. Effects of Cognitive-behavioral Treatment on Sex Offender Recidivism: Preliminary Results of a Longitudinal Study. *Criminal Justice and Behavior.* 21:28-54.

Marshall, W. L., C. M. Earls, Z. Segal, and J. Darke. 1983. A Behavioral Program for the Assessment and Treatment of Sexual Aggressors. In K. D. Craig and R. J. McMahon, eds. *Advances in Clinical Behavior Therapy.* New Yord: Brunner Mazel.

Motiuk, L. L. and F. J. Porporino. 1989. *Offender Risk/needs Assessment: A Study of Conditional Releases.* Ottawa: Solicitor General of Canada.

Nuffield, J. 1982. *Parole Decision-making in Canada: Research Towards Decision Guidelines.* Ottawa: Supply and Services Canada.

Pithers, W. D. 1990. Relapse Prevention with Sexual Aggressors: A Method for Maintaining Therapeutic Gain and Enhancing External Supervision. In W. L. Marshall, D. R. Laws, and H. E. Barbaree, eds. *Handbook of Sexual Assault: Issues, Theories, and Treatment of the Offender.* New York: Plenum.

Pithers, W. D., K. M. Kashima, G. F. Cumming, L. S. Beal, and M. M. Buell. 1988. Relapse Prevention of Sexual Aggression. In R. A. Prentky and V. L. Quinsey. Eds. *Human Sexual Aggression: Current Perspectives*. New York: New York Academy of Sciences.

Quinsey, V. L., ed. 1973. Methodological Issues in Evaluating the Effectiveness of Aversion Therapies for Institutionalized Child Molesters. *The Canadian Psychologist*. 14:350-361.

———. 1977. The Assessment and Treatment of Child Molesters: A Review. *Canadian Psychological Review*. 18:204-220.

———. 1980. The Base Rate Problem and the Prediction of Dangerousness: A Reappraisal. *Journal of Psychiatry and Law*. 8:329-340.

———. 1984. Sexual Aggression: Studies of Offenders Against Women. In D. Weisstub, ed. *Law and Mental Health: International Perspectives*. New York: Pergamon.

———. 1986. Men Who Have Sex with Children. In D. N. Weisstub, ed. *Law and Mental Health: International Perspectives*. New York: Pergamon.

Quinsey, V. L. and R. Ambtman. 1979. Variables Affecting Psychiatrists' and Teachers' Assessments of the Dangerousness of Mentally Ill Offenders. *Journal of Consulting and Clinical Psychology*. 47:353-362.

Quinsey, V. L. and T. C. Chaplin. 1988. Preventing Faking in Phallometric Assessments of Sexual Preference. In R. A Prentky and V. L. Quinsey, eds. *Human Sexual Aggression: Current Perspectives*. New York: New York Academy of Sciences.

Quinsey, V. L., T. C. Chaplin, A. M. Maguire, and D. Upfold. 1987. The Behavioral Treatment of Rapists and Child Molesters. In E. K. Morris and C. J. Braukmann, eds. *Behavioral Approaches to Crime and Delinquency: Application, Research, and Theory*. New York: Plenum.

Quinsey, V. L. and C. M. Earls. 1990. The Modification of Sexual Preferences. In W. L. Marshall, D. R. Laws, and H. E. Barbaree, eds. *The Handbook of Sexual Assault: Issues, Theories, and Treatment of the Offender*. New York: Plenum.

Quinsey, V. L. and D. R. Laws. 1990. Validity of Physiological Measures of Pedophilic Sexual Arousal in a Sexual Offender Population: A Critique of Hall, Proctor, and Nelson. *Journal of Consulting and Clinical Psychology*. 58.

Quinsey, V. L. and A. M. Maguire. 1986. Maximum Security Psychiatric Patients: Actuarial and Clinical Prediction of Dangerousness. *Journal of Interpersonal Violence*. 1:143-171.

Quinsey, V. L. and W. L. Marshall. 1983. Procedures for Reducing Inappropriate Sexual Arousal: An Evaluation Review. In J. G. Greer and I. R. Stuart, eds. *The Sexual Aggressor: Current Perspectives on Treatment.* New York: Van Nostrand Reinhold.

Quinsey, V. L., M. E. Rice, and G. T. Harris. (in press). Actuarial Prediction of Sexual Recidivism. *Journal of Interpersonal Violence.*

Quinsey, V. L., M. E. Rice, G. T. Harris, and M. L. Lalumiere. 1993. Assessing Treatment Efficacy in Outcome Studies of Sex Offenders. *Journal of Interpersonal Violence*. 8:512-523.

Quinsey, V. L. and W. D. Walker. 1992. Dealing with Dangerousness: Community Risk Management Strategies with Violent Offenders. In R. Peters, K. D. Craig, and V. L. Quinsey, eds. *Aggression and Violence Throughout the Lifespan.* Newbury Park, California: Sage.

Rice, M. E., G. T. Harris, and C. A. Cormier. 1992. An Evaluation of a Maximum Security Therapeutic Community for Psychopaths and Other Mentally Disordered Offenders. *Law and Human Behavior.* 16:399-412.

Rice, M. E., V. L. Quinsey, and G. T. Harris. 1991. Sexual Recidivism among Child Molesters Released from a Maximum Security Psychiatric Institution. *Journal of Consulting and Clinical Psychology.* 59:381-386.

Villeneuve, D. B. and V. L. Quinsey. (in press). Predictors of General and Violent Recidivism among Mentally Disordered Inmates. *Criminal Justice and Behavior.*

Webster, C. D., G. T. Harris, M. E. Rice, C. A. Cormier, and V. L. Quinsey. 1994. *The Violence Prediction Scheme: Assessing Dangerousness in High Risk Men.* Toronto: Centre of Criminology, University of Toronto.

Zamble, E. and F. J. Porporino. 1988. *Coping, Behavior, and Adaptation in Prison Inmates.* New York: Springer-Verlag.

Offender Employment and Training Programs: A Review of the Research

9

Douglas C. McDonald, Ph.D. [1]

Abt Associates Inc.

Cambridge, Massachusetts

Introduction

As the numbers of persons under correctional supervision in this country grows, so grows the challenge of integrating them into the community as law-abiding and productive citizens. Unfortunately, while their numbers swell, changes in the national and world economies are making it increasingly harder for persons lacking education and skills to find gainful employment in this country. In earlier centuries, and throughout a good part of this one, there were many opportunities for the uneducated and

---

[1]All views expressed here are the author's and do not necessarily reflect the views or positions held by Abt Associates, Inc., or any other organization or persons. The author is indebted to David Rodda, a colleague at Abt Associates, for his review memorandum on selected employment and training programs, done with support from the National Institute of Justice.

unskilled in cities and in the countryside. As machines were applied to tasks once requiring muscle and sometimes a modicum of skill, and as jobs once performed here were replaced by factories abroad, work that provided a route to prosperity for millions of illiterate immigrants has dwindled. The result of these and other changes is that there now exist large numbers of the poor who have a tenuous place in this economy, who are caught up in a variety of different pathologies, and who cycle in and out of the criminal justice system.

This essay explores the employment problems facing offenders and those institutions dedicated to getting them into the labor force. The first section examines briefly their employment and earnings; the second, the handicaps that offenders bring to the job market. The third describes briefly the development of offender employment and training programs during the past thirty years. The fourth section assesses the research on the first wave of offender and ex-offender programs, begun in the 1960s and 1970s, and the conclusions that we can draw from that research. Next, we examine a second wave of offender programs and evaluations of them, carried out in the 1980s, which were characterized by stronger research designs. The discussion then turns to an examination of more recent evaluations of employment and training programs designed not for offenders and ex-offenders specifically, but for various types of disadvantaged persons (which sometimes includes persons with criminal histories). We then consider why the research on employment and training programs has found so few program successes. Attention is given there to the larger socioeconomic dynamics in the economy and in the labor force. Finally, the paper ends with some suggestions for program managers who seek to provide effective employment and training programs for offenders.

This essay is limited to programs for adults, including young adults. Programs for juveniles who would not be in the adult criminal justice system are ignored; the principal objective for juveniles should not be to get them into jobs and careers. Moreover, the programs examined here are for persons who are under legal supervision in the community or who have been released from prisons or jails, even if they are not on probation or parole. Rather than distinguish between "offenders" and "ex-offenders," they are termed "offenders" here, regardless of their current legal status.

The Employment Plight of Offenders

The situation of most offenders, with respect to current employment and earnings and future prospects, is generally a dire one. Many are unemployed for large parts of the year, and most who do have jobs barely make enough to get them and their families out of poverty. The work they do tends to be concentrated in dead-end jobs with little stability and few or no benefits. Periods of employment are punctuated by spells of unemployment.

A 1986 survey of state correctional facilities—the most recent undertaken—found that most offenders (69 percent) reported being employed at the time of the arrest that led to their incarceration. Fifty-seven percent were employed full-time. Most were in low-wage jobs, however. Of those who were free for at least a year prior to arrest, 60 percent reported annual incomes of less than $10,000; a quarter of them reported making less than $3,000 a year (Innes 1988:2). A survey of jail inmates three years earlier reports similar findings. Fifty-three percent of all surveyed inmates were employed at the time of arrest. Among those who had been free for a year or more, 70 percent earned less than $10,000; 33 percent less than $3,000 (Baunach 1985:3).

Nationwide data are not available for probation and parole populations, but similar conditions likely could be found among those as well. In his study of parolees released from Federal prisons during 1978-1979, Beck found that 25 percent were unemployed twelve months after release, which was four times the unemployment rate of the nation's labor force as a whole. Among those who were employed, many did not enjoy a spell of continuous full-time work: on average, they reported working about 184 days during that 12 months. Moreover, 50 percent earned $6,025 or less during the twelve months, indicating that at least half lived in poverty (1981:4).

If one can extrapolate from these figures to all persons under community supervision, and if we assume that their experience in the labor market is roughly the same now as it was a decade ago—perhaps a questionable assumption, it appears that substantial proportions of offenders are able to get a job of some kind, even full-time jobs. However, it is likely that many (the majority?) of those who get jobs are employed for short periods of time, followed by spells of unemployment, and they "churn" in and out of the job market—and perhaps criminality—as well.

Why offenders are concentrated in the low-wage end of the labor market, if employed at all, is a matter of some contention. In some measure, it is a consequence of their relatively meager stock of "human capital"—those resources that persons bring to the job market. To the extent that this explains offenders' marginal position, their place in the labor market can be enhanced by improving their "capital" by training and education.

However, their marginal position is also affected by the nature and distribution of employment opportunities—which is to say, the structure of the job market.

Some analysts argue that the U.S. labor market is segmented into at least two different submarkets (for example, Doeringer and Piore, 1975). The "primary" labor market consists of the better paid, steady, and preferred jobs, in which employees have job stability, advancement opportunities, and employment relationships governed by a more or less explicit system of industrial rules. In contrast, the "secondary" labor market consists of jobs that are low-paying, unstable, dead-end, and marked by frequent layoffs and discharges. A large proportion of employed offenders who have jobs work in this latter segment, which may account for the instability of their employment and their generally low earnings. It is likely that they are consigned to this part of the market not only because of their poor skills but also because they face institutional barriers that keep them out of the better jobs—licensing and bonding requirements, for example. To the extent that offenders' marginal positions are determined by the quality of available jobs, and by the barriers to entering the primary labor market, efforts to improve their position by enhancing their skills and human capital will have limited success.

Programs seeking to improve the employment prospects of offenders therefore face several distinct but related challenges: helping offenders to find employment, to find jobs that pay decent wages, to stay on the job, and upon losing their job to get employed again. This suggests that employment and training programs cannot simply focus on training or job-readiness services to assist offenders in finding a job. Just getting a job often is not sufficient to gain stability, and programs should not close their books once the offender is placed on somebody's payroll.

Offenders' Handicaps in the Job Market

Many offenders not only lack employable skills, but also have deficient educations, problems with drugs, alcohol, and mental illness, and have few domestic resources upon which to rely. Most lack even a high school diploma, having dropped out before they acquired basic skills. A 1986 survey of state prisoners found that 62 percent had less then twelve years of schooling (Innes, 1988:2). More recent data from Massachusetts tells an even worse story: 79 percent of all inmates in that state's prisons on the first day in 1993 failed to complete high school (White 1993).

Because success in the labor market and educational achievement are linked, having dropped out of school saddles offenders with a substantial handicap. Many offenders also lack employable skills—or, at least, skills that they can rely upon to earn more than minimum wage. Moreover, for many, their willingness to work also is undercut by what might be called the culture of nonwork: the shared sentiment that working long hours for low pay is for "chumps."

A large—and probably growing—proportion also have problems with drugs and alcohol that interfere with their ability to perform well on a job, day after day. Although it is impossible to determine how many of the 3 million offenders under parole and probation supervision at any one time are using drugs, assorted evidence suggests that the numbers are substantial. For example, a study by Wish, Cuadrano, and Martorana of an intensive supervision probation program in Brooklyn found a high rate of recent drug use (68 percent) among those tested (1987). Probation officials in Massachusetts estimate that approximately 70 percent of all probationers have "serious" substance abuse problems, including alcohol (Corbett, 1990). The director of probation in the District of Columbia similarly estimates that over 70 percent of his adult probationers are "drug-involved" (Schuman, 1990). The Maryland Division of Parole and Probation reported that clients already identified by special condition as needing substance abuse treatment services comprise an estimated 40 to 45 percent of all new cases each year. Georgia's Probation Division estimates that approximately 80 percent of its probation population has some involvement with abuse of alcohol and/or drugs (American Probation and Parole Association and National Association of Probation Executives, 1988:42, 31).

In the past two decades, the domestic lives of the poor also have deteriorated, so that many offenders have few or no resources at home to help them through hard times. Consequently, finding shelter is often a problem. Finally, a substantial number also suffer from some form of mental illness; estimates of those in prison who have some symptoms of mental illness range from between 6 to 8 percent to around a third of all prisoners, depending upon the criterion used to classify mental illness. We know of no such estimates for the populations of probationers and parolees.

The bottom line is that many offenders not only have an employment (or unemployment) problem, but, also, a number of other difficulties that handicap their ability to find and keep a job that pays well. Strengthening their ability to get and keep a job often requires enhancing their education and technical skills but also getting other difficulties under control.

Employment and Training Programs for Offenders and Ex-offenders

Government programs to bring ex-offenders into the labor market began in the early 1960s, with the passage of the Manpower Demonstration and Training Act of 1962 (MDTA) and its subsequent amendments, and the Economic Opportunity Act of 1964. For the purposes of our discussion here, three different waves of manpower programs and studies during the past three decades can be distinguished. The first included studies of programs for offenders that were largely funded by the Federal government following the passage of these two acts of Congress. These programs proliferated in the 1960s and 1970s. The second wave began in 1972 while first-wave programs that were still alive brought in stronger tests of programs. By the early 1980s, Federal support for offender employment and training programs ended, as did research attention to these programs. However, a third wave of studies began on employment and training programs targeted at disadvantaged populations more generally. Although they have been administered outside the criminal justice system, evaluations of these programs can tell us something about the effectiveness of different employment and training approaches for offenders.

The various manpower programs established and evaluated during these thirty years have pursued a number of different approaches to improving the employment prospects of offenders in the community. These have included on-the-job training; classroom vocational training; work experience—including subsidized (or "supported") work; various types of job development programs; job placement assistance; "employability development" programs, including coaching for interviews, pre-vocational training, counseling, and other efforts to make clients "job ready"; financial assistance and counseling; and comprehensive services, sometimes in sheltered residential environments.

Although these approaches differ in important ways, they generally share the objective of developing "human capital." That is, they have sought to improve clients rather than restructure the job market, by removing social, institutional, and political barriers to full participation.

The First Wave: Early Studies of Community-based Criminal Justice Manpower Programs

For approximately two decades following enactment in 1962 of the Federal MDTA, a stated aim of public policy was to bring criminal offenders into the legitimate labor force by means of skills training and other types of employment assistance. Hundreds of employment and training programs for offenders and ex-offenders were created for those in various stages of the criminal process. Several were prison programs, because the original MDTA legislation restricted Federal funding to such programs. Some were embedded in pretrial diversion programs, others in parole and probation settings.

Although studies of many of these programs claimed to find positive results in terms of employment and reduced criminality, many suffered from weak research designs. During the 1970s and early 1980s, five reviews of these accumulated studies were published, in which the authors evaluated and synthesized the various findings: Taggert (1972), Mullen et al. at Abt Associates (1974), Toborg et al. (1977) at the Lazar Institute, Rovner-Pieczenik (1973), at the now-defunct Criminal Justice Research, Inc., and Wilson, Lenihan, and Goolkasian (1981), who surveyed for the National Institute of Justice both the findings of prior research as well as the experience of seventy-five different programs, only some of which had been formally evaluated.

Analyzing studies of manpower programs in all criminal justice environments, Taggert generally drew negative conclusions, finding "no proof that any single manpower service has had more than a marginal impact on its recipients, and no proof that any combination of services can make a substantial contribution" (1972:96). Rovner-Pieczenik's review of diversion programs was more optimistic, even though she recognized that the weak research designs raised questions about the validity of the positive results reported by evaluators (1973). Mullen and her colleagues (1974) were less sanguine.

> At best, research efforts to date have indicated that if participation in a diversion alternative has an effect on recidivism, it is probably of limited duration and generally small magnitude. . . Although attempts have been made to measure the effects. . . there is very little evidence that the outcomes achieved would not have occurred in the absence of intervention (1974:36-38).

With the exception of a few studies conducted since then (discussed next), this conclusion remains essentially true today for offender employment and training programs generally.

> It is possible that many of the programs worked better than these reviewers thought, and that the real problem was with inadequate research studies. To be sure, our ability to draw strong conclusions from most of the evaluations is weakened by the existence of several shortcomings of research methods that are all too common.

First, many studies base their assessment of program success by comparing the postprogram performance of successful program graduates with the performance of those who dropped out of the program or who were not selected to participate. Because programs usually screen aggressively for good candidates, it is hard to know if the success of program participants reflects the impact of the program or the ability of the screeners to identify people who were most likely to succeed. Those who performed well after graduating from the program may have done so even if they had not participated in the program. Moreover, evaluations that compare successful completers with dropouts may be biased in favor of finding positive program effects. Unfortunately, evaluations based on comparisons of possibly nonequivalent groups are very common, not only in studies of employment and training programs but many other types of treatment programs as well.

Second, some studies compare the performance of participants before and after program participation, and conclude that any improvement is evidence that the program had a positive effect. This inference is unwarranted, because the observed improvement may have occurred in the absence of program participation. Some studies have reported finding improvements in earnings, for example, before and after program participation, but also have found equivalent improvements in otherwise similar populations who were not given employment services (*see* for example, Baker and Sadd, 1979; Bloom et al., 1994). This suggests that one should be very cautious in interpreting the meaning of changes in participants' earnings and employment status before and after program participation.

Moreover, it is difficult to know from what program failures resulted. Did they flow from a design flaw—mistaken assumptions about how to improve offenders' employability, or a poorly conceived program model? Did they result not from a flawed designed but from poor implementation of the designers' plans? Or did they fail because of general problems in the larger environment, such as a tight labor market? Unfortunately, we are left with a very limited understanding of which approaches in this first wave of offender employment and training programs worked, for whom, and for what reasons.

The Second Wave: Controlled Experimental Evaluations of Offender Programs

Recognizing the difficulties of evaluating these programs, funding agencies were persuaded that stronger research designs were needed, and a number of controlled experiments were undertaken. The earliest was the Vera Institute of Justice's evaluation of the Wildcat Services Corporation, a "supported work" program begun in 1972 for chronically unemployed ex-offenders and former heroin addicts (Friedman, 1978). The supported work model involved closely supervised employment on work crews consisting entirely of Wildcat employees; wages were subsidized; participants did real work but were sheltered from the full demands of the workplace; stress was gradually increased; and counseling was available after hours, if needed. The hope was that this experience of working at a (nearly) real job would accustom these hard-to-employ persons to the demands of the working world and to the discipline of full-time work. Moreover, supported work was explicitly designed as a form of training rather than as make-work employment. Participants were expected to find a job within a year and a half.

Vera researchers imposed an experimental design to test the program's efficacy on ex-addicts, and a random assignment procedure was followed to create two comparison groups: one of subjects admitted to Wildcat, the other of those not admitted. The performance of subjects in both groups was monitored for three years. Researchers found that program participation increased employment stability and earning capacity dramatically in the early years. This impact diminished over the three years, but remained significantly positive at the end of the three-year follow-up period. Participants also were arrested less often in the first year, but the difference had evaporated by the end of the third. No significant difference in drug or alcohol use was detected (Friedman, 1978).

Because of these positive findings, the supported work demonstration was expanded nationwide by the Manpower Demonstration Research Corporation (MDRC) to include other hard-core unemployed populations, but the results of the controlled experiment were generally disappointing. At the end of three years, no impact was found for ex-offenders or youths on their employment, earnings, or recidivism. For ex-heroin addicts, there were short-term differences in earnings, employment, welfare dependency—largely because of the stipend participants earned while in the program—and drug use, but at the end of three years, these differences disappeared (Manpower Demonstration Research Corporation, 1980). However, for certain types of ex-addicts, there was evidence that the program worked. Older offenders and those with families fared better with respect to employment, crime commission, and drug use. Perhaps they were better prepared to take advantage of the program (Piliavin and Gartner, 1981:xii).

Why did the Wildcat experiment appear to have a lasting effect on employment and earnings, while the MDRC experiment generally failed to do so? One is that MDRC was more insistent on cutting people out of the program after twelve or eighteen months, depending upon the site, while the Wildcat program was more permissive, continuing people in the program for longer periods if they were not able to find paying work. Because the supported work stipends were counted as earnings, this may have contributed to the positive results reported by the researchers. There were also some differences in the types of participants selected for the program. The research design used for the Wildcat experiment also may have introduced a bias in favor of the program. Another possible explanation is that the labor market was considerably healthier in the early 1970s—when Wildcat was begun—compared with the mid- to late-1970s, when the MDRC subjects were being evaluated.

The Vera Institute also conducted an experimental test of another employment and vocational development program for criminal defendants diverted from prosecution—the Court Employment Project. Researchers found that participants' earnings and employment improved, but this improvement was seen also among subjects not admitted to the program (that is, those who were assigned to the control group). The researchers concluded, consequently, that the program was having no apparent effect on offenders' employment prospects (Baker and Sadd, 1979).

Another form of assistance—financial aid to released prisoners to help them through the transition—was tested in a controlled experiment in Baltimore in the mid-1970s, called the Living Insurance for Ex-Prisoners (LIFE) program. Four groups of offenders were created by random assignments: three experimental groups and one control group. One of the experimental groups consisted of subjects given financial aid; subjects in the second received job placement and vocational counseling; and subjects in the third group received all three types of assistance. Those receiving financial aid were found to have lower arrest rates than subjects in all other groups, including control subjects, but none of the experimental groups fared better than controls in finding employment (Lenihan, 1977).

A subsequent nationwide replication of this program, the Transitional Aid Research Project (TARP), was designed as an experiment having five groups: four different experimental groups receiving different combinations and amounts of aid and job placement services, and a control group receiving neither aid nor services. Job placement services alone were found to have no effect on employment. As in the LIFE experiment, researchers found that transitional aid reduced re-arrest rates, but they also found that the payments increased unemployment (because they created a disincentive to find work). The net effect of these two dynamics was to cancel out the positive effects, leaving no differences in recidivism among experimentals and controls (Rossi, Berk, Lenihan, 1980).

In short, several different approaches to improving the employment and earnings prospects of offenders have been tried but have had only modest successes at best. There is evidence that supported work was successful for limited segments of the offender populations, and perhaps the LIFE participants as well (who differed in some ways from those in the later TARP experiment). How well either of these types of programs would perform in today's climate, with a different type of offender having problems with drugs other than heroin, only can be guessed.

The Third Wave: Programs for Other Disadvantaged Populations

With the termination in 1982 of Federal funding authorized by the Comprehensive Employment and Training Act (CETA), ex-offender employment and training programs mostly disappeared. This collapse of public support for offender employment and training programs occurred at roughly the same time that Federal policy turned away from offender rehabilitation objectives more generally. In place of rehabilitation, policy-makers sought to reduce crime by deterring and incapacitating offenders (by imposing prison sentences), and hoped to achieve the same among probationers and parolees by intensifying surveillance of them.

Although funding for manpower programs targeting ex-offenders declined in the late 1970s and early 1980s, manpower programs for various disadvantaged populations were funded and have been evaluated. Ex-offenders were not specifically targeted by these programs, but many of the participants in the eligible disadvantaged groups did have arrest records and were probably similar to those who, in an earlier decade, would have encountered manpower services in criminal justice settings. Research on these programs is suggestive, but the generalizability of the findings to ex-offender populations is unknown.

For example, the Job Corps, begun in 1969, provides a comprehensive array of manpower services to extremely disadvantaged youths in a rural residential setting. Evaluators at Mathematica Policy Research, using a strong quasi-experimental design rather than an experimental one, found participants had higher earnings and lower rates of crime (Mallar et al., 1982). Although this finding has been widely touted as a major success story, its utility for offenders is questionable. Some of the program's success resulted from enrolling youths in the military, which is not an option for many convicted persons. Violent offenders were screened out. The rural location of the residential programs may work against integrating offenders into their home communities.

Following the termination of the CETA program, the largest amount of federal employment and training funds were channeled through the Job Training Partnership Act (JTPA). Programs sponsored by the JTPA provide a variety of services: on-the-job training; classroom vocational instruction; and a combination of other services, including job search assistance, and basic education. With government sponsorship, Abt Associates conducted a controlled experiment at sixteen different sites, and found mixed results. JTPA programs were found to produce modest positive effects on earnings for adults through a thirty-month follow-up period; the effects were larger for women than for men. Moreover, these gains exceeded the costs of the program for these adults. However, no positive effects attributable to the program were found for out-of-school youths, including a subgroup of these youths who had arrest records. Nor was there evidence of a positive effect on subsequent arrests in any subgroup (Bloom et al., 1994).

Another program, JOBSTART, reported greater success. This program for dropout youths offers comprehensive services similar to those delivered in the Job Corps, but in a nonresidential setting. An experimental evaluation of the program found that among a subgroup of young men having arrest records, the program appears to have produced a substantial increase in earnings, as well as positive effects on rearrests and drug use. One of the most successful sites, the Center for Employment and Training in San Jose, California, was especially aggressive in job placement, and provided other services as well (Cave et al., 1993). This is an important finding:

focusing on job placement rather than training or job-readiness preparation might be a more direct way of improving employment prospects.

Why So Few Successes?

Why these employment and training programs generally have produced such meager returns is not well understood. In the criminal justice arena, these failures might be explained by the coercive environment in which these programs exist, and perhaps by the difficulty of working with clients who are manipulative and suspicious of social service agencies, and who suffer from a number of severe handicaps, including substance abuse, mental illness, chaotic family lives, and poverty. These cannot be the only reasons, however, because studies of programs operating outside the criminal justice system also fail to find strong impacts.

It is possible that none of the interventions have been intensive enough to make a significant difference. Nearly all the persons served by these programs suffer from multiple deficits and problems that are many years in the making. Ex-offenders are especially handicapped, and have few personal and social resources upon which to build. As the author of a recent Department of Labor paper remarks, "An intervention lasting three or four months is not going to be able to turn around sixteen years of accumulated problems" (U.S. Department of Labor, 1994:8).

How intensive must a training program be to have a substantial effect? One difficulty with determining this is the high cost of implementing very intensive training programs. Heckman (1994) estimates that to get a $1,000 increase in annual earnings requires at least an investment of $10,000 in training. (Many of the programs evaluated have failed to earn that return.) At this optimistic rate of return, training will cost in the area of $50,000 per client to yield an increase of about $5,000 per year in earnings. It is difficult to know how large an improvement in earning power has to be with offenders to keep them on the straight and narrow, but it is probably more than a few thousand dollars a year. At $50,000-plus per head for training, the cost of training programs for a half-million or so offenders per year will be exceedingly high (about $25 billion).

Another reason that these various employment and training programs have produced such modest results for offenders may be that offenders also are mired in a variety of other problems—drug abuse, housing instability, troubled family lives, and mental illness. The accumulated effect of these various problems is that the focus on employment and training is insufficient to help them overcome the problems that interfere with getting work and also training for work.

The lack of program success also may be explained in part by the nearly exclusive focus of the programs on developing offenders' "human capital," rather than attempting to change the nature of the labor market that may be blocking their entry. It is interesting that one program that reported successes aimed not to build human capital by training, but instead focused on job placement.

One aspect of the inhospitable job market that offenders face, which may account for some measure of the programs' apparent failure to have strong effects, is the general shrinking of wages and employment prospects for all uneducated and unskilled persons. Since 1973, opportunities for legitimate income have declined as a result of changes in the composition of work in the U.S. economy, especially for men with less education and fewer skills, and for youths generally. Between 1979 and 1985, the American economy generated a net gain of 8 million new wage and salary jobs, even while losing more than 1.7 million jobs in the manufacturing sector (U.S. Department of Labor, 1987). However, as much as half of these new jobs may have developed in the low-wage and part-time end of the service and retail trade sectors (Bluestone and Harrison, 1986). The decline of manufacturing jobs has had an especially devastating effect on persons lacking education and skills.

Consequently, among the unskilled and uneducated, real wages have declined precipitously. For example, real average incomes (that is, adjusted for inflation) for males not completing high school have declined about 40 percent since 1973. Opportunities for upward mobility on the job have diminished; more persons have dropped out of the legitimate labor force altogether; marriage rates have dropped; the number of single heads of households has increased; and the proportions of individuals and families living in poverty have risen. About 50 percent of high-school dropouts are unemployed; among black dropout youths, the rate is about 70 percent. The plight of those with records of arrests and convictions is severe, in part because of the barriers to employment that such records create. In the face of these declining employment prospects for unskilled offenders, it is not surprising that employment and training programs for offenders have fared so poorly.

In general, research on employment and training programs support the general proposition that increased earnings, by whatever legitimate means (such as stipends while in a supported work program or a training program, or wages paid on the job), have a positive effect in reducing criminality. To be sure, this is not found in all studies, but the general statement is probably true for many offenders. The fundamental problem is how to get offenders jobs, and stable ones—or, at least, a string of jobs that leave as little time unemployed as possible.

Some Suggestions for Program Managers and Policymakers

Although a cyclical upturn in the economy will improve employment and earnings prospects for some, there is little on the horizon that leads us to expect substantial improvements for those in the low wage "secondary" labor market—or for offenders who hope to move into that market. Rather than passively accept defeat, however, policy makers and program managers seeking to integrate offenders into the world of legitimate employment will continue to explore new approaches. What follows are some suggestions.

Focus, to the extent possible, on placing offenders in jobs. Job developers should cultivate relationships with local employers to learn of their labor needs and openings. Admittedly, such strategies will be more successful in areas where the local economy is healthy.

Provide continuing services, even after the first job is obtained. Because many offenders will find jobs that are unstable and short-termed, the challenge facing the offender and employment and training programs will be to string together a sequence of jobs, as well as learning how to "churn" successfully. As Heckman remarks of youth generally, "Churning is a form of learning and most youth who are in deadend jobs work and search their way out of them" (1994:106). Offenders have generally worse prospects than all youths, but it is nonetheless important to recognize that employment instability is a feature of any job market, and not necessarily evidence of an offender's personal defects.

Tighten the linkages between prison and community-based programs. Where persons are released from prison, a well-administered system of bringing persons into employment and training programs soon after hitting the street will increase the likelihood of post-release success.

Assess offenders to determine their readiness for employment, as well as to identify other problems that may obstruct their attempts to enter the labor market. If offenders are found to have serious substance abuse problems, symptoms of mental illness, housing or domestic problems, or serious health problems, ancillary services should be made available to alleviate these problems. Ideally, efforts to get them into the job market should be made as soon as possible, even if the other problems are not fully alleviated, because having a job may assist in resolving these other personal problems.

Consider other changes in the structure of the job market to facilitate the employment and improve the earnings not only of offenders but of other poor people, as well. For example, the earned income tax credit could be expanded to subsidize the wages of the working poor so that they can live better within their means. Other types of wage subsidies might be considered.

The federal government should reassert its role in supporting experimentation. In the Violent Crime Control and Law Enforcement Act of 1994, Congress ordered the creation of a new office in the U.S. Department of Justice to encourage and support job training and placement programs in state and local governments for paroled prisoners and probationers. Although the magnitude of this assistance is not yet known, this might herald the turnaround of a situation that has prevailed during the past decade and a half.

Whether programs are federally supported or not, administrators and policy makers should recognize that, with an organized attempt to learn from experimentation, our ability to develop progressively more effective programs is hamstrung. The experience of the first two decades following the Manpower Demonstration and Training Act should be sobering: hundreds of programs were developed by thousands of intelligent and hard-working persons. Very few of them designed the programs in a way that permitted good evaluation. The legacy of their efforts consequently evaporated within months after their programs died for lack of funding. Unless we design programs explicitly as tests of various employment and training approaches, we will spend large amounts of money and even more precious human resources, and still not know at the end of the day what works, and for which types of people.

References

American Probation and Parole Association and National Association of Probation Executives. 1988. *National Narcotics Intervention Project Strategy Briefs.* A collection of descriptions of BJA-supported programs collected by Timothy Matthews. Lexington, Kentucky: Council of State Governments.

Baker, Sally Hillsman and Susan Sadd. 1979. *The Court Employment Project Evaluation.* New York: Vera Institute of Justice.

Baunach, Phyllis Jo. 1985. "Jail Inmates 1983." Washington, D.C.: Bureau of Justice Statistics.

Beck, James L. 1981. Employment, Community Treatment Center Placement, and Recidivism: A Study of Released Federal Offenders. *Federal Probation*. 44:4.

Bloom, Howard S., Larry L. Orr, George Cave, Stephen H. Bell, Fred Doolittle, Winston Lin. 1994. *The National JTPA Study, Overview: Impacts, Benefits and Costs of Title II-A*. Cambridge, Massachusetts: Abt Associates Inc.

Bluestone, Barry and Bennett Harrison. 1986. *The Great American Job Machine*. Report prepared for the U.S. Congress, Joint Economic Committee.

Cave, George, Hans Bos, Fred Doolittle, and Cyril Toussaint. 1993. *JOBSTART: Final Report on a Program for School Dropouts*. New York: Manpower Demonstration Research Corporation.

Corbett, Ronald. 1990. (Massachusetts Department of Probation). Interview with author, March 19, 1990.

Doeringer, Peter B. and Michael J. Piore. 1975. Unemployment and the "dual labor market." *The Public Interest*. 38:67-79.

Friedman, Lucy. 1978. *The Wildcat Evaluation: An Early Test of Support Work in Drug Abuse Rehabilitation*. Rockville, Maryland: National Institute on Drug Abuse.

Heckman, James J. 1994. Is Job Training Oversold? *The Public Interest*: 115:91-115.

Innes, Christopher A. 1988. Profile of State Prison Inmates, 1986. Washington, D.C.: Bureau of Justice Statistics.

Lenihan, Kenneth. 1977. *Unlocking the Second Gate*. R&D Monograph 45. Washington, D.C.: U.S. Department of Labor.

Mallar, Charles, Stuart Kerachsky, Craig Thornton, and David Long. 1982. *Third Follow-up Report of the Evaluation of the Economic Impact of the Job Corps Program*. Princeton, New Jersey: Mathematica Policy Research, Inc.

Manpower Demonstration Research Corporation. 1980. *Summary and Findings of the National Supported Work Demonstration*. Cambridge, Massachusetts: Ballinger Publishing Company.

Mullen, Joan, Kenneth Carlson, Ralph Earle, Carol Blew, and Linda Li. 1974. *Pre-Trial Services: An Evaluation of Policy Related Research*. Cambridge, Massachusetts: Abt Associates Inc.

Piliavin, Irving and Rosemary Gartner. 1981. *The Impact of Supported Work on Ex-Offenders*. New York: Manpower Demonstration Research Corporation.

Rossi, Peter H., Richard A. Berk, and Kenneth J. Lenihan. 1980. *Money, Work, and Crime*. New York: Academic Press.

Rovner-Pieczenik, Roberta. 1973. *The First Decade of Experience: A Synthesis of Manpower Research and Development Projects in Criminal Justice and Corrections*. Cambridge, Massachusetts: Criminal Justice Research, Inc.

Schuman, Allan. 1990. (Director of Social Services Division of the D.C. Superior Court). Interview with author, March 21.

Taggert, Robert. 1977. *The Prison of Unemployment*. Baltimore: Johns Hopkins University Press.

Toborg, Mary, Lawrence J. Center, Raymond H. Milkman, and Dennis W. Davis. 1978. *The Transition from Prison to Employment: An Assessment of Community-Based Assistance Programs*. Washington, D.C.: The National Institute of Law Enforcement and Criminal Justice.

U.S. Department of Labor. 1987. *Monthly Labor Review* (Bureau of Labor Statistics), April, Table 20.

———. 1994. Future Direction for Youth Demonstrations. Unpublished paper.

White, Michael A. 1993. *A Statistical Description of Residents of Massachusetts Correctional Institutions on January 1, 1993*. Boston: Massachusetts Department of Correction.

Wilson, Cicero, Kenneth J. Lenihan, and Gail A. Goolkasian. 1981. *Employment Services for Ex-Offenders*. Washington, D.C.: National Institute of Justice.

Wish, Eric D., M. Cuadrano, and J. A. Martorana. 1987. Estimates of Drug Use in Intensive Supervision Probationers: Results from a Pilot Study. *Federal Probation*. 51:1.

Section 4:

Bridging the Gap Between Research and Practice

Closing Comments

10

Hubert G. Locke, Ph.D.

Southern Illinois University, Carbondale, Illinois
Professor and Conference Chair
Graduate School of Public Affairs
University of Washington, Seattle

Two decades ago, in the space of two years, two events occurred that have been crucial for the field of corrections. Frequent reference has been made throughout this meeting to the first event: the publication by Robert Martinson of his provocative article, "What Works? - Questions and Answers about Prison Reform," which appeared in the Spring 1974 issue of *The Public Interest*. The second event took place two years later; it was the first International Conference for Socially Handicapped and Stigmatized Persons which met in London in 1976 and was the forerunner to this meeting. For a full generation now, the Martinson-perspective has been a major factor in the shaping of public policy, at least in the United States, with respect to the issue of rehabilitation and recidivism in corrections. What are the prospects, after two decades in which, in this country, prison-building has been the fastest growing industry in the nation, that the perspectives presented and discussed at this meeting might begin to influence the public discourse and, eventually, public policy on this critical issue?

The United States is a nation of contrasts and contradictions. We have the highest prison population of any nation in the world, but we also have developed, according to Dr. Neudek, more alternative community-based programs for offenders than any other country. These two approaches have been forced, by the politics of the era, to compete against one another when common sense would suggest that prisons and community-based alternatives ought to complement one another: prisons for persons who pose a clear danger to society; community-based programs for those who do not. At this point, at least in the resource allocation process, community-based programs are losing out badly to new prison construction.

As is now well known, Martinson's position with respect to the issue of what works in corrections was both poorly stated and greatly distorted. His oft-quoted summary that "with few and isolated exceptions, the rehabilitative efforts that have been reported so far had no appreciable effect on recidivism" was modified even in his original article by the statement that "it is just possible that some of our treatment programs are working to some extent, but that our research is so bad that it is incapable of telling" (Martinson, Palmer and Adams, *Rehabilitation, Recidivism and Research*, National Council on Crime and Delinquency, 1976, p. 49).

Subsequently, the question of methodology—not program content nor effectiveness—became the principal focus in the Martinson debate: The question was not whether anything works or does not work, but whether our research has been sophisticated and rigorous enough to tell us what does or does not work. Martinson's critics were also quick to note that his initial comments focused chiefly on whether "any treatment methods were of value, not for particular types of offenders, but for all or nearly all offenders. . . Rather than asking what works for offenders as a whole, the critics argued, we must increasingly ask which method works best for which offenders and under what conditions" (Martinson, et al., p. 42).

It is precisely these questions that have been the focal point of this meeting. Two decades after Martinson, it is clear that either we know much more than we knew then or that we can substantiate what we know with far greater empirical validity.

1. From Dr. Anglin and his colleagues at the University of California, Los Angeles, we learn that there are both research findings and clinical experience that indicate that "treatment for substance-abusing offenders in community-based programs can reduce substance abuse, criminal behavior, and recidivism, whether the offender enters treatment voluntarily or under some form of coercion." Given the high volume of crimes committed by drug-dependent offenders, if policy makers acted on this one insight alone, a significant change could occur in dealing with the general problem of crime for, as Dr. Anglin and his colleagues put it, "a consistent finding is that as levels of drug use decline, so also does criminal activity."

2. Drs. Harris and Rice offer us the broader observation that "there is now sufficient evidence to make the strong statement that treatment for offenders can reduce criminal recidivism as well as have other positive effects. Programs that are highly structured and behavioral or cognitive-behavioral, that are run in the community rather than in an institution, that are run with integrity and enthusiasm, that target high-, rather than low-, risk offenders, that are intensive in terms of number of hours and overall length of program can be expected to be considerably more effective than others." With respect to mentally disordered offenders, Harris and Rice indicate the state of empirical knowledge is less specific; nevertheless, they assert that we can deduce certain principles of effective service for such persons, and that such principles enacted in a "faithfully implemented psychosocial program" would likely be less expensive and more cost effective than traditional custodial hospitalization.

3. Professor Quinsey warns us that, with respect to sex offenders, we must proceed with the utmost caution since the public has a zero tolerance for mistakes in this area and since "even with the best system of assessment, treatment, and management, some sex offenders will inevitably recidivate while under supervision." What Quinsey advises are efforts to more accurately appraise risk and to link risk factors with dispositional decisions, a base from which he then proceeds to offer a number of acute diagnostic and treatment principles.

4. Professor Fagan makes substantially similar observations regarding the treatment of violent offenders, pointing out that while "no strong assertions about program effectiveness can be made . . . there are several trends regarding intervention that are noteworthy, including that fact that programs emphasizing therapeutic integrity yield better results than eclectic treatments; and behavioral or cognitive or life skills based interventions, or some combination of such, are more effective than other approaches."

5. Dr. McDonald reviewed the studies of community-based programs designed to integrate unskilled and unemployed offenders into the legitimate work force, and finds that such programs have fared poorly. He notes that in the socioeconomic climate of the past two decades in which these programs have had to operate, it is perhaps not surprising that these programs have not done better but, drawing upon that body of experience, he makes a number of highly useful suggestions for program managers and policy makers that might improve employment prospects for both youth and adult offenders.

6. Finally, Dr. Gendreau, who started us off, also summed up the state of knowledge in a most eloquent and concise fashion. He reminds us that programs of high quality are shown to reduce recidivism from 10 percent to as high as 60 percent. Further, and of critical importance to the public policy debate, he points out that public opinion surveys continue to show strong public support for the goal of rehabilitation in corrections.

So it is that our knowledge base with respect to what works and what does not work in corrections, while far from complete, is much greater than it was two decades ago. It is certainly extensive enough for us to assert that what passes for public policy these days in countries like the United States, where prevailing policy proceeds as if these insights were totally unknown, makes a travesty of both knowledge and common sense.

Given these circumstances, let us return to the question asked at the outset: What are the prospects that the insights and perspectives presented at this meeting might come to influence the public debate and public policy on the critical issue of criminal recidivism and rehabilitation?

Here, it may be instructive to note, from a policy perspective, that decision makers did not immediately rush to put Martinson's views into practice. In *The Public Interest* article, Martinson himself tells the story of being asked to undertake a study in 1966 by the New York State Governor's Special Committee on Criminal Offenders, and that by 1970 the state had changed its mind about the worth and utility of the data Martinson and his colleagues had gathered. By 1972, Martinson laments, "fully a year after I had reedited the study for final publication—the state had not only failed to publish it, but also had refused to give me permission to publish it on my own." The article might never have seen the light of day except for the fact that it was subpoenaed in a case before one of the local trial courts.

There is an important lesson here. Martinson's study was a prelude to one of the most conservative eras in American politics, one in which policy makers in many political jurisdictions were looking for reasons to repudiate the putative liberal policies of previous decades. The study confirmed what a cadre of reactionary policy makers wanted to hear, at a time in which the sentiments within the professional corrections community still ran toward a philosophy of rehabilitation rather than retribution.

Currently, it is reactionary politics that still holds sway over the public policy process, at least in this nation and certainly regarding issues of crime and corrections. It may seem to be the least favorable climate in which to try and effect change toward more sensible and effective policies in this field. But this author remains a fervent believer in the capacity of an enlightened electorate to make sound and wise political choices. This especially is to be the case with respect to this issue of crime and corrections, in spite of the emotionalism bordering on hysteria that can become attached to this issue and in spite of the, at times, blatantly irresponsible treatment it receives by the media.

Thoughtful citizens, when confronted with the realities of what we are doing in corrections today, with what it is costing this nation to do what we are doing today, and how little in the way of public safety or personal security we are getting for what we are doing today, can be persuaded that there are more sensible and more effective ways to get the job done! Dr. Prendergast may be right, but it may also be that we are about to reach the nadir of public cynicism with respect to this issue, that the predictable failures of such demonic policies as "three-strikes-and-you're-out" soon will prove to be more than a fundamentally decent-minded citizenry bargained for, and that the pendulum will begin to swing toward more workable solutions.

Public policy experts argue that policy is best made by an incremental process. The best policy, they suggest, addresses a problem in small cumulative segments, trying a relatively minor or modest change or intervention, testing or evaluating the impact of that change, and calculating and initiating the next cautious step. Whatever may be said for this approach to public policy formation, it is not the way in which criminal justice policy in general or corrections policy in particular have been developed over the course of this century.

Both areas—criminal justice policy and corrections policy—have been marked by sea changes, especially in the past half-century. The body politic seems not to be content with gradual, incremental change; instead, our societies have lunged dramatically from one side of the policy fence to the other; from rehabilitation to retribution, from concern with prisoners' rights to concern about victims' rights, from indeterminate to determinate to mandatory sentencing, from maximum use of probation and parole to "three-strikes-and-you're-out."

In one sense, each of these policy stances represents ideological positions competing in the public arena for attention and influence. In democratic societies, that is how it ought to be; except, in this instance, ideology ought to be informed by the knowledge that arises out of experience and the testing or the evaluation of experience. This is what this conference has been about—we have spent the past two and a half days examining bodies of knowledge that are derived from the rigorous testing of various experiments and experiences that permit us to say with a considerable degree of confidence what will and what will not work in efforts to rehabilitate criminal offenders. The question is how to get this knowledge not only into practice but also into the policy arena so that the maximum resources our various societies have to bring to bear on this problem can be mobilized and directed in what we believe will be more effective ways.

The first task is the easier one: getting knowledge into practice. Many of the practitioners here are already on the cutting edge of developments that have been discussed in this meeting; others will take back new insights learned here and, hopefully, put them into practice. Gradually, it is to be hoped that communities will come to see and appreciate the outcomes of your efforts: that there are more practical, cost-effective, publicly safe and, for those still concerned about such matters, humane ways of going about the business of dealing with criminal offenders.

Practitioners understandably may be reluctant to invite researchers to evaluate their programs. This may be especially true if the program is new or experimental. The practitioner may have secured the funds or gained permission to initiate a new program based on all sorts of promises, expectations, and assurances. It may not seem to be in one's best interest, therefore, to find out whether it is working or not! But if we are to turn around the policy debate, we need a constant improvement and expansion of our fund of knowledge, and that can happen when practitioners invite and welcome competent researchers to look over what they are doing.

The second task is admittedly the more difficult, translating what we know into effective public policy. There is no magic bullet for this one. However, if it is to happen, it will be because you men and women seize the march in the policy debate. The academics among us must give more aid and support to those policy makers in our midst who are looking for sensible alternatives to our present turmoil; it no longer suffices for us to do our research, disseminate it in our professional journals where it can be read by our peers, and leave it to chance that some enterprising legislative aide will stumble across our findings while searching for answers to an elective official's inquiries. Likewise, the practitioners must seize every opportunity possible to help educate the public—opportunities to speak to groups of all sorts, shapes and sizes; to write op ed pieces; to develop relationships with local media; to testify at legislative hearings; to engage volunteers wherever feasible so that they can get first-hand exposure to effective programs—in short, to do whatever it is possible to do in order to change the climate of public thinking.

Jim Lawrence, the president of this international body representing over 250 agencies and some 1,500 residential and community-based programs, has said that "in a time when countries around the world are burdened with increasing numbers of violent and special need offenders, it is in the public's best interest to search out new ways to reduce crime among these offenders." The programs in which you are engaged are showing us those ways. Let us hope an aware and enlightened public will press for their expansion as sensible alternatives to our present institutional and policy failures. It is a difficult challenge we face, to be sure, but that is nothing new for you men and women. You certainly would not be in the business you are if you were not adept at dealing with difficult people under difficult circumstances in difficult situations. The policy challenge to you is the most difficult of all: persuading and convincing a scared, skeptical public that there are better ways to deal with our fears for our public safety. This author wishes you the very best in your efforts; a sane and sensible future for our societies depends on the outcomes of your work. Do not fail us!

INDEX

F

P

S

T